Blockchain Scalability

Wuhui Chen • Zibin Zheng • Huawei Huang
Editors

Blockchain Scalability

 Springer

Editors
Wuhui Chen (iD)
GuangDong Engineering Technology
Research Center of Blockchain
Sun Yat-sen University
Guangdong, China

Zibin Zheng
GuangDong Engineering Technology
Research Center of Blockchain
Sun Yat-sen University
Guangdong, China

Huawei Huang
GuangDong Engineering Technology
Research Center of Blockchain
Sun Yat-sen University
Guangdong, China

ISBN 978-981-99-1061-8   ISBN 978-981-99-1059-5   (eBook)
https://doi.org/10.1007/978-981-99-1059-5

This Springer imprint is published by the registered company Springer Nature Singapore Pte Ltd.
The registered company address is: 152 Beach Road, #21-01/04 Gateway East, Singapore 189721,
Singapore

Preface

Blockchain technology has been the subject of extensive attention from government, enterprise, and academia due to its potential to create a trusted, decentralized environment for a variety of applications. However, the current blockchain faces a significant scalability bottleneck that limits its ability to meet the demands of large-scale practical applications. The bottleneck is mainly characterized by low performance efficiency and difficulty in functional extension, which pose significant challenges for realizing the full potential of blockchain technology.

Over the past few years, substantial progress has been made in blockchain scalability technologies. Various methods have been developed to improve the performance of blockchain or enable cross-chain technology for interoperability. However, the research in this field is still in its early stages of development.

This book aims to provide a comprehensive and state-of-the-art resource for researchers, engineers, policymakers, and students interested in understanding and addressing the scalability bottleneck problem in blockchain technology. The book adopts an approach that is based on the existing large-scale application scenarios, which provides readers with a comprehensive analysis of blockchain scalability issues, key technologies, and future directions. The book covers various areas related to blockchain scalability, including the root of blockchain scalability problems, mainstream blockchain performance, the classification of existing scalability problem solutions, exciting sharding-based approaches, open issues, and future directions to scale blockchain.

The book's comprehensive coverage of blockchain scalability issues and solutions makes it a valuable resource for anyone interested in understanding and addressing the scalability bottleneck problem in blockchain technology. We hope that this book will contribute to the realization of the full potential of blockchain technology by providing a holistic view of the challenges and opportunities in this field.

Guangdong, China

Wuhui Chen
Zibin Zheng
Huawei Huang

Acknowledgments

We would like to express our sincere appreciation to all those who have contributed to the completion of this book on blockchain scalability.

First, we extend our gratitude to the contributors who have shared their valuable expertise and insights on this complex and rapidly evolving topic. Their contributions have been instrumental in creating a comprehensive and up-to-date resource on the subject.

We are also grateful to the editorial team at Springer for their guidance and support throughout the publishing process. Their professionalism, expertise, and commitment to excellence have been crucial in making this book a reality.

Finally, we express our appreciation to the readers of this book. We hope that the book will be a valuable resource for researchers, engineers, policymakers, and others working in the area of blockchain scalability. We also hope that the book will inspire further research and innovation in this exciting and important field.

We acknowledge that the subject of blockchain and its applications is complex and rapidly evolving, and that there are many potential conflicts of interest that may arise in the course of researching, writing, and publishing a book on this topic. We have made every effort to disclose any conflicts of interest that we are aware of, and we welcome feedback and input from readers and other stakeholders on any potential biases or conflicts that may be present in the work. This book is partially supported by the National Key R&D Program of China (No. 2020YFB1006001), the National Natural Science Foundation of China under project (62032025, 62272496, 62172453), Fundamental Research Funds for the Central Universities, Sun Yat-sen University (Grant No. 23lgbj019), the National Natural Science Foundation of Guangdong province (2022A1515010154), the Major Key Project of PCL (PCL2021A06), the Program for Guangdong Introducing Innovative and Entrepreneurial Teams (2017ZT07X355), and the Pearl River Talent Recruitment Program (No. 2019QN01X130).

Contents

1 **Blockchain Scalability Fundamentals** 1
Huawei Huang, Wei Kong, Sicong Zhou, Zibin Zheng, and Song Guo

2 **Overview to Blockchain Scalability Challenges and Solutions** 51
Qiheng Zhou, Huawei Huang, Zibin Zheng, and Jing Bian

3 **On-Chain and Off-Chain Scalability Techniques** 81
Ting Cai, Wuhui Chen, Kostas E. Psannis, Sotirios K. Goudos,
Yang Yu, Zibin Zheng, and Shaohua Wan

4 **Layered Sharding on Open Blockchain** 97
Zicong Hong, Song Guo, Peng Li, and Wuhui Chen

5 **Sharding-Based Scalable Consortium Blockchain** 119
Peilin Zheng, Quanqing Xu, Zibin Zheng, Zhiyuan Zhou, Ying Yan,
and Hui Zhang

6 **State Sharding for Permissioned Blockchain** 143
Peilin Zheng, Quanqing Xu, Xiapu Luo, Zibin Zheng, Weilin Zheng,
Xu Chen, Zhiyuan Zhou, Ying Yan, and Hui Zhang

7 **Elastic Resource Allocation in Sharding-Based Blockchains** 165
Huawei Huang, Zhengyu Yue, Xiaowen Peng, Liuding He,
Wuhui Chen, Hong-Ning Dai, Zibin Zheng, and Song Guo

8 **Dynamic Sharding: A Trade-OFF Between Security
and Scalability** 193
Jianting Zhang, Zicong Hong, Xiaoyu Qiu, Yufeng Zhan, Song Guo,
and Wuhui Chen

9 **A Scalable and Secure Framework for 5G Networks Applications** 223
Sicong Zhou, Huawei Huang, Wuhui Chen, Pan Zhou, Zibin Zheng,
and Song Guo

Chapter 1
Blockchain Scalability Fundamentals

Huawei Huang, Wei Kong, Sicong Zhou, Zibin Zheng, and Song Guo

1.1 Overview

Centralized security mechanisms are prone to Single Point of Failure, meaning that once a centralized component is compromised, the whole system would cease to function. The decentralization of blockchain can eliminate such concern without the need of a trusted third party. With the benefit of decentralized characteristics, blockchains have been deeply diving into multiple applications that are closely related to every aspect of our daily life, such as cryptocurrencies, business applications, smart city, Internet-of-Things (IoT) applications, and etc. The blockchain

H. Huang · Z. Zheng (✉)
GuangDong Engineering Technology Research Center of Blockchain, Sun Yat-sen University, Guangdong, China
e-mail: huanghw28@mail.sysu.edu.cn; zhzibin@mail.sysu.edu.cn

W. Kong · S. Zhou
School of Computer Science and Engineering, Sun Yat-Sen University, Guangzhou, China

S. Guo (✉)
Department of Computing, The Hong Kong Polytechnic University, Hung Hom, Hong Kong, China
e-mail: song.guo@polyu.edu.hk

© The Author(s), under exclusive license to Springer Nature Singapore Pte Ltd. 2023
W. Chen et al. (eds.), *Blockchain Scalability*,
https://doi.org/10.1007/978-981-99-1059-5_1

theory and technology will bring substantial innovations, incentives, and a great number of application scenarios in diverse fields.

We have found that a survey of the state-of-the-art theories, modelings and useful tools that can (i) improve the performance of blockchains, and (ii) help better understand blockchains, is still missing. As a result, we made in-depth investigations on these directions and presented in this chapter includes the following contributions.

- We introduces the preliminaries of blockchains.
- We then present a comprehensive investigation on the state-of-the-art theoretical modelings, analytics models, performance measurements, and useful experiment tools for blockchains, blockchain networks, and blockchain systems.
- Several promising directions and open issues for future studies are also envisioned finally.

1.2 Preliminaries of Blockchains

Blockchain is a promising paradigm for content distribution and distributed consensus over P2P networks. In this section, we present the basic concepts, definitions and terminologies of blockchains appeared in this chapter. Due to the frequent use of acronyms in this book, we include an acronym table, i.e., Table 1 in the online supplementary material.

1.2.1 Prime Blockchain Platforms

1.2.1.1 Bitcoin

Bitcoin is viewed as the blockchain system that executes the first cryptocurrency. It builds upon two major techniques, i.e., *Nakamoto Consensus* and *UTXO Model*, which are introduced as follows.

Nakamoto Consensus To achieve an agreement of blocks, Bitcoin adopts the Nakamoto Consensus, in which miners generate new blocks by solving a puzzle. In such a puzzle-solving process, also referred to as mining, miners need to calculate a nonce value that fits the required difficulty level. Through changing the difficulty, Bitcoin system can maintain a stable rate of block-generation, which is about one block per 10 minutes. When a miner generates a new block, it broadcasts this message to all the other miners in the network. If others receive this new block, they add this block to their local chain. If all of the other miners receive this new block timely, the length of the main chain increases by one. However, because of the network delays, not always all the other miners can receive a new block in time. When a miner generates a block before it receives the previous one, a fork yields. Bitcoin addresses this issue by following the rule of longest chain.

UTXO Model The Unspent Transaction Output (UTXO) model is adopted by cryptocurrencies like Bitcoin, and other popular blockchain systems [1, 2]. A UTXO is a set of digital money, each represents a chain of ownership between the owners and the receivers based on the cryptography technologies. In a blockchain, the overall UTXOs form a set, in which each element denotes the unspent output of a transaction, and can be used as an input for a future transaction. A client may own multiple UTXOs, and the total coin of this client is calculated by summing up all associated UTXOs. Using this model, blockchains can prevent the double-spend [3] attacks efficiently.

1.2.1.2   Ethereum

Ethereum [4] is an open-source blockchain platform enabling the function of smart contract. As the token in Ethereum, *Ether* is rewarded to the miners who conducted computation to secure the consensus of the blockchain. Ethereum executes on decentralized Ethereum Virtual Machines (EVMs), in which scripts are running on a network consisting of public Ethereum nodes. Comparing with Bitcoin, the EVM's instruction set is believed Turing-complete. Ethereum also introduces an internal pricing mechanism, called *gas*. A unit of gas measures the amount of computational effort needed to execute operations in a transaction. Thus, gas mechanism is useful to restrain the spam in smart contracts. Ethereum 2.0 is an upgraded version based on the original Ethereum. The upgrades include a transition from PoW to Proof-of-Stake (PoS), and a throughput-improving based on sharding technologies. The comparison between Bitcoin & Ethereum is summarized in Table 1.1.

Account/Balance Model Unlike Bitcoin where states are composed by UTXOs, Ethereum adopts a more common and straightforward model that is used by banks, the Account/Balance Model. In every account, an incrementing counter of transaction execution, nonce, is implemented to prevent double spending attacks, which serves as a complement for the model's simple structure. There are basically 2 types of accounts, *external owned accounts* (EOAs) and *contract accounts* (CAs), each controlled by private keys and contract codes, respectively.

Table 1.1 Comparison between Bitcoin and Ethereum

	State model	Consensus protocols	Throughput
Bitcoin	UTXO	PoW	3 to 7 TPS[5]
Ethereum1.0	Account/balance	PoW	7 to 15 TPS[5]
Ethereum2.0	Account/balance	PoS sharding	Unknown

1.2.1.3 Hyperledger Fabric

Hyperledger Fabric [6] is a popular permissioned blockchain platform for industrial use. In industry, goals are quite different from cryptocurrency systems. Greater significance is attached to lower maintenance cost, higher throughput performance and permission control. For a node in a permissioned setting, other nodes, though untrusted, the identities are known. With different levels of trust among users, different consensus protocols can be customized for fault tolerant.

1.2.1.4 EOSIO

EOSIO [7] is another popular blockchain platform released by a company *block.one* on 2018. Different from Bitcoin and Ethereum, the smart contracts of EOSIO don't need to pay transaction fees. Its throughput is claimed to reach millions of transactions per second. Furthermore, EOSIO also enables low block-confirmatoin latency, low-overhead BFT finality, and etc. These excellent features has attracted a large-number of users and developers to quickly and easily deploy decentralized applications in a governed blockchain. For example, in total 89,800,000 EOSIO blocks have been generated in less than one and a half years since its first launching.

1.2.2 Consensus Mechanism

The consensus mechanism in blockchains is for fault-tolerant to achieve an agreement on the same state of the blockchain network, such as a single state of all transactions in a cryptocurrency blockchain. Popular proof-based consensus protocols include PoW and PoS. In PoW, miners compete with each other to solve a puzzle that is difficult to produce a result but easy to verify the result by others. Once a miner yields a required nonce value through a huge number of attempts, it gets paid a certain cryptocurrencies for creating a new block. In contrast, PoS doesn't have miners. Instead, the new block is forged by *validators* selected randomly within a committee. The probability to be chosen as a validator is linearly related to the size of its stake. PoW and PoS are both adopted as consensus protocols for the security of cryptocurrencies. The former is based on the CPU power, and the latter on the coin age. Therefore, PoS is with lower energy-cost and less likely to be attacked by the 51% attack.

1.2.3 Scalability of Blockchains

Blockchain as a distributed and public database of transactions has become a platform for decentralized applications. Despite its increasing popularity, blockchain technology faces the scalability problem: throughput does not scale with the increasing network size. Thus, scalable blockchain protocols that can solve the scalability issues are still in an urgent need. Many different directions, such as *Off-chain*, *DAG*, and *Sharding* techniques, have been exploited to address the scalability of blockchains. Here, we present several representative terms related to scalability.

1.2.3.1   Off-Chain Techniques

Contrary to the on-chain transactions that are dealt with on the blockchain and visible to all nodes of the blockchain network, the off-chain transactions are processed outside the blockchain through a third-party guarantor who endorses the correctness of the transaction. The on-chain transactions incur longer latencies since the confirmation of an on-chain transaction has to take different steps. In contrast, the off-chain techniques can instantly execute the off-chain transactions because those transactions don't need to wait on the queue as on an on-chain network.

1.2.3.2   DAG

Mathematically, a DAG is a finite directed graph where no directed cycles exist. In the context of blockchain, DAG is viewed as a revolutionized technology that can upgrade blockchain to a new generation. This is because DAG is blockless, and all transactions link to multiple other transactions following a topological order on a DAG network. Thus, data can move directly between network participants. This results in a faster, cheaper and more scalable solution for blockchains. In fact, the bottleneck of blockchains mainly relies on the structure of blocks. Thus, probably the blockless DAG could be a promising solution to improve the scalability of blockchains substantially.

1.2.3.3   Sharding Technique

The consensus protocol of Bitcoin, i.e., Nakamoto Consensus, has significant drawbacks on the performance of transaction throughput and network scalability. To address these issues, *sharding* technique is one of the outstanding approaches, which improves the throughput and scalability by partitioning the blockchain network into several small shards such that each can process a bunch of unconfirmed transactions in parallel to generate medium blocks. Such medium blocks are then merged together in a final block. Basically, sharding technique includes *Network Sharding*, *Transaction Sharding* and *State Sharding*.

1.2.3.4 Cross-Shard Transactions

One shortcoming of sharding technique is that the malicious network nodes residing in the same shard may collude with each other, resulting in security issues. Therefore, the sharding-based protocols exploits *reshuffling* strategy to address such security threats. However, reshuffling brings the *cross-shard* data migration. Thus, how to efficiently handle the cross-shard transactions becomes an emerging topic in the context of sharding blockchain.

1.3 Theories to Improving the Performance of Blockchains

1.3.1 Latest Theories to Improving Blockchain Performance

Summary of this subsection is included in Table 1.2.

1.3.1.1 Throughput and Latency

Aiming to reduce the confirmation latency of transactions to milliseconds, Hari et al. [8] proposed a high-throughput, low-latency, deterministic confirmation mechanism called ACCEL for accelerating Bitcoin's block confirmation. The key findings include how to identify the singular blocks, and how to use singular blocks to reduce the confirmation delay. Once the confirmation delay is reduced, the throughput increases accordingly.

Two obstacles have hindered the scalability of the cryptocurrency systems. The first one is the low throughput, and the other one is the requirement for every node to duplicate the communication, storage, and state representation of the entire blockchain network. Wang and Wang [9] studied how to solve the above obstacles. Without weakening decentralization and security, the proposed Monoxide technique offers a linear scale-out ability by partitioning the workload. And they preserved the simplicity of the blockchain system and amplified its capacity. The authors also proposed a novel *Chu-ko-nu* mining mechanism, which ensures the cross-zone atomicity, efficiency and security of the blockchain system with thousands of independent zones. Then, the authors have conducted experiments to evaluate the scalability performance of the proposed Monoxide with respect to TPS, the overheads of cross-zone transactions, the confirmation latency of transactions, etc.

To bitcoin, low *throughput* and long *transaction confirmation latency* are two critical bottleneck metrics. To overcome these two bottlenecks, Yang et al. [10] designed a new blockchain protocol called Prism, which achieves a scalable throughput as high as 70,000 transactions per second, while ensuring a full security of bitcoin. The project of Prism is open-sourced in Github. The instances of Prism can be flexibly deployed on commercial cloud platform such as AWS. However, the

Table 1.2 Latest theories of improving the performance of blockchains

Emphasis	Ref.	Recognition	Challenge	Methodology
Throughput and latency	[8]	ACCEL: reduce the confirmation delay of blocks	Most of the blockchain applications desire fast confirmation of their transactions	Authors proposed a high-throughput, low-latency, deterministic confirmation mechanism, aiming to accelerate Bitcoin's block confirmation.
	[9]	Monoxide	Scalability issues, and efficient processing of cross-shard transactions	The proposed Monoxide offers a linear scale-out by partitioning workloads. Particularly, *Chu-ko-nu* mining mechanism enables the cross-zone atomicity, efficiency and security of the system.
	[10]	Prism	Low transaction throughput and large transaction confirmation of bitcoin	Authors proposed a new blockchain protocol, i.e., Prism, aiming to achieve a scalable throughput with a full security of bitcoin.
	[11]	GARET	How to place transactions to shards considering the complexity of transactions or the workload generated by transactions	Authors proposed a gas consumption-aware relocation mechanism for improving throughput in sharding-based Ethereum.

(continued)

Table 1.2 (continued)

Emphasis	Ref.	Recognition	Challenge	Methodology
Storage efficiency	[12]	Erasure code-based	How to reduce the storage consumption of blockchains	Authors proposed a new type of low-storage blockchain nodes using erasure code theory to reduce the storage space of blockchains.
	[13]	Jidar: data-reduction strategy	How to reduce the data consumption of bitcoin's blocks	Authors proposed a data reduction strategy for Bitcoin namely Jidar, in which each node only has to store the transactions of interest and the related Merkle branches from the complete blocks.
	[14]	_Segment blockchain_	To reduce the storage of blockchain systems while maintaining the decentralization without sacrificing security	Authors proposed a data-reduced storage mechanism named _segment blockchain_ such that each node only has to store a segment of the blockchain.
Reliability analysis	[15]	Availability of blockchains	The availability of read and write on blockchains is uneven	Authors studied the availability for blockchain-based systems, where the read and write availability is conflict to each other.
	[16]	Reliability prediction	The reliability of blockchain peers is unknown	Authors proposed H-BRP to predict the reliability of blockchain peers by extracting their reliability parameters.

authors also admitted that although the proposed Prism has a high throughput, its confirming latency still maintains as large as 10 seconds since there is only a single *voter chain* in Prism. A promising solution is to introduce a large number of such voter chains, each of which is not necessarily secure. Even though every voter chain is under attacking with a probability as high as 30%, the successful rate of attacking a half number of all voter chains is still theoretically very low. Thus, the authors believed that using multiple voter chains would be a good solution to reducing the confirmation latency while not sacrificing system security.

Considering that Ethereum simply allocates transactions to shards according to their account addresses rather than relying on the workload or the complexity of transactions, the resource consumption of transactions in each shard is unbalanced. In consequence, the network transaction throughput is affected and becomes low. To solve this problem, Woo et al. [11] proposed a heuristic algorithm named GARET, which is a gas consumption-aware relocation mechanism for improving throughput in sharding-based Ethereum environments. In particular, the proposed GARET can relocate transaction workloads of each shard according to the gas consumption. The experiment results show that GARET achieves a higher transactions throughput and a lower transaction latency compared with existing techniques.

1.3.1.2 Storage Efficiency

The transactions generated at real-time make the size of blockchains keep growing. For example, the storage efficiency of original-version Bitcoin has received much criticism since it requires to store the full transaction history in each Bitcoin peer. Although some revised protocols advocate that only the full-size nodes store the entire copy of whole ledger, the transactions still consume a large storage space in those full-size nodes. To alleviate this problem, several pioneer studies proposed storage-efficient solutions for blockchain networks. For example, By exploiting the erasure code-based approach, Perard et al. [12] proposed a low-storage blockchain mechanism, aiming to achieve a low requirement of storage for blockchains. The new low-storage nodes only have to store the linearly encoded fragments of each block. The original blockchain data can be easily recovered by retrieving fragments from other nodes under the erasure-code framework. Thus, this type of blockchain nodes allows blockchain clients to reduce the storage capacity. The authors also tested their system on the low-configuration Raspberry Pi to show the effectiveness, which demonstrates the possibility towards running blockchains on IoT devices.

Then, Dai et al. [13] proposed Jidar, which is a data reduction strategy for Bitcoin. In Jidar, each node only has to store the transactions of interest and the related Merkle branches from the complete blocks. All nodes verify transactions collaboratively by a query mechanism. This approach seems very promising to the storage efficiency of Bitcoin. Their experiments show that the proposed Jidar can reduce the storage overhead of each peer to about 1% comparing with the original Bitcoin.

Under the similar idea, Xu et al. [14] reduced the storage of blockchains using a *segment blockchain* mechanism, in which each node only needs to store a piece of blockchain segment. The authors also proved that the proposed mechanism endures a failure probability $(\phi/n)^m$ if an adversary party commits a collusion with less than a number ϕ of nodes and each segment is stored by a number m of nodes. This theoretical result is useful for the storage design of blockchains when developing a particular segment mechanism towards data-heavy distributed applications.

1.3.1.3   Reliability of Blockchains

As a decentralized mechanism for data protection, the reliability of blockchains plays an important role in data falsification. The following works studied the fundamental supporting mechanisms to achieve data falsification prevention. The availability of blockchains is a key factor for blockchain-based distributed applications (DApps). However, such availability guarantees of blockchain systems are unknown. To this end, Weber et al. [15] studied the availability limitations of two popular blockchains, i.e., Bitcoin and Ethereum. The authors found that the availability of reading and writing operations are conflict to each other. Through measuring and analyzing the transactions of Ethereum, they observed that the DApps could be stuck in an uncertain state while transactions are pending in a blockchain system. This observation suggests that maybe blockchains should support some built-in transaction-abort options for DApps. The authors finally presented techniques that can alleviate the availability limitations of Ethereum and Bitcoin blockchains.

In public blockchains, the system clients join the blockchain network basically through a third-party peer. Thus, the reliability of the selected blockchain peer is critical to the security of clients in terms of both resource-efficiency and monetary issues. To enable clients evaluate and choose the reliable blockchain peers, Zheng et al. [16] proposed a hybrid reliability prediction model for blockchains named H-BRP, which is able to predict the reliability of blockchain peers by extracting their reliability parameters.

1.3.2   Scalability-Improving Solutions

One of the critical bottlenecks of today's blockchain systems is the scalability. For example, the throughput of a blockchain is not scalable when the network size grows. To address this dilemma, a number of scalability approaches have been proposed. In this part, we conduct an overview of the most recent solutions with respect to Sharding techniques, interoperability among multiple blockchains, and other solutions. We summarize this subsection in Table 1.3.

Table 1.3 Latest scalability solutions to improving the performance of blockchains

Emphasis	Ref.	Recognition	Methodology
Solutions to sharding blockchains	[1]	Elastico	Authors proposed a new distributed agreement protocol for the permission-less blockchains, called Elastico, which is viewed as the first secure candidate for a sharding protocol towards the open public blockchains.
	[9]	Monoxide	The proposed Monoxide enables the system to handle transactions through a number of independent zones. This scheme is essentially following the principle of sharding mechanism.
	[17]	Rapidchain	Authors proposed a new sharding-based protocol for public blockchains that achieves non-linearly increase of intra-committee communications with the number of committee members.
	[18]	SharPer	Authors proposed a permissioned blockchain system named *SharPer*, which adopts sharding techniques to improve scalability of cross-shard transactions.
	[19]	D-GAS	Authors proposed a dynamic load balancing mechanism for Ethereum shards, i.e., D-GAS. It reallocates Tx accounts by their gas consumption on each shard.
	[20]	NRSS	Authors proposed a node-rating based new Sharding scheme, i.e., NRSS, for blockchains, aiming to improve the throughput of committees.
	[21]	OptChain	Authors proposed a new sharding paradigm, called OptChain, mainly used for optimizing the placement of transactions into shards.

(continued)

Table 1.3 (continued)

Emphasis	Ref.	Recognition	Methodology
	[22]	Sharding-based scaling system	Authors proposed an efficient shard-formation protocol that assigns nodes into shards securely, and a distributed transaction protocol that can guard against malicious Byzantine fault coordinators.
	[23]	SSChain	Authors proposed a non-reshuffling structure called SSChain, which supports both transaction sharding and state sharding while eliminating huge data-migration across shards.
	[24]	Eumonia	Authors proposed Eumonia, which is a permissionless parallel-chain protocol for realizing a global ordering of blocks.
	[25]	Vulnerability of Sybil attacks	Authors systematically analyzed the vulnerability of Sybil attacks in protocol Elastico.
	[26]	n/2 BFT Sharding approach	Authors proposed a new blockchain sharding approach that can tolerate up to 1/2 of the Byzantine nodes within a shard.
	[27]	CycLedger	Authors proposed a protocol CycLedger to pave a way towards scalability, security and incentive for sharding blockchains.
Interoperability of multiple-chain systems	[28]	Interoperability architecture	Authors proposed a novel interoperability architecture that supports the cross-chain cooperations among multiple blockchains, and a novel Monitor Multiplexing Reading (MMR) method for the passive cross-chain communications.
	[29]	HyperService	Authors proposed a programming platform that provides interoperability and programmability over multiple heterogeneous blockchains.

[30]	Protocol *Move*	Authors proposed a programming model for smart-contract developers to create DApps that can interoperate and scale in a multiple-chain environment.
[31]	Cross-cryptocurrency TX protocol	Authors proposed a decentralized cryptocurrency exchange protocol enabling cross-cryptocurrency transactions based on smart contracts deployed on Ethereum.
[32]	Cross-chain comm.	Authors conducted a systematic classification of cross-chain communication protocols.

1.3.2.1 Solutions to Sharding Blockchains

Bitcoin's transaction throughput does not scale well. The solutions that use classical Byzantine consensus protocols do not work in an open environment like cryptocurrencies. To solve the above problems, Luu et al. [1] proposed a new distributed agreement protocol for the permission-less blockchains, called *Elastico*, which is viewed as the first secure candidate for a sharding protocol towards the open public blockchains that tolerate a constant fraction of byzantine-fault network nodes. The key idea in Elastico is to partition the network into smaller committees, each of which processes a disjoint set of transactions or a *shard*. The number of committees grows linearly in the total computational power of the network. Using Elastico, the blockchain's transaction throughput increases almost linearly with the computational power of the network.

Some early-stage sharding blockchain protocols (e.g., Elastico) improve the scalability by enforcing multiple groups of committees work in parallel. However, this manner still requires a large amount of communication for verifying every transaction linearly increasing with the number of nodes within a committee. Thus, the benefit of sharding policy was not fully employed. As an improved solution, Zamani et al. [17] proposed a Byzantine-resilient sharding-based protocol, namely Rapidchain, for permissionless blockchains. Taking the advantage of block pipelining, RapidChain improves the throughput by using a sound intra-committee consensus. The authors also developed an efficient cross-shard verification method to avoid the broadcast messages flooding in the holistic network.

To enforce the throughput scaling with the network size, Gao et al. [33] proposed a scalable blockchain protocol, which leverages both sharding and Proof-of-Stake consensus techniques. Their experiments were performed in an Amazon EC2-based simulation network. Although the results showed that the throughput of the proposed protocol increases following the network size, the performance was still not so high, for example, the maximum throughput was 36 transactions per second and the transaction latency was around 27 seconds.

Aiming to improve the efficiency of cross-shard transactions, Amiri et al. [18] proposed a permissioned blockchain system named *SharPer*, which is strive for the scalability of blockchains by dividing and reallocating different data shards to various network clusters. The major contributions of the proposed SharPer include the related algorithm and protocol associated to such SharPer model. In the Amiri previous work, they have already proposed a permissioned blockchain, upon which the authors extended it by introducing a consensus protocol in the processing of both intra-shard and cross-shard transactions. Finally, SharPer was devised by adopting sharding techniques. One of the important contributions is that SharPer can be used in the networks where there are a high percentage of non-faulty nodes. Furthermore, SharPer also contributes a flattened consensus protocol w.r.t the order of cross-shard transactions among all involved clusters.

Considering that the Ethereum places each group of transactions on a shard by their account addresses, the workloads and complexity of transactions in shards are apparently unbalanced. This manner further damages the network throughput.

To address this uneven problem, Kim et al. [19] proposed D-GAS, which is a dynamic load balancing mechanism for Ethereum shards. Using such D-GAS, the transaction workloads of accounts on each shard can be reallocated according to their gas consumption. The target is to maximize the throughput of those transactions. The evaluation results showed that the proposed D-GAS achieved at most a 12% superiority of transaction throughput and a 74% lower transaction latency comparing with other existing techniques.

The random sharding strategy causes imbalanced performance gaps among different committees in a blockchain network. Those gaps yield a bottleneck of transaction throughput. Thus, Wang et al. [20] proposed a new sharding policy for blockchains named NRSS, which exploits node rating to assess network nodes according to their performance of transaction verifications. After such evaluation, all network nodes will be reallocated to different committees aiming at filling the previous imbalanced performance gaps. Through the experiments conducted on a local blockchain system, the results showed that NRSS improves throughput by around 32% under sharding techniques.

Sharding has been proposed to mainly improve the scalability and the throughput performance of blockchains. A good sharding policy should minimize the cross-shard communications as much as possible. A classic design of sharding is the *Transactions Sharding*. However, such Transactions Sharding exploits the *random sharding* policy, which leads to a dilemma that most transactions are cross-shard. To this end, Nguyen et al. [21] proposed a new sharding paradigm differing from the random sharding, called OptChain, which can minimize the number of cross-shard transactions. The authors achieved their goal through the following two aspects. First they designed two metrics, named T2S-score (Transaction-to-Shard) and L2S-score (Latency-to-Shard), respectively. T2S-score aims to measure how likely a transaction should be placed into a shard, while L2S-score is used to measure the confirmation latency when placing a transaction into a shard. Next, they utilized a well-known PageRank analysis to calculate T2S-score and proposed a mathematical model to estimate L2S-score. Finally, how does the proposed OptChain place transactions into shards based on the combination of T2S and L2S scores? In brief, they introduced another metric composed of both T2S and L2S, called *temporal fitness* score. For a given transaction u and a shard S_i, OptChain figures the temporal fitness score for the pair $\langle u, S_i \rangle$. Then, OptChain just puts transaction u into the shard that is with the highest temporal fitness score.

Similar to [21], Dang et al. [22] proposed a new shard-formation protocol, in which the nodes of different shards are re-assigned into different committees to reach a certain safety degree. In addition, they also proposed a coordination protocol to handle the cross-shard transactions towards guarding against the Byzantine-fault malicious coordinators. The experiment results showed that the throughput achieves a few thousands of TPS in both a local cluster with 100 nodes and a large-scale Google cloud platform testbed.

Considering that the reshuffling operations lead to huge data migration in the sharding-based protocols, Chen et al. [23] devised a non-reshuffling structure called SSChain. Such new sharding-based protocol can avoid the overhead of data migration while enabling both transaction sharding and state sharding. Their evaluation results showed that SSChain achieves at least 6500 TPS in a network with 1800 nodes and no periodical data-migration needed.

Multiple chains can help increase the throughput of the blockchain. However, one issue under multiple-chain system must be solved. That is, the logical ordering of blocks generated should be guaranteed, because the correct logical order is critical to the confirmation of transactions. To this end, Niu et al. [24] proposed Eumonia, which is a permissionless parallel-chain protocol towards a global ordering of blocks. The authors implemented Eunomia by exploiting a fine-grained UTXO sharding model, in which the conflicted transactions can be well handled, and such protocol is proved as Simple Payment Verification (SPV) friendly.

Although the sharding techniques have received much interests recently, it should be noticed that the committee organization is easily to attract Sybil attacks, in which a malicious node can compromise the consensus by creating multiple dummy committee members in the vote phase of the consensus protocol. To address such Sybil attacks, Rajab et al. [25] systematically formulated a model and performed an analysis w.r.t the vulnerability of Sybil attacks in the pioneer sharding protocol Elastico [1]. The authors found that the blockchain nodes that have high hash-computing power are capable to manipulate Elastico protocol using a large number of Sybil IDs. The other two conditions of Sybil attacks were derived and evaluated by numerical simulations.

The traditional Sharding blockchain protocols can only endure up to 1/3 Byzantine-fault nodes within a shard. This weak BFT feature makes the number of nodes inside a shard cannot be small to ensure the shard functions securely. To improve the sustainability of blockchain sharding, Xu et al. [26] proposed a new BFT sharding approach that can tolerate at most 1/2 Byzantine-fault nodes existing inside a shard. This approach benefits the throughput of decentralized databases.

Although the existing sharding-based protocols, e.g., Elastico, OminiLedger and RapaidChain, have gained a lot of attention, they still have some drawbacks. For example, the mutual connections among all honest nodes require a big amount of communication resources. Furthermore, there is no an incentive mechanism driven nodes to participate in sharding protocol actively. To solve those problems, Zhang et al. [27] proposed *CycLedger*, which is a protocol designed for the sharding-based distributed ledger towards scalability, reliable security, and incentives. Such the proposed CycLedger is able to select a leader and a subset of nodes for each committee that handle the intra-shard consensus and the synchronization with other committees. A semi-commitment strategy and a recovery processing scheme were also proposed to deal with system crashing. In addition, the authors also proposed a reputation-based incentive policy to encourage nodes behaving honestly.

1.3.2.2 Multiple-Chain and Cross-Chain: Interoperability Amongst Multiple Blockchains

The interoperability of blockchains plays a significant role for the cross-chain transactions. Such interoperability mainly includes the effective communications and data exchange amongst multiple blockchains, as shown in Fig. 1.1. A lot of theoretical and practical issues of this direction need urgent solutions. Some representative studies are reviewed as follows.

To enable rich functionalities and capabilities for the future blockchain ecosystems, Jin et al. [28] proposed a novel interoperability architecture that supports the cross-chain cooperation among multiple blockchains, such as bitcoin and Ethereum. The authors classified the interoperability of multiple-chain ecosystems into passive and active modes, which are shown in Fig. 1.2. Then, the authors introduced a particular method, called Monitor Multiplexing Reading (MMR), dedicated to the passive cross-chain communications.

Following the widespread adoption of smart contracts, the roles of blockchains have been upgraded from token exchanges into programmable state machines. Thus,

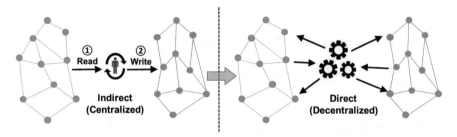

Fig. 1.1 The illustration of interoperability across blockchains [28]. The left figure demonstrates the indirect way of interoperability that requires a centralized third party. The right figure demonstrates the direct way of interoperability without the presence of any third party

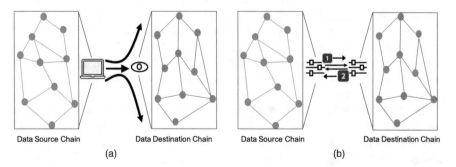

Fig. 1.2 The interoperability of blockchains [28]. Passive mode is shown in the left figure, in which the source chain is monitored by the destination chain instead of actively sending information to the destination chain as shown in the right figure. (**a**) Passive mode. (**b**) Active mode

the blockchain interoperability must evolve accordingly. To help realize such new type of interoperability among multiple heterogeneous blockchains, Liu et al. [29] proposed HyperService, which includes two major components, i.e., a programming framework allowing developers to create cross-chain applications; and a universal interoperability protocol towards secure implementation of DApps on blockchains. The authors implemented a 35,000-line prototype to prove the practicality of HyperService. Using the prototype, the end-to-end delays of cross-chain DApps, and the aggregated platform throughput can be measured conveniently.

In an ecosystem that consists of multiple blockchains, interoperability among those difference blockchains is an essential issue. To help the smart-contract developers build DApps, Fynn et al. [30] proposed a practical *Move* protocol that works for multiple blockchains. The basic idea of such protocol is to support a move operation enabling to move objects and smart contracts from one blockchain to another. Recently, to enable cross-cryptocurrency transactions, Tian et al. [31] proposed a decentralized cryptocurrency exchange strategy implemented on Ethereum through smart contracts. Additionally, a great number of studies of cross-chain communications are included in [32], in which readers can find a systematic classification of cross-chain communication protocols.

1.3.3 New Protocols and Infrastructures

This subsection is summarized in Table 1.4.

1.3.3.1 New Protocols for Blockchains

David et al. [34] proposed a provably secure PoS protocol named *Ouroboros Praos*, which particularly exploits forward secure digital signatures and a verifiable random function such that the proposed Ouroboros Praos can endure any corruption towards any participants from an adversary in a given message delivery delay.

In blockchain systems, a node only connects to a small number of neighbor nodes. Mutual communications are achieved by gossip-like P2P messages. Based on such P2P gossip communications, Buchman et al. [35] proposed a new protocol named Tendermint, which serves as a new termination mechanism for simplifying BFT consensus protocol.

In Monoxide proposed by Wang and Wang [9], the authors have devised a novel proof-of-work scheme, named *Chu-ko-nu mining*. This new proof protocol encourages a miner to create multiple blocks in different zones simultaneously with a single PoW solving effort. This mechanism makes the effective mining power in each zone is almost equal to the level of the total physical mining power in the entire network. Thus, Chu-ko-nu mining increases the attack threshold for each zone to 50%. Furthermore, Chu-ko-nu mining can improve the energy consumption spent

Table 1.4 New protocols and infrastructures to improving the performance of blockchains

Emphasis	Ref.	Recognition	Methodology
New protocols	[34]	Ouroboros praos	Authors proposed a new secure proof-of-stake protocol named *Ouroboros Praos*, which is proved secure in the semi-synchronous adversarial setting.
	[35]	Tendermint	Authors proposed a new BFT consensus protocol for the wide area network organized by the gossip-based P2P network under adversarial conditions.
	[9]	Chu-ko-nu mining	Authors proposed a novel proof-of-work scheme, named *Chu-ko-nu mining*, which incentivizes miners to create multiple blocks in different zones with only a single PoW mining.
	[36]	Proof-of-trust (PoT)	Authors proposed a novel proof-of-trust consensus for the online services of crowdsourcing.
New infrastructures and architectures	[37]	StreamChain	Authors proposed to shift the block-based distributed ledgers to a new paradigm of *stream transaction processing* to achieve a low end-to-end latencies without much affecting throughput.
	[38]	CAPER: cross-app trans. handling	Authors proposed a permissioned blockchain named CAPER that can well manage both the internal and the cross-application transactions for distributed applications.
	[39]	Optimal mining for miners	Authors proposed an edge computing-based blockchain network architecture, aiming to allocate optimal computational resources for miners.
	[40]	AxeChain: useful mining	Authors proposed a new framework for practical PoW blockchains called AxeChain, which can spend computing power of blockchains to solve arbitrary practical problems submitted by system clients.
	[41]	Non-linear blockchain system	Authors explored three major metrics of blockchains, and devised a non-linear blockchain system.

on mining new blocks because a lot of more blocks can be produced in each round of normal PoW mining.

The online services of crowdsourcing face a challenge to find a suitable consensus protocol. By leveraging the advantages of the blockchain such as the traceability of service contracts, Zou et al. [36] proposed a new consensus protocol, named *Proof-of-Trust* (PoT) consensus, for crowdsourcing and the general online service industries. Basically, such PoT consensus protocol leverages a trust management of all service participants, and it works as a hybrid blockchain architecture in which a consortium blockchain integrates with a public service network.

1.3.3.2   New Infrastructures and Architectures for Blockchains

Conventionally, block-based data structure is adopted by permissionless blockchain systems as blocks can efficiently amortize the cost of cryptography. However, the benefits of blocks are saturated in today's permissioned blockchains since the block-processing introduces large batching latencies. To the distributed ledgers that are neither geo-distributed nor Pow-required, István et al. [37] proposed to shift the traditional block-based data structure into the paradigm of *stream-like transaction processing*. The premier advantage of such paradigm shift is to largely shrink the end-to-end latencies for permissioned blockchains. The authors developed a prototype of their concept based on Hyperledger Fabric. The results showed that the end-to-end latencies achieved sub-10 ms and the throughput was close to 1500 TPS.

Permissioned blockchains have a number of limitations, such as poor performance, privacy leaking, and inefficient cross-application transaction handling mechanism. To address those issues, Amiri et al. [38] proposed CAPER, which a permissioned blockchain that can well deal with the cross-application transactions for distributed applications. In particular, CAPER constructs its blockchain ledger using DAG and handles the cross-application transactions by adopting three specific consensus protocols, i.e., a global consensus using a separate set of orders, a hierarchical consensus protocol, and a *one-level* consensus protocol. Then, Chang et al. [39] proposed an edge computing-based blockchain architecture, in which edge-computing providers supply computational resources for blockchain miners. The authors then formulated a two-phase stackelberg game for the proposed architecture, aiming to find the Stackelberg equilibrium of the theoretical optimal mining scheme. Next, Zheng et al. [40] proposed a new infrastructure for practical PoW blockchains called AxeChain, which aims to exploit the precious computing power of miners to solve arbitrary practical problems submitted by system users. The authors also analyzed the trade-off between energy consumption and security guarantees of such AxeChain. This study opens up a new direction for pursing high energy efficiency of meaningful PoW protocols.

With the non-linear (e.g., graphical) structure adopted by blockchain networks, researchers are becoming interested in the performance improvement brought by new data structures. To find insights under such non-linear blockchain systems,

Chen et al. [41] performed a systematic analysis by taking three critical metrics into account, i.e., *full verification*, *scalability*, and *finality-duration*. The authors revealed that it is impossible to achieve a blockchain that enables those three metrics at the same time. Any blockchain designers must consider the trade-off among such three properties.

1.4   Various Modelings and Techniques for Better Understanding Blockchains

We summarize various analytical models for blockchain networks in Tables 1.5 and 1.6.

1.4.1   Graph-Based Theories

The graphs are widely used in blockchain networks. For example, Merkel Tree has been adopted by Bitcoin, and several blockchain protocols, such as Ghost [42], Phantom [43], and Conflux [44], constructed their blocks using the directed acyclic graph (DAG) technique. Different from those generalized graph structures, we review the most recent studies that exploit the graph theories for better understanding blockchains in this part.

Since the transactions in blockchains are easily structured into graphs, the graph theories and graph-based data mining techniques are viewed as good tools to discover the interesting findings beyond the graphs of blockchain networks. Some representative recent studies are reviewed as follows.

Leveraging the techniques of graph analysis, Chen et al. [45] characterized three major activities on Ethereum, i.e., money transfer, the creation of smart contracts, and the invocation of smart contracts. The major contribution is that it performed the first systematic investigation and proposed new approaches based on cross-graph analysis, which can address two security issues existing in Ethereum: attack forensics and anomaly detection. Particularly, w.r.t the graph theory, the authors mainly concentrated on the following two aspects:

1. *Graph Construction*: They identified four types of transactions that are not related to money transfer, smart contract creation, or smart contract invocation.
2. *Graph Analysis*: Then, they divided the remaining transactions into three groups according to the activities they triggered, i.e., money flow graph (MFG), smart contract creation graph (CCG) and contract invocation graph (CIG).

Via this manner, the authors delivered many useful insights of transactions that are helpful to address the security issues of Ethereum.

Table 1.5 Various modelings, techniques and theories for better understanding blockchains

Category	Emphasis	Ref.	Metrics	Methodology and implications
Graph-based theoriess	Transactions mining	[45]	Cross-graph analysis of Ethereum	Via graph analysis, authors extracted three major activities, i.e., money transfer, smart contracts creation, and smart contracts invocation.
		[49]	Features of transaction graphs	Proposed an extendable and computationally efficient method for graph representation learning on Blockchains.
		[50]	Market manipulation patterns	Authors exploited the graph-based data-mining approach to reveal the market manipulation evidence of Bitcoin.
		[53]	Clustering coefficient, assortativity of TX graph	Authors exploited the graph-based analysis to reveal the abnormal transactions of EOSIO.
	Token networks	[51]	Token-transfer distributions	Authors studied the token networks through analyzing smart contracts of Ethereum blockchain based on graph analysis.
		[46, 47]	Extreme chainlet activity	Authors proposed graph-based analysis models for assessing the financial investment risk of Bitcoin.

Stochastic modelings	Blockchain network analysis	[54]	Block completion rates, and the probability of a successful adversarial attack	Authors derived stochastic models to capture critical blockchain properties, and to evaluate the impact of blockchain propagation latency on key performance metrics. This study provides us useful insights of design issues of blockchain networks.
	Stability analysis	[55]	Time to consistency, cycle length, consistency fraction, age of information	Authors proposed a network model which can identify the stochastic stability of blockchain systems.
	Failure probability analysis	[56–58]	Failure probability of a committee, sums of upper-bounded hypergeometric and binomial distributions for each epoch	Authors proposed a probabilistic model to derive the security analysis under Sharding blockchain protocols. This study can tell how to keep the failure probability smaller than a defined threshold for a specific sharding protocol.
Queueing theories	Mining procedure and block-generation	[59, 60]	The average number of TX in the arrival queue and in a block, and average confirmation time of TX	Authors developed a Markovian batch-service queueing system to express the mining process and the generation of new blocks in miners pool.
	Block-confirmation time	[61]	The residual lifetime of a block till the next block is confirmed	Authors proposed a theoretical framework to deeply understand the transaction confirmation time, by integrating the queueing theory and machine learning techniques.
	Synchronization process of Bitcoin network	[62]	Stationary queue-length distribution	Authors proposed an infinite-server model with random fluid limit for Bitcoin network.

(continued)

Table 1.5 (continued)

Category	Emphasis	Ref.	Metrics	Methodology and implications
	Mining resources allocation	[63]	Mining resource for miners, queueing stability	Authors proposed a Lyapunov optimization-based queueing analytical model to study the allocation of mining resources for the PoW-based blockchain networks.
	Blockchain's theoretical working principles	[64]	number of TX per block, mining interval of each block, memory pool size, waiting time, number of unconfirmed TX	Authors proposed a queueing theory-based model to have a better understanding the theoretical working principle of blockchain networks.

Table 1.6 Various analytics models for better understanding blockchain networks

Emphasis	Ref.	Metrics	Methodology and implications
Applicability of blockchains	[65]	Public verifiability, transparency, privacy, integrity, redundancy, and trust anchor	Authors proposed the first structured analytical methodology that can help decide whether a particular application system indeed needs a blockchain, either a permissioned or permissionless, as its technical solution.
	[66]	Scalability, efficiency and privacy issues in cloud for blockchains	Authors proposes a novel upper bound privacy leakage based approach to identify intermediate data sets partitioned and distributed in cloud for encryption. This approach can significantly improve the scalability and efficiency of data processing for privacy preserving in cloud.
Exploration of ethereum transactions	[67]	Temporal information and the multiplicity features of Ethereum transactions	Authors proposed an analytical model based on the multiplex network theory for understanding Ethereum transactions.
	[68]	Pending time of Ethereum transactions	Authors conducted a characterization study of the Ethereum by focusing on the pending time, and attempted to find the correlation between pending time and fee-related parameters of Ethereum.
Modeling the competition over multiple miners	[69]	Competing mining resources of miners of a cryptocurrency blockchain	Authors exploited the Game Theory to find a Nash equilibria while peers are competing mining resources.
A neat bound of consistency latency	[70]	Consistency of a PoW blockchain	Authors derived a neat bound of mining latencies that helps understand the consistency of Nakamoto's blockchain consensus in asynchronous networks.

(continued)

Table 1.6 (continued)

Emphasis	Ref.	Metrics	Methodology and implications
Network connectivity	[71]	Consensus security	Authors proposed an analytical model to evaluate the impact of network connectivity on the consensus security of PoW blockchain under different adversary models.
How ethereum responds to sharding	[72]	Balance among shards, number of TX that would involve multiple shards, the amount of data relocated across shards	Authors studied how sharding impact Ethereum by firstly modeling Ethereum through graph modeling, and then assessing the three metrics mentioned when partitioning the graph.
Required properties of sharding protocols	[73]	Consistency and scalability	Authors proposed an analytical model to evaluate whether a protocol for sharded distributed ledgers fulfills necessary properties.
Vulnerability by forking attacks	[74]	Hashrate power, net cost of an attack	Authors proposed fine-grained vulnerability analytical model of blockchain networks incurred by intentional forking attacks taking the advantages of large deviation theory.
Counterattack to double-spend attacks	[3]	Robustness parameter, vulnerability probability	Authors studied how to defense and even counterattack the double-spend attacks in PoW blockchains.
Limitations of PBFT-based blockchains	[75]	Performance of blockchain applications, Persistence, Possibility of forks	Authors studied and identified several misalignments between the requirements of permissioned blockchains and the classic BFT protocols.
Unified analysis of different PoX consensus schemes	[76]	Resource sensitivity, system convergence, and resource Fairness	Authors proposed a new Markov model to unify the analysis of the steady-state for weighted resource distribution of different PoX-based Blockchains.

Similarly, by processing Bitcoin transaction history, Akcora et al. [46] and Dixon et al. [47] modeled the transfer network into an extreme transaction graph. Through the analysis of chainlet activities [48] in the constructed graph, they proposed to use GARCH-based forecasting models to identify the financial risk of Bitcoin market for cryptocurrency users.

An emerging research direction associated with blockchain-based cryptocurrencies is to understand the network dynamics behind graphs of those blockchains, such as the transaction graph. This is because people are wondering what the connection between the price of a cryptocurrency and the dynamics of the overlying transaction graph is. To answer such a question, Abay et al. [49] proposed Chainnet, which is a computationally lightweight method to learning the graph features of blockchains. The authors also disclosed several insightful findings. For example, it is the topological feature of transaction graph that impacts the prediction of Bitcoin price dynamics, rather than the degree distribution of the transaction graph.

Furthermore, utilizing the Mt. Gox transaction history, Chen et al. [50] also exploited the graph-based data-mining approach to dig the market manipulation of Bitcoin. The authors constructed three graphs, i.e., extreme high graph (EHG), extreme low graph (ELG), and normal graph (NMG), based on the initial processing of transaction dataset. Then, they discovered many correlations between market manipulation patterns and the price of Bitcoin.

On the other direction, based on *address graphs*, Victor et al. [51] studied the ERC20 token networks through analyzing smart contracts of Ethereum blockchain. Different from other graph-based approaches, the authors focused on their attention on the address graphs, i.e., token networks. With all network addresses, each token network is viewed as an overlay graph of the entire Ethereum network addresses. Similar to [45], the authors presented the relationship between transactions by exploiting graph-based analysis, in which the arrows can denote the invoking functions between transactions and smart contracts, and the token transfers between transactions as well. The findings presented by this study help us have a well understanding of token networks in terms of time-varying characteristics, such as the usage patterns of the blockchain system. An interesting finding is that around 90% of all transfers stem from the top 1000 token contracts. That is to say, only less than 10% of token recipients have transferred their tokens. This finding is contrary to the viewpoint proposed by Somin et al. [52], where Somin et al. showed that the full transfers seem to obey a power-law distribution. However, the study [51] indicated that those transfers in token networks likely do not follow a power law. The authors attributed such the observations to the following three possible reasons: (1) most of the token users don't have incentives to transfer their tokens. Instead, they just simply hold tokens; (2) the majority of inactive tokens are treated as something like unwanted spam; (3) a small portion, i.e., approximately 8%, of users intended to sell their tokens to a market exchange.

Recently, Zhao et al. [53] explored the account creation, account vote, money transfer and contract authorization activities of early-stage EOSIO transactions through graph-based metric analysis. Their study revealed abnormal transactions like voting gangs and frauds.

1.4.2 Stochastic Modelings

The latencies of block transfer and processing are generally existing in blockchain networks since the large number of miner nodes are geographically distributed. Such delays increase the probability of forking and the vulnerability to malicious attacks. Thus, it is critical to know how would the network dynamics caused by the block propagation latencies and the fluctuation of hashing power of miners impact the blockchain performance such as block generation rate. To find the connection between those factors, Papadis et al. [54] developed stochastic models to derive the blockchain evolution in a wide-area network. Their results showed us practical insights for the design issues of blockchains, for example, how to change the difficulty of mining in the PoW consensus while guaranteeing an expected block generation rate or an immunity level of adversarial attacks. The authors then performed analytical studies and simulations to evaluate the accuracy of their models. This stochastic analysis opens up a door for us to have a deeper understanding of dynamics in a blockchain network.

Towards the stability and scalability of blockchain systems, Gopalan et al. [55] also proposed a stochastic model for a blockchain system. During their modeling, a structural asymptotic property called *one-endedness* was identified. The authors also proved that a blockchain system is one-ended if it is stochastically stable. The upper and lower bounds of the stability region were also studied. The authors found that the stability bounds are closely related to the conductance of the P2P blockchain network. Those findings are very insightful such that researchers can assess the scalability of blockchain systems deployed on large-scale P2P networks.

Although Sharding protocol is viewed as a very promising solution to solving the scalability of blockchains and adopted by multiple well-known blockchains such as RapidChain [17], OmniLedger [2], and Monoxide [9], the failure probability for a committee under Sharding protocol is still unknown. To fill this gap, Hafid et al. [56–58] proposed a stochastic model to capture the security analysis under Sharding-based blockchains using a probabilistic approach. With the proposed mathematical model, the upper bound of the failure probability was derived for a committee. In particular, three probability inequalities were used in their model, i.e., Chebyshev, Hoeffding, and Chvátal. The authors claim that the proposed stochastic model can be used to analyze the security of any Sharding-based protocol.

1.4.3 Queueing Theories for Blockchain Systems

In blockchain networks, several stages of mining processing and the generation of new blocks can be formulated as queueing systems, such as the transaction-arrival queue, the transaction-confirmation queue, and the block-verification queue. Thus, a growing number of studies are exploiting the queueing theory to disclose the mining and consensus mechanisms of blockchains. Some recent representative works are reviewed as follows.

To develop a queueing theory of blockchain systems, Li et al. [59, 60] devised a batch-service queueing system to describe the mining and the creating of new blocks in miners' pool. For the blockchain queueing system, the authors exploited the type GI/M/1 continuous-time Markov process. Then, they derived the stable condition and the stationary probability matrix of the queueing system utilizing the matrix-geometric techniques.

Then, viewing that the confirmation delay of Bitcoin transactions are larger than conventional credit card systems, Ricci et al. [61] proposed a theoretical framework integrating the queueing theory and machine learning techniques to have a deep understanding towards the transaction confirmation time. The reason the authors chose the queueing theory for their study is that a queueing model is suitable to see insights into how the different blockchain parameters affect the transaction latencies. Their measurement results showed that the Bitcoin users experience a delay that is slightly larger than the residual time of a block confirmation.

Frolkova et al. [62] formulated the synchronization process of Bitcoin network as an infinite-server model. The authors derived a closed-form for the model that can be used to capture the queue stationary distribution. Furthermore, they also proposed a random-style fluid limit under service latencies.

On the other hand, to evaluate and optimize the performance of blockchain-based systems, Memon et al. [64] proposed a simulation model by exploiting queueing theory. In the proposed model, the authors constructed an M/M/1 queue for the memory pool, and an M/M/c queue for the mining pool, respectively. This model can capture multiple critical statistics metrics of blockchain networks, such as the number of transactions every new block, the mining interval of a block, transactions throughput, and the waiting time in memory pool, etc.

Next, Fang et al. [63] proposed a queueing analytical model to allocate mining resources for the general PoW-based blockchain networks. The authors formulated the queueing model using Lyapunov optimization techniques. Based on such stochastic theory, a dynamic allocation algorithm was designed to find a trade-off between mining energy and queueing delay. Different from the aforementioned work [59–61], the proposed Lyapunov-based algorithm does not need to make any statistical assumptions on the arrivals and services.

1.4.4 Analytical Models for Blockchain Networks

This subsection is summarized in Table 1.6.

For the people considering whether a blockchain system is needed for his/her business, a notable fact is that blockchain is not always applicable to all real-life use cases. To help analyze whether blockchain is appropriate to a specific application scenario, Wust et al. [65] provided the first structured analytical methodology and applied it to analyzing three representative scenarios, i.e., supply chain management, interbank payments, and decentralized autonomous organizations. The other article [66] proposes a novel upper bound privacy leakage based approach to identify intermediate data sets partitioned and distributed in cloud for encryption. This approach can significantly improve the scalability and efficiency of data processing for privacy preserving in cloud. This study provides insights of scalability, efficiency and privacy issues in cloud for blockchain.

Although Ethereum has gained much popularity since its debut in 2014, the systematically analysis of Ethereum transactions still suffers from insufficient explorations. Therefore, Lin et al. [67] proposed to model the transactions using the techniques of multiplex network. The authors then devised several random-walk strategies for graph representation of the transactions network. This study could help us better understand the temporal data and the multiplicity features of Ethereum transactions.

To better understand the network features of an Ethereum transaction, Sousa et al. [68] focused on the pending time, which is defined as the latency counting from the time a transaction is observed to the time this transaction is packed into the blockchain. The authors tried to find the correlations between such pending time with the fee-related parameters such as gas and gas price. Surprisingly, their data-driven empirical analysis results showed that the correlation between those two factors has no clear clue. This finding is counterintuitive.

To achieve a consensus about the state of blockchains, miners have to compete with each other by invoking a certain proof mechanism, say PoW. Such competition among miners is the key module to public blockchains such as Bitcoin. To model the competition over multiple miners of a cryptocurrency blockchain, Altman et al. [69] exploited the Game Theory to find a Nash equilibria while peers are competing mining resources. The proposed approach help researchers well understand such competition. However, the authors also mentioned that they didn't study the punishment and cooperation between miners over the repeated games. Those open topics will be very interesting for future studies.

Besides competitions among individual miners, there are also competitions among mining pools. Malicious pools can pull off DDoS attacks to overload the victim pools' manager with invalid share submissions. The delay in verifying extra share submissions potentially impairs the hash power of the victim pool and thus undermines the potential reward for pool miners. Knowing that the chance of getting a reward is smaller, miners in the victim pools would migrate to another mining pools, which would further weaken the victim pools. To better understand this kind of competition, Wu et al. [77] proposed a stochastic game-theoretic model in a two-mining-pool case. The authors used Q-learning algorithm to find the Nash equilibrium and maximize the long-term payoffs. The experiment showed that the smaller mining pool is more likely to attack the larger one. Also, mining pools tend to adopt lower attack level when the DDoS attack cost increases.

To ensure the consistency of PoW blockchain in an asynchronous network, Zhao et al. [70] performed an analysis and derived a neat bound around $\frac{2\mu}{\ln(\mu/\nu)}$, where $\mu + \nu = 1$, with μ and ν denoting the fraction of computation power dominated by the honest and adversarial miners, respectively. Such a neat bound of mining latencies is helpful to us to well understand the consistency of Nakamoto's blockchain consensus in asynchronous networks.

Bitcoin's consensus security is built upon the assumption of honest-majority. Under this assumption, the blockchain system is thought secure only if the majority of miners are honest while voting towards a global consensus. Recent researches believe that network connectivity, the forks of a blockchain, and the strategy of mining are major factors that impact the security of consensus in Bitcoin blockchain. To provide pioneering concrete modelings and analysis, Xiao et al. [71] proposed an analytical model to evaluate the network connectivity on the consensus security of PoW blockchains. To validate the effectiveness of the proposed analytical model, the authors applied it to two adversary scenarios, i.e., *honest-but-potentially-colluding*, and *selfish mining* models.

Although Sharding is viewed as a prevalent technique for improving the scalability to blockchain systems, several essential questions are: what we can expect from and what price is required to pay for introducing Sharding technique to Ethereum? To answer those questions, Fynn et al. [72] studied how sharding works for Ethereum by modeling Ethereum into a graph. Via partitioning the graph, they evaluated the trade-off between the edge-cut and balance. Several practical insights have been disclosed. For example, three major components, e..g, computation, storage and bandwidth, are playing a critical role when partitioning Ethereum; A good design of incentives is also necessary for adopting sharding mechanism.

As mentioned multiple times, sharding technique is viewed as a promising solution to improving the scalability of blockchains. However, the properties of a sharded blockchain under a fully adaptive adversary are still unknown. To this end, Avarikioti et al. [73] defined the *consistency* and *scalability* for sharded blockchain protocol. The limitations of security and efficiency of sharding protocols were also derived. Then, they analyzed these two properties on the context of multiple popular sharding-based protocols such as *OmniLedger*, *RapidChain*, *Elastico*, and *Monoxide*. Several interesting conclusions have been drawn. For example, the authors thought that Elastico and Momoxide failed to guarantee the balance between consistency and scalability properties, while OmniLedger and RapidChain fulfill all requirements of a robust sharded blockchain protocol.

Forking attacks has become the normal threats faced by the blockchain market. The related existing studies mainly focus on the detection of such attacks through transactions. However, this manner cannot prevent the forking attacks from happening. To resist the forking attacks, Wang et al. [74] studied the fine-grained vulnerability of blockchain networks caused by intentional forks using the large deviation theory. This study can help set the robustness parameters for a blockchain network since the vulnerability analysis provides the correlation between robust level and the vulnerability probability. In detail, the authors found that it is much more cost-efficient to set the robust level parameters than to spend the computational capability used to lower the attack probability.

The existing economic analysis [78] reported that the attacks towards PoW mining-based blockchain systems can be cheap under a specific condition when renting sufficient hashrate capability. Moroz et al. [3] studied how to defense the double-spend attacks in an interesting reverse direction. The authors found that the counterattack of victims can lead to a classic game-theoretic *War of Attrition* model. This study showed us the double-spend attacks on some PoW-based blockchains are actually cheap. However, the defense or even counterattack to such double-spend attacks is possible when victims are owning the same capacity as the attacker.

Although BFT protocols have attracted a lot of attention, there are still a number of fundamental limitations unaddressed while running blockchain applications based on the classical BFT protocols. Those limitations include one related to low performance issues, and two correlated to the gaps between the state machine replication and blockchain models (i.e., the lack of strong persistence guarantees and the occurrence of forks). To identify those limitations, Bessani et al. [75] first studied them using a digital coin blockchain App called SmartCoin, and a popular BFT replication library called BFT-SMART, then they discussed how to tackle these limitations in a protocol-agnostic manner. The authors also implemented an experimental platform of permissioned blockchain, namely SmartChain. Their evaluation results showed that SmartChain can address the limitations aforementioned and significantly improve the performance of a blockchain application.

The Nakamoto protocol is designed to solve the Byzantine Generals Problem for permissionless Blockchains. However, a general analytical model is still missing for capturing the steady-state profit of each miner against the competitors. To this end, Yu et al. [76] studied the weighted resource distribution of proof-based consensus engines, referred to as Proof-of-X (PoX), in large-scale networks. The proposed Markov model attempts to unify the analysis of different PoX mechanisms considering three new unified metrics, i.e., resource sensitivity, system convergence, and resource fairness.

1.4.5 Data Analytics for Cryptocurrency Blockchains

This subsection is summarized in Table 1.7.

1.4.5.1 Market Risks Detection

As aforementioned, Akcora et al. [46] proposed a graph-based predictive model to forecast the investment risk of Bitcoin market. On the other hand, with the tremendously increasing price of cryptocurrencies such as Bitcoin, hackers are imminently utilizing any available computational resources to participate in mining. Thus, any web users face severe risks from the cryptocurrency-hungry hackers. For example, the *cryptojacking* attacks [87] have raised growing attention. In such type of attacks, a mining script is embedded secretly by a hacker without notice from the user. When the script is loaded, the mining will begin in the background of the system and a large portion of hardware resources are requisitioned for mining. To tackle the cryptojacking attacks, Tahir et al. [79] proposed a machine learning-based

Table 1.7 Data analytics for better understanding cryptocurrency blockchains

Emphasis	Ref.	Metrics	Methodology and implications
Cryptojacking detection	[79]	Hardware performance counters	Authors proposed a machine learning-based solution to prevent cryptojacking attacks.
	[80]	Various system resource utilization	Authors proposed an in-browser cryptojacking detection approach (CapJack), based on the latest CapsNet.
Market-manipulation mining	[50]	Various graph characteristics of transaction graph	Authors proposed a mining approach using the exchanges collected from the transaction networks.
Predicting volatility of Bitcoin price	[47]	Various graph characteristics of extreme chainlets	Authors proposed a graph-based analytic model to predict the intraday financial risk of Bitcoin market.
Money-laundering detection	[81]	Various graph characteristics of transaction graph	Authors exploited machine learning models to detect potential money laundering activities from Bitcoin transactions.
Ponzi-scheme detection	[82]	Factors that affect scam persistence	Authors analyzed the demand and supply perspectives of Ponzi schemes on Bitcoin ecosystem.
	[83, 84]	Account and code features of smart contracts	Authors detected Ponzi schemes for Ethereum based on data mining and machine learning approaches.
Design problem of cryptoeconomic systems	[85]	Price of XNS token, Subsidy of App developers	Authors presented a practical evidence-based example to show how data science and stochastic modeling can be applied to designing cryptoeconomic blockchains.
Pricing mining hardware	[86]	Miner revenue, ASIC value	Authors studied the correlation between the price of mining hardware (ASIC) and the value volatility of underlying cryptocurrency.

solution, which leverages the hardware performance counters as the critical features and can achieve a high accuracy while classifying the parasitic miners. The authors also built their approach into a browser extension towards the widespread real-time protection for web users. Similarly, Ning et al. [80] proposed *CapJack*, which is an in-browser cryptojacking detector based on deep capsule network (CapsNet) [88] technology.

As mentioned previously, to detect potential manipulation of Bitcoin market, Chen et al. [50] proposed a graph-based mining to study the evidence from the transaction network built based on Mt. Gox transaction history. The findings of this study suggests that the cryptocurrency market requires regulation.

To predict drastic price fluctuation of Bitcoin, Dixon et al. [47] studied the impact of extreme transaction graph (ETG) activity on the intraday dynamics of the Bitcoin prices. The authors utilized chainlets [48] (sub graphs of transaction graph) for developing their predictive models.

1.4.5.2 Ponzi Schemes Detection

Ponzi scheme [89], as a classic scam, is taking advantages of mainstream blockchains such as Ethereum. Data mining technologies [90] are widely used for detecting Ponzi schemes. For example, several representative studies are reviewed as follows. Vasek et al. [82] analyzed the demand and supply Ponzi schemes on Bitcoin ecosystem. The authors were interested at the reasons that make those Ponzi frauds succeeded in attracting victims, and the lifetime of those scams. To detect such Ponzi schemes towards a healthier blockchain economic environment, Chen et al. [83, 84] proposed a machine learning-based classification model by exploiting data mining on smart contracts of Ethereum. The experimental results showed that the proposed detection model can even identify Ponzi schemes at the very beginning when those schemes are created.

1.4.5.3 Money-Laundering Detection

Although Bitcoin has received enormous attention, it is also criticized for being carried out criminal financial activities such as ponzi schemes and money laundering. For example, Seo et al. [91] mentioned that money laundering conducted in the underground market can be detected using the Bitcoin mixing services. However, they didn't present an essential anti-money laundering strategy. In contrast, utilizing a transaction dataset collected over three years, Hu et al. [81] performed in-depth detection for discovering money laundering activities on Bitcoin network. To identify the money laundering transactions from the regular ones, the authors proposed four types of classifiers based on the graph features appeared on the transaction graph, i.e., immediate neighbors, deepwalk embeddings, node2vec embeddings and decision tree-based.

1.4.5.4 Portrait of Cryptoeconomic Systems

It is not common to introduce data science and stochastic simulation modelings into the design problem of cryptoeconomic engineering. Laskowski et al. [85] presented a practical evidence-based example to show how this manner can be applied to designing cryptoeconomic blockchains.

Yaish et al. [86] discussed the relationship between the cryptocurrency mining and the market price of the special hardware (ASICs) that supports PoW consensus. The authors showed that the decreasing volatility of Bitcoin's price has a counterintuitive negative impact to the value of mining hardware. This is because miners are not financially incentivized to participate in mining, when Bitcoin becomes widely adopted thus making its volatility decrease. This study also revealed that a mining hardware ASIC could be imitated by bonds and underlying cryptocurrencies such as bitcoins.

1.5 Useful Measurements, Datasets and Experiment Tools for Blockchains

Measurements are summarized in Table 1.8, and datasets are summarized in Table 1.9.

1.5.1 Performance Measurements and Datasets for Blockchains

Although diverse blockchains have been proposed in recent years, very few efforts have been devoted to measuring the performance of different blockchain systems. Thus, this part reviews the representative studies of performance measurements for blockchains. The measurement metrics include throughput, security, scalability, etc.

As a pioneer work in this direction, Gervais et al. [92] proposed a quantitative framework, using which they studied the security and performance of several PoW blockchains, such as Bitcoin, Litecoin, Dogecoin and Ethereum. The authors focused on multiple metrics of security model, e.g., stale block rate, mining power, mining costs, the number of block confirmations, propagation ability, and the impact of eclipse attacks. They also conducted extensive simulations for the four blockchains aforementioned with respect to the impact of block interval, the impact of block size, and throughput. Via the evaluation of network parameters about the security of PoW blockchains, researchers can compare the security performance objectively, and thus help them appropriately make optimal adversarial strategies and the security provisions of PoW blockchains.

Table 1.8 Various performance measurements of blockchains

Ref.	Target blockchains	Metrics	Implementation/experiments/methodology
[9]	General mining-based blockchains, e.g., bitcoin and ethereum	TPS, the overheads of cross-zone transactions, the confirmation latency of transactions, etc.	Monoxide was implemented utilizing C++. RocksDB was used to store blocks and TX. The real-world testing system was deployed on a distributed configuration consisting of 1200 virtual machines, with each owning 8 cores and 32 GB memory. In total 48,000 blockchain nodes were exploited in the testbed.
[10]	General blockchains	Throughput and confirmation latency, scalability under different number of clients, forking rate, and resource utilization (CPU, network bandwidth)	Prism testbed is deployed on Amazon EC2 instances each with 16 CPU cores, 16 GB RAM, 400 GB NVMe SSD, and a 10 Gbps network interface. In total 100 Prism client instances are connected into a topology in random 4-regular graph.
[11]	Ethereum	TX throughput, the makespan of transaction latency	The proposed GARET algorithm was measured to outperform existing techniques by up to 12% in TX throughput, and decrease the makespan of TX latency by about 74% under various conditions in sharding ethereum.
[92]	Bitcoin, litecoin, dogecoin, ethereum	Block interval, block size, and throughput	Proposed a quantitative framework, using which they studied the security and performance of several PoW blockchains. Via the evaluation of network parameters about the security of PoW blockchains, researchers can make trade-offs between the security provisions and performance objectively.
[93]	Hyperledger fabric	Execution time, latency, throughput, scalability vs the number of blockchain nodes	Presented the performance measurement and analysis towards Hyperledger Fabric version 0.6 and version 1.0.

Ref.	Target blockchains	Metrics	Implementation/experiments/methodology
[94]	Ethereum, parity, CITA, hyperledger fabric	TPS, average response delay, transactions per CPU, TX per memory second, TX per disk I/O and TX per network data	Proposed a scalable framework for monitoring the real-time performance blockchain systems. The authors evaluated four popular blockchain systems, i.e., ethereum, parity, CITA and hyperledger fabric.
[95]	Private blockchains	Throughput and latency, scalability, fault tolerance and security, and other micro measurements, e.g., CPU utilization, network utilization, etc.	The authors proposed blockbench for measuring and analyzing the multiple performance of private blockchain systems. Through this blockbench, the authors revealed several insightful bottlenecks and trade-offs while designing the software of blockchains.
[96]	Ethereum	Network size and geographic distribution of ethereum network nodes	Proposed a network monitoring tool named NodeFinder, which is designed to find the unusual network properties of ethereum network nodes in the underlying P2P network perspective.
[97]	Bitcoin network	TPS, network latency, number of forks, and mining rewards	The authors proposed a local Bitcoin network simulator to study the performance of bitcoin under different network conditions including various topologies, network latencies, packet loss rates, and mining difficulties.

Table 1.9 Blockchain dataset frameworks and evaluation tools

Recognition	Target	Ref.	Utilization
XBlock-ETH	Ethereum	[102]	Authors released a new open-source dataset framework for analysis of ethereum, i.e., XBlock-ETH, which includes multiple types of ethereum datasets such as transactions, smart contracts and tokens.
XBlock-EOS	EOS	[103]	Authors proposed a new dataset framework dedicated to EOSIO, named XBlock-EOS, to show how to perform comprehensive statistics and exploration of EOSIO datasets.
BlockSci	General blockchains	[104]	Authors proposed an open-source software platform, named BlockSci, for the analysis of blockchains.
Blockbench	General blockchains	[95]	Authors proposed a benchmarking framework for measuring the data processing capability and performance of different layers of a blockchain system.
NodeFinder	Etheruem nodes	[96]	Authors proposed a measuring tool named NodeFinder, to investigate the opaque network characteristics of ethereum network nodes.
Network simulator for bitcoin	Bitcoin	[97]	Authors proposed a configurable network simulator for the performance measurements of bitcoin using lightweight virtualization technologies.

Nasir et al. [93] conducted performance measurements and discussion of two versions of Hyperledger Fabric. The authors focused on the metrics including execution time, transaction latency, throughput and the scalability versus the number of nodes in blockchain platforms. Several useful insights have been revealed for the two versions of Hyperledger Fabric. As already mentioned previously in [9], the authors evaluated their proposed Monoxide w.r.t the metrics including the scalability of TPS as the number of network zones increase, the overhead of both cross-zone transactions and storage size, the confirmation latency of transactions, and the orphan rate of blocks. In [10], the authors performed rich measurements for their proposed new blockchain protocol Prism under limited network bandwidth and CPU resources. The performance evaluated includes the distribution of block propagation delays, the relationship between block size and mining rate, block size versus assembly time, the expected time to reach consensus on block hash, the expected time to reach consensus on blocks, etc.

Later, Zheng et al. [94] proposed a scalable framework for monitoring the real-time performance blockchain systems. This work has evaluated four popular blockchain systems, i.e., Ethereum, Parity [98], Cryptape Inter-enterprise Trust Automation (CITA) [99] and Hyperledger Fabric [100], in terms of several metrics including *transactions per second*, *average response delay*, *transactions per CPU*, *transactions per memory second*, *transactions per disk I/O* and *transactions per network data*. Such comprehensive performance evaluation results offered us rich viewpoints on the 4 popular blockchain systems. Their experimental logs and technique report [101] can be accessed from http://xblock.pro. Recently, Zheng et al. [102] extended their work and released a new open-source dataset framework, called XBlock-ETH, for the data-driven analysis of Ethereum. XBlock-ETH contains multiple types of Ethereum data such as transactions, smart contracts and tokens. Thus, researchers can extract and explore the data of Ethereum using XBlock-ETH. The authors first collected and cleaned the most recent on-chain dataset from Ethereum. Then, they presented how to perform basic exploration of these datasets to make them best. Like their previous work, those datasets and processing codes can be found from the webpage *xblock.pro* aforementioned. In the other similar work [103] of the same team, authors proposed another new dataset framework dedicated to EOSIO, named XBlock-EOS, which also includes multiple types of rich on-chain/off-chain datasets such as transactions, blocks, smart contracts, internal/external EOS transfer events, tokens, accounts and resource management. To show how to utilize the proposed framework, the authors presented comprehensive statistics and explorations using those datasets, for example, blockchain analysis, smart contract analysis, and cryptocurrency analysis. Finally, this study also discussed future directions of XBlock-EOS in the topics including: (i) data analysis based on off-chain data to provide off-chain user behavior for blockchain developers, (ii) exploring new features of EOSIO data that are different from those of Ethereum, and (iii) conducting a joint analysis of EOSIO with other blockchains.

1.5.2 Useful Evaluation Tools for Blockchains

Kalodner et al. [104] proposed BlockSci, which is designed as an open-source software platform for blockchain analysis. Under the architecture of BlockSci, the raw blockchain data is parsed to produce the core blockchain data including transaction graph, indexes and scripts, which are then provided to the analysis library. Together with the auxiliary data including P2P data, price data and user tags, a client can either directly query or read through a Jupyter notebook interface.

To evaluate the performance of private blockchains, Dinh et al. [95] proposed a benchmarking framework, named Blockbench, which can measure the data processing capability and the performance of various layers of a blockchain system. Using such Blockbench, the authors then performed detailed measurements and analysis of three blockchains, i.e., Ethereum, Parity and Hyperledger. The results disclosed some useful experiences of those three blockchain systems. For example, today's blockchains are not scalable w.r.t data processing workloads, and several bottlenecks should be considered while designing different layers of blockchain in the software engineering perspective.

Ethereum has received enormous attention on the mining challenges, the analytics of smart contracts, and the management of block mining. However, not so many efforts have been spent on the information dissemination in the perspective of P2P networks. To fill this gap, Kim et al. [96] proposed a measuring tool named NodeFinder, which aims to discover the opaque network properties of Ethereum network nodes. Through a three-month long data collection on the P2P network, the authors analyzed and found several unprecedented differences of Ethereum network comparing with other popular P2P networks like BitTorrent, Bitcoin and Gnutella in terms of network size and geographic distribution.

Recently, by exploiting lightweight virtualization technologies, Alsahan et al. [97] developed a configurable network simulator for the performance measurements of Bitcoin. The proposed simulator allows users to configure diverse network conditions, such as blockchain network topology, link delays, and mining difficulties, to emulate the real-world operation environment. Using this simulator, experiments can be performed to measure Bitcoin network under various network conditions. It also supports conducting the tests of security attacks and point of failure simulations. The authors also made this simulator open-source on Github.

1.6 Open Issues and Future Directions

In this section, we envision the open issues and promising directions for future studies.

1.6.1 Performance-Improving Issues

1.6.1.1 Scalability Issues

Scalability is still a severe challenge for most of the blockchain systems. For example, the PBFT consensus protocols issue a $O(n^2)$ number of messages, where n is the number of participants. The large number of messages makes the scalability unrealistic. Therefore, new distributed practical byzantine protocols and theoretical modelings of scalability solutions, such as sidechain, subchain, off-chain, sharding technique, DAG, and even chain-less proposals, are in an urgent need for scalable blockchains.

1.6.1.2 Resilient Mechanisms for Sharding Technique

The sharding technique includes three typical categories, i.e., transaction sharding, network sharding, and state sharding. Via the extensive review on the existing studies of sharding techniques, we found that the resilient mechanisms for sharding blockchains are still missing. Particularly to the state sharding, once the failures occurred on blockchain nodes, how to ensure the correct recovery of the real-time running states in the failed blockchain node(s) is critical to the resilience and robustness of the blockchain.

1.6.1.3 Cross-Shard Performance

Although a number of committee-based sharding protocols [2, 9, 17, 105] have been proposed, those protocols can only endure at most 1/3 adversaries. Thus, more robust byzantine agreement protocols need to be devised. Furthermore, all the sharding-based protocols incur additional cross-shard traffics and latencies because of the cross-shard transactions. Therefore, the cross-shard performance in terms of throughput, latency and other metrics, has to be well guaranteed in future studies. On the other hand, the cross-shard transactions are inherent for the cross-shard protocols. Thus, the pros and cons of such the correlation between different shards are worthy investigating using certain modelings and theories such as graph-based analysis.

1.6.1.4 Cross-Chain Transaction Accelerating Mechanisms

On cross-chain operations, [28] is essentially a pioneer step towards practical blockchain-based ecosystems. Following this roadmap paved by Jin et al. [28], we are exciting to anticipate the subsequent related investigations will appear soon in the near future. For example, although the inter-chain transaction experiments achieve an initial success, we believe that the secure cross-chain transaction accelerating mechanisms are still on the way. In addition, further improvements are still required for the interoperability among multiple blockchains, such as decentralized load balancing smart contracts for sharded blockchains.

1.6.1.5   Ordering Blocks for Multiple-Chain Protocols

Although multiple-chain techniques can improve the throughput by exploiting the parallel mining of multiple chain instances, how to construct and manage the blocks in all chains in a globally consistent order is still a challenge to the multiple-chain based scalability protocols and solutions.

1.6.1.6   Hardware-Assisted Accelerating Solutions for Blockchain Networks

To improve the performance of blockchains, for example, to reduce the latency of transaction confirmation, some advanced network technologies, such as RDMA (Remote Direct Memory Access) and high-speed network cards, can be exploited in accelerating the data-access among miners in blockchain networks.

1.6.1.7   Performance Optimization in Different Blockchain Network Layers

The blockchain network is built over the P2P networks, which include several typical layers, such as mac layer, routing layer, network layer, and application layer. The BFT-based protocols are essentially working for the network layer. In fact, performance improvements can be achieved by proposing various protocols, algorithms, and theoretical models for other layers of the blockchain network.

1.6.1.8   Blockchain-Assisted BigData Networks

Although big data and blockchain have several performance metrics that are contrary to each other. For example, big data is a centralized management technology with an emphasize on the privacy-preserving oriented to diverse computing environments. The data processed by big data technology should ensure nonredundancy and unstructured architecture in a large-scale computing network. In contrast, blockchain technology builds on a decentralized, transparent and immutable architecture, in which data type is simple, data is structured and highly redundant. Furthermore, the performance of blockchains require scalability and the off-chain computing paradigm. Thus, how to integrate those two technologies together and pursue the mutual benefit for each other is an open issue that is worthy in-depth studies. For example, the potential research topics include how to design a suitable new blockchain architecture for big data technologies, and how to break the isolated data islands using blockchains while guaranteeing the privacy issues of big data.

1.6.2   Issues for Better Understanding Blockchains Further

Although the state-of-the-art studies have reviewed a lot of modelings and theories for better understanding blockchains, more sophisticated approaches and insightful mechanisms are still needed to help researchers gain a new level of perception over the high-performance blockchain systems. Some interesting directions are summarized here for inspiring more subsequent investigations.

- Exploiting more general queueing theories to capture the real-world arrival process of transactions, mining new blocks, and other queueing-related blockchain phases.
- Performing priority-based service policies while dealing with transactions and new blocks, to meet a predefined security or regulation level.
- Developing more general probabilistic models to characterize the correlations among the multiple performance parameters of blockchain systems.

1.6.3   Security Issues of Blockchains

1.6.3.1   Privacy-Preserving for Blockchains

From the previous overview, we observe that most of the existing works under this category are discussing the blockchain-based security and privacy-preserving applications. The fact is that the security and privacy are also the critical issues of the blockchain itself. For example, the privacy of transactions could be hacked by attackers. However, dedicated studies focusing on those issues are still insufficient.

1.6.3.2   Anti-cryptojacking Mechanisms for Malicious Miners

The Cryptojacking Miners are reportedly existing in web browsers according to [79]. This type of malicious codes is commandeering the hardware resources such as computational capability and memory of web users. Thus, the anti-cryptojacking mechanisms and strategies are necessary to develop for protecting normal browser users.

1.6.3.3   Security Issues of Cryptocurrency Blockchains

The security issues of cryptocurrency blockchains, such as double-spend attacks, frauds in smart contracts, have arisen growing attention from both industrial and academic fields. However, little efforts have been committed to the theoretical investigations towards the security issues of cryptocurrency blockchains. For example, the exploration of punishment and cooperation between miners over multiple chains is an interesting topic for cryptocurrency blockchains. Thus, we expect to see broader perspectives of modeling the behaviors of both attackers and counterattackers in the context of monetary blockchain attacks.

1.6.4   Powerful Experimental Platforms for Blockchains

To most of the beginners in the field of the blockchain, they have a problem about lack of powerful simulation/emulation tools for verifying their new ideas or protocols. Therefore, the powerful simulation/emulation platforms that are easy to deploy scalable testbeds for the experiments would be very helpful to the research community.

Tailor-made experiment platforms based on existing blockchain systems are also needed. Building a blockchain system from scratch, or learning from the implementation of existing blockchain systems by reading codes, these are some time-consuming yet not rewarding tasks for researchers. A platform that enable us to tweak a variety of aspects of interest in existing blockchain systems can potentially be very helpful to the research community as well.

1.7   Conclusion

Through investigations, we found that a dedicated survey focusing on the theoretical modelings, analytical models and useful experiment tools for blockchains is still missing. To fill this gap, we then conducted a comprehensive survey of the state-of-the-art on blockchains, particularly in the perspectives of theories, modelings, and measurement/evaluation tools. The taxonomy of each topic presented in this chapter tried to convey the new protocols, ideas, and solutions that can improve the scalability of blockchains, and help people better understand the blockchains in a further level. We believe our work provides a timely guidance on the theoretical insights of blockchains for researchers, engineers, educators, and generalized readers.

Acknowledgments This work was supported in part by the Key-Area Research and Development Program of Guangdong Province (No. 2019B020214006), the National Natural Science Foundation of China (No. 62032025, No. 61902445, No. 61872310), the Fundamental Research Funds for the Central Universities of China (No.19lgpy222), the Guangdong Basic and Applied Basic Research Foundation (No. 2019A1515011798), the Hong Kong RGC Research Impact Fund (RIF) (No. R5060-19, No. R5034-18), General Research Fund (GRF) (No. 152221/19E), and the Collaborative Research Fund (CRF) (No. C5026-18G).

References

1. Luu L, Narayanan V, Zheng C, Baweja K, Gilbert S, Saxena P (2016) A secure sharding protocol for open blockchains. In: Proceedings of the 2016 ACM SIGSAC conference on computer and communications security, pp 17–30
2. Kokoris-Kogias E, Jovanovic P, Gasser L, Gailly N, Syta E, Ford B (2018) Omniledger: a secure, scale-out, decentralized ledger via sharding. In: 2018 IEEE symposium on security and privacy (SP). IEEE, Piscataway, pp 583–598
3. Moroz DJ, Aronoff DJ, Narula N, Parkes DC (2020) Double-spend counterattacks: threat of retaliation in proof-of-work systems
4. Wood G, et al (2014) Ethereum: a secure decentralised generalised transaction ledger. Ethereum project yellow paper 151:1–32
5. Ethereum sharding. https://eth.wiki/sharding/Sharding-FAQs
6. Hyperledger fabric website. https://hyperledger-fabric.readthedocs.io/en/release-1.4/write_first_app.html
7. EOSIO (2020). https://eos.io/
8. Hari A, Kodialam M, Lakshman T (2019) Accel: accelerating the bitcoin blockchain for high-throughput, low-latency applications. In: IEEE conference on computer communications (INFOCOM'19). IEEE, Piscataway, pp 2368–2376
9. Wang J, Wang H (2019) Monoxide: scale out blockchains with asynchronous consensus zones. In: Proceedings of 16th USENIX symposium on networked systems design and implementation (NSDI), pp 95–112
10. Yang L, Bagaria V, Wang G, Alizadeh M, Tse D, Fanti G, Viswanath P (2019) Prism: scaling bitcoin by 10,000 x. arXiv:190911261
11. Woo S, Song J, Kim S, Kim Y, Park S (2020) GARET: improving throughput using gas consumption-aware relocation in ethereum sharding environments. Cluster Comput. 23:2235–2247
12. Perard D, Lacan J, Bachy Y, Detchart J (2018) Erasure code-based low storage blockchain node. In: 2018 IEEE international conference on internet of things (iThings) and IEEE green computing and communications (GreenCom) and IEEE cyber, physical and social computing (CPSCom) and IEEE smart data (SmartData). IEEE, Piscataway, pp 1622–1627
13. Dai X, Xiao J, Yang W, Wang C, Jin H (2019) Jidar: a jigsaw-like data reduction approach without trust assumptions for bitcoin system. In: IEEE 39th international conference on distributed computing systems (ICDCS). IEEE, Piscataway, pp 1317–1326
14. Xu Y, Huang Y (2020) Segment blockchain: a size reduced storage mechanism for blockchain. IEEE Access 8:17434–17441
15. Weber I, Gramoli V, Ponomarev A, Staples M, Holz R, Tran AB, Rimba P (2017) On availability for blockchain-based systems. In: 2017 IEEE 36th symposium on reliable distributed systems (SRDS). IEEE, Piscataway, pp 64–73
16. Zheng P, Zheng Z, Chen L (2019) Selecting reliable blockchain peers via hybrid blockchain reliability prediction. arXiv:191014614
17. Zamani M, Movahedi M, Raykova M (2018) Rapidchain: scaling blockchain via full sharding. In: Proceedings of the 2018 ACM SIGSAC conference on computer and communications security, pp 931–948

18. Amiri MJ, Agrawal D, Abbadi AE (2019) Sharper: sharding permissioned blockchains over network clusters. arXiv:191000765

19. Kim S, Song J, Woo S, Kim Y, Park S (2019) Gas consumption-aware dynamic load balancing in ethereum sharding environments. In: IEEE 4th International Workshops on foundations and applications of self* systems (FAS*W). IEEE, Piscataway, pp 188–193

20. Wang J, Zhou Y, Li X, Xu T, Qiu T (2019) A node rating based sharding scheme for blockchain. In: Proceedings of IEEE 25th international conference on parallel and distributed systems (ICPADS). IEEE, Piscataway, pp 302–309

21. Nguyen LN, Nguyen TD, Dinh TN, Thai MT (2019) Optchain: optimal transactions placement for scalable blockchain sharding. In: Proceedings of IEEE 39th international conference on distributed computing systems (ICDCS), pp 525–535

22. Dang H, Dinh TTA, Loghin D, Chang EC, Lin Q, Ooi BC (2019) Towards scaling blockchain systems via sharding. In: Proceedings of the 2019 international conference on management of data, pp 123–140

23. Chen H, Wang Y (2019) SSChain: a full sharding protocol for public blockchain without data migration overhead. Pervasive Mobile Comput 59:101055

24. Niu J (2019) Eunomia: a permissionless parallel chain protocol based on logical clock. arXiv:190807567

25. Rajab T, Manshaei MH, Dakhilalian M, Jadliwala M, Rahman MA (2020) On the feasibility of sybil attacks in shard-based permissionless blockchains. arXiv:200206531

26. Xu Y, Huang Y (2020) An n/2 byzantine node tolerate blockchain sharding approach. arXiv:200105240

27. Zhang M, Li J, Chen Z, Chen H, Deng X (2020) Cycledger: a scalable and secure parallel protocol for distributed ledger via sharding. arXiv:200106778

28. Jin H, Dai X, Xiao J (2018) Towards a novel architecture for enabling interoperability amongst multiple blockchains. In: 2018 IEEE 38th international conference on distributed computing systems (ICDCS). IEEE, Piscataway, pp 1203–1211

29. Liu Z, Xiang Y, Shi J, Gao P, Wang H, Xiao X, Wen B, Hu YC (2019) Hyperservice: interoperability and programmability across heterogeneous blockchains. In: Proceedings of the 2019 ACM SIGSAC conference on computer and communications security, pp 549–566

30. Fynn E, Bessani A, Pedone F (2020) Smart contracts on the move. arXiv:200405933

31. Tian H, Xue K, Li S, Xu J, Liu J, Zhao J (2020) Enabling cross-chain transactions: a decentralized cryptocurrency exchange protocol. arXiv:200503199

32. Zamyatin A, Al-Bassam M, Zindros D, Kokoris-Kogias E, Moreno-Sanchez P, Kiayias A, Knottenbelt WJ (2019) SoK: communication across distributed ledgers. Tech. Rep., IACR Cryptology ePrint Archive, 2019:1128

33. Gao Y, Kawai S, Nobuhara H (2019) Scalable blockchain protocol based on proof of stake and sharding. J Adv Comput Intell Intell Inf 23(5):856–863. https://doi.org/10.20965/jaciii.2019.p0856

34. David B, Gaži P, Kiayias A, Russell A (2018) Ouroboros praos: an adaptively-secure, semi-synchronous proof-of-stake blockchain. In: Annual international conference on the theory and applications of cryptographic techniques. Springer, Berlin, pp 66–98

35. Buchman E, Kwon J, Milosevic Z (2018) The latest gossip on bft consensus. arXiv:180704938

36. Zou J, Ye B, Qu L, Wang Y, Orgun MA, Li L (2018) A proof-of-trust consensus protocol for enhancing accountability in crowdsourcing services. IEEE Trans Serv Comput 12:429–445

37. István Z, Sorniotti A, Vukolić M (2018) Streamchain: do blockchains need blocks? In: Proceedings of the 2nd workshop on scalable and resilient infrastructures for distributed ledgers, pp 1–6

38. Amiri MJ, Agrawal D, Abbadi AE (2019) Caper: a cross-application permissioned blockchain. Proc VLDB Endowment 12(11):1385–1398

39. Chang Z, Guo W, Guo X, Zhou Z, Ristaniemi T (2020) Incentive mechanism for edge computing-based blockchain. IEEE Trans Ind Inf 16(11):7105–7114. https://doi.org/10.1109/TII.2020.2973248

40. Zheng W, Chen X, Zheng Z, Luo X, Cui J (2020) AxeChain: a secure and decentralized blockchain for solving easily-verifiable problems. arXiv:200313999
41. Chen L, Xu L, Gao Z, Kasichainula K, Shi W (2020) Nonlinear blockchain scalability: a game-theoretic perspective. arXiv:200108231
42. Sompolinsky Y, Zohar A (2015) Secure high-rate transaction processing in bitcoin. In: International Conference on Financial Cryptography and Data Security. Springer, Berlin, pp 507–527
43. Sompolinsky Y, Zohar A (2018) Phantom: a scalable blockdag protocol. IACR Cryptology ePrint Archive 2018:104
44. Li C, Li P, Zhou D, Xu W, Long F, Yao A (2018) Scaling nakamoto consensus to thousands of transactions per second. arXiv:180503870
45. Chen T, Zhu Y, Li Z, Chen J, Li X, Luo X, Lin X, Zhange X (2018) Understanding ethereum via graph analysis. In: Proceedings of IEEE conference on computer communications (INFOCOM). IEEE, Piscataway, pp 1484–1492
46. Akcora CG, Dixon MF, Gel YR, Kantarcioglu M (2018) Bitcoin risk modeling with blockchain graphs. Econ Lett 173:138–142
47. Dixon MF, Akcora CG, Gel YR, Kantarcioglu M (2019) Blockchain analytics for intraday financial risk modeling. Digit Financ 1(1–4):67–89
48. Akcora CG, Dey AK, Gel YR, Kantarcioglu M (2018) Forecasting bitcoin price with graph chainlets. In: Pacific-Asia conference on knowledge discovery and data mining. Springer, Berlin, pp 765–776
49. Abay NC, Akcora CG, Gel YR, Kantarcioglu M, Islambekov UD, Tian Y, Thuraisingham B (2019) Chainnet: learning on blockchain graphs with topological features. In: IEEE international conference on data mining (ICDM), pp 946–951
50. Chen W, Wu J, Zheng Z, Chen C, Zhou Y (2019) Market manipulation of bitcoin: evidence from mining the Mt. Gox transaction network. In: Proceedings of IEEE conference on computer communications (INFOCOM), pp 964–972
51. Victor F, Lüders BK (2019) Measuring ethereum-based ERC20 token networks. In: International conference on financial cryptography and data security. Springer, Berlin, pp 113–129
52. Somin S, Gordon G, Altshuler Y (2018) Network analysis of ERC20 tokens trading on ethereum blockchain. In: International conference on complex systems. Springer, Berlin, pp 439–450
53. Zhao Y, Liu J, Han Q, Zheng W, Wu J (2020) Exploring eosio via graph characterization. arXiv:200410017
54. Papadis N, Borst S, Walid A, Grissa M, Tassiulas L (2018) Stochastic models and wide-area network measurements for blockchain design and analysis. In: Proceedings of IEEE conference on computer communications (INFOCOM). IEEE, Piscataway, pp 2546–2554
55. Gopalan A, Sankararaman A, Walid A, Vishwanath S (2020) Stability and scalability of blockchain systems. arXiv:200202567
56. Hafid A, Hafid AS, Samih M (2019) A probabilistic security analysis of sharding-based blockchain protocols. In: Proceedings of international congress on blockchain and applications (Blockchain), pp 55–60
57. Hafid A, Hafid AS, Samih M (2019) A methodology for a probabilistic security analysis of sharding-based blockchain protocols. In: Proceedings of international congress on blockchain and applications. Springer, Berlin, pp 101–109
58. Hafid A, Hafid AS, Samih M (2019) New mathematical model to analyze security of sharding-based blockchain protocols. IEEE Access 7:185447–185457
59. Li QL, Ma JY, Chang YX (2018) Blockchain queue theory. In: International conference on computational social networks. Springer, Berlin, pp 25–40
60. Li QL, Ma JY, Chang YX, Ma FQ, Yu HB (2019) Markov processes in blockchain systems. Comput Soc Netw 6(1):1–28
61. Ricci S, Ferreira E, Menasche DS, Ziviani A, Souza JE, Vieira AB (2019) Learning blockchain delays: a queueing theory approach. ACM SIGMETRICS Perform Eval Rev 46(3):122–125

62. Frolkova M, Mandjes M (2019) A bitcoin-inspired infinite-server model with a random fluid limit. Stoch Models 35(1):1–32
63. Fang M, Liu J (2020) Toward low-cost and stable blockchain networks. arXiv:200208027
64. Memon RA, Li JP, Ahmed J (2019) Simulation model for blockchain systems using queuing theory. Electronics 8(2):234
65. Wüst K, Gervais A (2018) Do you need a blockchain? In: 2018 crypto valley conference on blockchain technology (CVCBT). IEEE, Piscataway, pp 45–54
66. Zhang X, Liu C, Nepal S, Pandey S, Chen J (2013) A privacy leakage upper bound constraint-based approach for cost-effective privacy preserving of intermediate data sets in cloud. IEEE Trans Parallel Distrib Syst 24(6):1192–1202
67. Lin D, Wu J, Yuan Q, Zheng Z (2020) Modeling and understanding ethereum transaction records via a complex network approach. IEEE Trans Circuits Syst II: Exp Briefs 67(11):2737–2741
68. Sousa JEA, Oliveira V, Valadares J, Vieira AB, Bernardino HS, Dias G (2019) An analysis of the fees and pending time correlation in ethereum. In: Proceedings of LANOMS, IFIP, pp 1–7
69. Altman E, Menasché D, Reiffers A, Datar M, Dhamal S, Touati C, El-Azouzi R (2019) Blockchain competition between miners: a game theoretic perspective. Front Blockchain 2:26
70. Zhao J, Tang J, Li Z, Wang H, Lam KY, Xue k (2020) An analysis of blockchain consistency in asynchronous networks: deriving a neat bound. In: Proceedings of IEEE international conference on distributed computing systems (ICDCS), pp 1–10
71. Xiao Y, Zhang N, Lou W, Hou YT (2020) Modeling the impact of network connectivity on consensus security of proof-of-work blockchain. In: IEEE conference on computer communications (INFOCOM'20), pp 1–9
72. Fynn E, Pedone F (2018) Challenges and pitfalls of partitioning blockchains. In: 2018 48th annual IEEE/IFIP international conference on dependable systems and networks workshops (DSN-W). IEEE, Piscataway, pp 128–133
73. Avarikioti Z, Kokoris-Kogias E, Wattenhofer R (2019) Divide and scale: formalization of distributed ledger sharding protocols. arXiv:191010434
74. Wang S, Wang C, Hu Q (2019) Corking by forking: vulnerability analysis of blockchain. In: Proceedings of IEEE conference on computer communications (INFOCOM). IEEE, Piscataway, pp 829–837
75. Bessani A, Alchieri E, Sousa J, Oliveira A, Pedone F (2020) From byzantine replication to blockchain: consensus is only the beginning. arXiv:200414527
76. Yu G, Zha X, Wang X, Ni W, Yu K, Zhang JA, Liu RP (2020) A unified analytical model for proof-of-x schemes. Comput Secur 96:101934
77. Wu S, Chen Y, Li M, Luo X, Liu Z, Liu L (2020) Survive and thrive: a stochastic game for DDoS attacks in bitcoin mining pools. IEEE/ACM Trans Netw 28(2):874–887
78. Budish E (2018) The economic limits of bitcoin and the blockchain. Tech. Rep., National Bureau of Economic Research
79. Tahir R, Durrani S, Ahmed F, Saeed H, Zaffar F, Ilyas S (2019) The browsers strike back: countering cryptojacking and parasitic miners on the web. In: Proceedings of IEEE conference on computer communications (INFOCOM). IEEE, Piscataway, pp 703–711
80. Ning R, Wang C, Xin C, Li J, Zhu L, Wu H (2019) CapJack: capture in-browser crypto-jacking by deep capsule network through behavioral analysis. In: Proceedings of IEEE conference on computer communications (INFOCOM). IEEE, Piscataway, pp 1873–1881
81. Hu Y, Seneviratne S, Thilakarathna K, Fukuda K, Seneviratne A (2019) Characterizing and detecting money laundering activities on the bitcoin network. arXiv:191212060
82. Vasek M, Moore T (2018) Analyzing the bitcoin ponzi scheme ecosystem. In: International conference on financial cryptography and data security. Springer, Berlin, pp 101–112
83. Chen W, Zheng Z, Cui J, Ngai E, Zheng P, Zhou Y (2018) Detecting ponzi schemes on ethereum: towards healthier blockchain technology. In: Proceedings of the 2018 world wide web conference (WWW), pp 1409–1418

84. Chen W, Zheng Z, Ngai ECH, Zheng P, Zhou Y (2019) Exploiting blockchain data to detect smart ponzi schemes on ethereum. IEEE Access 7:37575–37586
85. Laskowski M, Zargham M, Turesson H, Kim HM, Barlin M, Kabanov D, Dhaliwal E (2020) Evidence based decision making in blockchain economic systems: from theory to practice. arXiv:200103020
86. Yaish A, Zohar A (2020) Pricing ASICs for cryptocurrency mining. arXiv:200211064
87. Eskandari S, Leoutsarakos A, Mursch T, Clark J (2018) A first look at browser-based cryptojacking. In: IEEE European symposium on security and privacy workshops (EuroS&PW). IEEE, Piscataway, pp 58–66
88. Sabour S, Frosst N, Hinton GE (2017) Dynamic routing between capsules. In: Advances in neural information processing systems, pp 3856–3866
89. Bartoletti M, Carta S, Cimoli T, Saia R (2020) Dissecting ponzi schemes on ethereum: identification, analysis, and impact. Future Gener Comput Syst 102:259–277
90. Bartoletti M, Pes B, Serusi S (2018) Data mining for detecting bitcoin ponzi schemes. In: 2018 crypto valley conference on blockchain technology (CVCBT). IEEE, Piscataway, pp 75–84
91. Seo J, Park M, Oh H, Lee K (2018) Money laundering in the bitcoin network: perspective of mixing services. In: Proceedings of IEEE international conference on information and communication technology convergence (ICTC), pp 1403–1405
92. Gervais A, Karame GO, Wüst K, Glykantzis V, Ritzdorf H, Capkun S (2016) On the security and performance of proof of work blockchains. In: Proceedings of the 2016 ACM SIGSAC conference on computer and communications security, pp 3–16
93. Nasir Q, Qasse IA, Abu Talib M, Nassif AB (2018) Performance analysis of hyperledger fabric platforms. Secur Commun Netw
94. Zheng P, Zheng Z, Luo X, Chen X, Liu X (2018) A detailed and real-time performance monitoring framework for blockchain systems. In: Proceedings of IEEE/ACM 40th international conference on software engineering: software engineering in practice track (ICSE-SEIP), pp 134–143
95. Dinh TTA, Wang J, Chen G, Liu R, Ooi BC, Tan KL (2017) Blockbench: a framework for analyzing private blockchains. In: Proceedings of the 2017 ACM international conference on management of data, pp 1085–1100
96. Kim SK, Ma Z, Murali S, Mason J, Miller A, Bailey M (2018) Measuring ethereum network peers. In: Proceedings of the internet measurement conference (IMC'18), pp 91–104
97. Alsahan L, Lasla N, Abdallah MM (2020) Local bitcoin network simulator for performance evaluation using lightweight virtualization. In: Proceedings of IEEE international conference on informatics, IoT, and enabling technologies, pp 1–6
98. Parity documentation. https://paritytech.github.io/wiki
99. Cita technical whitepaper. https://github.com/cryptape/cita
100. Androulaki E, Barger A, Bortnikov V, Cachin C, Christidis K, De Caro A, Enyeart D, Ferris C, Laventman G, Manevich Y, et al (2018) Hyperledger fabric: a distributed operating system for permissioned blockchains. In: Proceedings of the thirteenth Eurosys conference, pp 1–15
101. Xblock (2020) Performance monitoring. http://xblock.pro/performance/
102. Zheng P, Zheng Z, Dai Hn (2019) XBlock-ETH: extracting and exploring blockchain data from etherem. arXiv:191100169
103. Zheng W, Zheng Z, Dai HN, Chen X, Zheng P (2020) XBlock-EOS: extracting and exploring blockchain data from EOSIO. arXiv:200311967
104. Kalodner H, Goldfeder S, Chator A, Möser M, Narayanan A (2017) BlockSci: design and applications of a blockchain analysis platform. arXiv:170902489
105. Miller A, Xia Y, Croman K, Shi E, Song D (2016) The honey badger of BFT protocols. In: Proceedings of the 2016 ACM SIGSAC conference on computer and communications security (CCS), pp 31–42

Chapter 2
Overview to Blockchain Scalability Challenges and Solutions

Qiheng Zhou, Huawei Huang, Zibin Zheng, and Jing Bian

2.1 Overview

The rapid development of blockchain technology has drawn growing attention.When the number of users of blockchain systems increases extensively, the scalability issues of major public-chain [1] platforms (e.g. Bitcoin and Ethereum) have arisen and greatly affected the development of blockchain (Fig. 2.1).

In order to improve the scalability of the blockchain, many companies and research teams have proposed a large number of different solutions. We classify them according to the hierarchical structure of blockchain. In detail, the hierarchical structure mainly includes two layers. Layer1 concentrates on the on-chain design of blockchain including the structure of blocks, consensus algorithm and also the specific structure of the main-chain. On the other hand, Layer2 focuses on off-chain methods, which intends to reduce the burden of the main-chain, such as executing some transactions off-chain and moving some complex computational tasks to an off-chain platform. Although the existing solutions somewhat improve the scalability, it should be noticed that most of these solutions sacrifice the most

Received December 27, 2019, accepted January 12, 2020, date of publication January 17, 2020, date of current version January 27, 2020. Digital Object Identifier https://doi.org/10.1109/ACCESS.2020.2967218

Q. Zhou · J. Bian
School of Computer Science and Engineering, Sun Yat-sen University, Guangzhou, China

National Engineering Research Center of Digital Life, Sun Yat-sen University, Guangzhou, China

H. Huang (✉) · Z. Zheng (✉)
GuangDong Engineering Technology Research Center of Blockchain, Sun Yat-sen University, Guangdong, China
e-mail: huanghw28@mail.sysu.edu.cn; zhzibin@mail.sysu.edu.cn

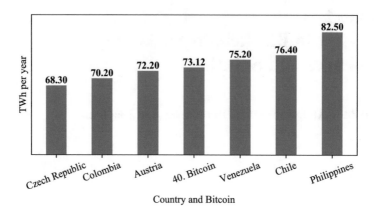

Fig. 2.1 Energy consumption by country and bitcoin: the number above the bar indicates the energy consumption and Bitcoin consumes 73.12 TWh per year, which ranks the 40th among all countries (https://digiconomist.net/bitcoin-energy-consumption)

fundamental property of blockchain, i.e., decentralization, and also bring new security issues.

In this chapter, we intend to provide some concrete facts to briefly explain the performance of several typical blockchains, then present and classify various existing scalability solutions towards blockchain. Finally, we discusse some open issues and future directions to scale blockchain.

2.2   Scalability Issue of Blockchain

With the domination of Bitcoin in cryptocurrency, the scalability issues of blockchain have been exposed, too. Kyle Croman et al. [2] analyzed several key metrics to measure the scalability of Bitcoin, including *maximum throughput, latency, bootstrap time* and *cost per confirmed transaction (CPCT)*. The maximum throughput and latency are the two most important performance metrics that have a significant impact on the user's quality of experience (QoE).

Among all metrics listed above, transaction throughput receives the most attention. It has been reported that Bitcoin's highest transaction throughput is 7 TPS (transaction-per-second) [3] while Visa can achieve more than 4000 TPS [4] Obviously, low throughput of Bitcoin cannot satisfy the large-scale trading scenarios.

In theory, transaction throughput is restrained by the block interval and the block size. A larger block can store more transactions, directly raising throughput, but it also causes an increase in block propagation time. To ensure the current block to be propagated to most peers in the whole network before the next block is generated, which is critical to reducing the probability of *fork*, the block size and the average block interval between two successive blocks should be well configured. In Bitcoin, the block interval is about 10 minutes, and the block size is around 1 MB [5], which limits the number of transactions that can be stored in each block. Thus, to maintain the block propagation time while increasing the block size, the average bandwidth of the whole system that determines the block propagation time becomes a performance bottleneck of the blockchain system.

Another metric, transaction confirmation latency that is the time for a transaction to be confirmed, also has a strong relation with user experience.

Due to the huge volume of Bitcoin transactions nowadays, the limited size of blocks is far from enough to deliver all transactions submitted by nodes. Under such a situation, miners tend to select transactions that are with high transaction fees. As a result, the transactions that are with a low bid have to wait until packaged, which leads to the longer transaction latency [44]. Ethereum, another popular PoW-featured blockchain (in its pre-2.0 version) makes this problem even severe since some popular decentralized applications (DApps) [45] in Ethereum have induced extensive congestion in the entire network. As we can see in Fig. 2.2, the total number of Ethereum transactions waiting to be confirmed in a certain period maintains a high level.

Besides the performance bottleneck of blockchain, we should also consider the capacity problem of blockchain seriously. As the scale of a blockchain growing rapidly, the storage required by all blocks grows accordingly. Therefore, the full nodes, which store all block data of the network, are required large storage capacity for each. Similarly, the Bootstrap time will increases linearly as the blockchain history grows, slowing down the process of new nodes joining into the system. All these restrictions degrade the availability and decentralization of a blockchain, and thus should be examined closely when developing a large-scale blockchain. Nowadays, more block compression methods have been proposed to reduce redundant data of blocks, which is beneficial for easing the capacity problem. At the same time, sharding techniques, partitioning the whole blockchain network

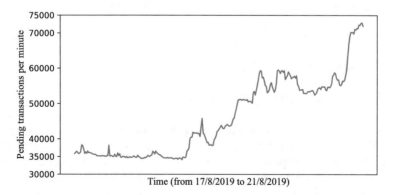

Fig. 2.2 Ethereum pending transactions queue: the number of ethereum pending transactions in a certain period (Etherscan.io)

into different shards, have been researched more detailed to solve the capacity problem of blockchain.

Meanwhile, many concerns have been raised about the energy consumption of Proof-of-work based blockchain systems, such as Bitcoin and Ethereum [46]. Miners in a PoW-featured blockchain are always competing with each other through calculating, which results in a large dissipation of electricity. Figure 2.1 shows the energy consumption of Bitcoin comparing with that of some countries/states, where we can find that the entire Bitcoin network consumes even more energy than many countries, such as Austria and Colombia, and barely ranks the 40th. Although PoW works securely, it's far from green enough to be a sustainable consensus mechanism for future blockchain.

Striving to improve the scalability of blockchains while maintaining security and decentralization, many existing approaches have been proposed by literature. We will review some mainstream solutions in the next section.

2.3   Taxonomy of the Approaches to Solving the Scalability of Blockchain

By Table 2.1, we classify the existing popular solutions of solving the scalability of blockchains into three layers: *Layer1 Layer2*, and *Layer0*.

Layer1 focuses on consensus, network and data structure of blockchain, all of which are executed on-chain. In contrast, Layer2 seeks the opportunity to scale out blockchain by off-chain methods such as off-chain channel [6, 8], side-chain [11, 12] and cross-chain protocols [13, 14]. Besides, we also present a Table 2.2 which shows the data of Transaction Per Second (TPS) and confirmation time of some representative scaling solutions.

In the subsequent parts of this section, we elaborate on these existing state-of-the-art solutions dedicated to improving the scalability of blockchains.

2.3.1   Layer1: On-Chain Solutions

2.3.1.1   Solutions Related to Block Data

As discussed in Section 2.2, the scalability problem has a certain relevance with block size. Obviously, increasing block size enables a block to include more transactions. Block compression can achieve the same effect and also reduce storage overhead. And, some other solutions explore methods to achieve data reduction are also proposed. In this section, we will introduce some approaches focused on these ideas.

Table 2.1 Taxonomy of the scalability solutions in different layers

Layer	Categories	Solutions
Layer2: *non on-chain*	Payment channel	Lightning network [6], DMC [7] Raiden network [8], Sprites [9]
	Side chain	Pegged sidechain [10], plasma [11] liquidity.network [12]
	Cross-chain	Cosmos [13], polkadot [14]
	Off-chain computation	Truebit [15], Arbitrum [16]
Layer1: *on-chain*	Block data	SegWit [17], bitcoin-cash [18] Compact block relay [19], Txilm [20] CUB [21], Jidar [22]
	Consensus	Bitcoin-NG [23], algorand [24] Snow white [25], Ouroboros [26, 27]
	Sharding	Elastico[28], OmniLedger[29] RapidChain[30], Monoxide[31]
	DAG	Inclusive[32], SPECTRE[33] PHANTOM[34], Conflux[35] Dagcoin[36], IOTA[37] Byteball[38], Nano[39]
Layer0	Data propagation	Erlay[40], Kadcast[41] Velocity[42], bloXroute[43]

Table 2.2 Comparsion of Transaction per second (TPS) and confirmation time among different solutions

Project	Technology	TPS (tx/sec)	Confirmation time
Ouroboros [26]	PoS	257.6	2 min
ByzCoin [4]	PBFT	1000	15–20 s
Algorand [24]	Byzantine agreement	875+	22 s
RapidChain [30]	Sharding	7380	8.7 s
Monoxide [31]	Sharding	11,694	13–21 s
Conflux [35]	DAG	6400	4.5–7.4 min

Segregated Witness The Segregated Witness (SegWit) [17] defined in BIP141 [47] is designed to prevent non-intentional Bitcoin transaction malleability and to alleviate blockchain size-limitation that reduces the transaction speed of Bitcoin. It achieves the goals by splitting the transaction into two segments, removing the unlocking signatures from the original transaction hashes, and the new *Witness* structure will contain both the scripts and signatures.

SegWit also defines a new way to calculate the maximum block-size by assigning a weight for each block. The new calculation is shown as follows.

$$BW = 3 \times BS + TS,$$

where BW is new defined Block weight and BS is Base size including the size of the original transaction serialization without any witness-related data. TS stands for Total size, which is the size of transaction serialization described in BIP144 [47] Block weight is limited under 4 MB, and theoretically allowing more transactions can be accommodated in one block, which slightly increases the scalability performance of blockchain.

An additional design of SegWit is to provide convenience for deploying Lightning Networks [6], which will be introduced in the Part(B) of this section.

Bitcoin-Cash In 2017, because of the scalability problem, Bitcoin experienced a hard fork [48] and was split into two blockchain branches, i.e., Bitcoin and Bitcoin-Cash. Bitcoin-Cash has increased its block size to 8 MB, which is much larger than the size of its previous version (only 1 MB in size). After that, Bitcoin-Cash was upgraded further, to expand the block size up to 32 MB. The average block interval of Bitcoin-Cash is still maintained at the original 10 minutes. In theory, the transaction throughput can be greatly increased. This has been verified in the stress test conducted in September 2018.

From the theoretical and practical points of view, improving the block size can scale-out the blockchain capacity directly. However, the infinite expansion enlarges the size of each block, which cannot be transferred easily due to the limitation of intra-blockchain bandwidth. Thus, only increasing the block size is not a sustainable solution. Some other studies [49, 50] also claim that larger blocks may lead to the problem of centralization since individual users in the network are not able to propagate blocks efficiently and also have difficulty in verifying a large number of transactions within a given interval. This will result in that only a centralized organization can act as a full node.

Block Compression To improve the throughput of blockchains, various solutions related to block compression have been proposed (e.g. Compact block relay [19] and Txilm [20]). All these methods share a similar idea that is to reduce some redundant data of a block that has been already stored in the *Mempool* of receivers.

Compact block relay was proposed in BIP152 [19] and altered the data structure of origin blocks in Bitcoin. A compact block contains the header of the block and some short transaction IDs (TXIDs) which will be used for matching transactions that are already available to the receivers.

Figure 2.3 shows the workflow of this protocol. BIP152 provides two modes for block relay. The essential part of the protocol is sending *cmpctblock* messages and receivers dealing with the messages. Node A send a compact block to Node B. The moment Node B receives the block, Node B should calculate TXIDs of the transactions in their Mempool and match each of them with TXIDs stored in the

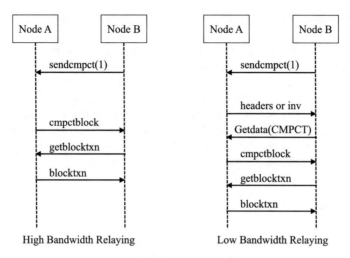

Fig. 2.3 Procedures of two modes of compact block relay

compact block. Then, if all unconfirmed transactions are available to Node *B*, the full block can be reconstructed. Otherwise, Node *B* should send a *getblocktxn* message to require the information of transactions they do not have and reconstruct the block after they receive all the data they need. The main difference between the provided two modes is that, in Low Bandwidth Relaying, the compact blocks are sent only if the receivers make requests.

Txilm is a protocol based on BIP152 [19] that compresses transactions in each block to save the bandwidth of the network. Txilm utilizes a short hash of TXID to represent a transaction, which achieves a greater result on block compression. However, hash collisions are more likely to occur when a short hash is used. Therefore, Txilm optimizes the protocol using sorted transactions based on TXIDs to reduce the probability of hash collision and prevent the system from Collision attack by adding "SALT" (e.g. CRC32-Merkle root) when computing the hash of TXIDs. Based on the protocol, 80 times of data reduction is realized in their simulations and thus increases the throughput of the blockchain.

Some other approaches [51, 52], concerned with data of the block is also proposed in recent years. All existing solutions make some contributions to increasing the transaction throughput of blockchain but demand more optimization to scale the blockchain system.

Storage Scheme Optimization Apart from block compression, there are some other solutions to reduce the storage pressure of each user.

CUB [21] proposes a scheme that assigns different nodes into a *Consensus Unit*. In each unit, each node stores part of the block data. The blocks of the whole chain are assigned to nodes in the unit to minimize the total query cost. They name this process as *block assignment problem* and propose algorithms to solve it, which reduces the storage overhead of each node while ensuring the throughput and latency.

Jidar [22] is a data reduction approach for Bitcoin system. The main idea of Jidar is to allow users only store relevant data they are interested in and thus releases the storage pressure of each node. When a new block is created, each node stores only a small part of the total data of a block, including relevant transactions and Merkle branch. Jidar adopts bloom filter to validate if the input of a transaction has been spent. Besides, if some users want to get all block data of the system, they can ask other nodes for data and cohere all fragments into complete blocks. However, incentive mechanisms are required to support this function.

2.3.1.2 Different Consensus Strategies

We then review different consensus strategies of blockchain and some optimizations proposed to improve the scalability of blockchain.

PoW (Proof of Work) Bitcoin, proposed in 2008, adopted the PoW to achieve consensus in a decentralized network [5]. Under PoW, participants, also called *miners*, need to solve a computational task in order to generate a new block. When the answer is found, the miner broadcasts a relevant message to the network for other miners to verify the new block. If the block is validated, it can be added into the chain and the miner who generates it will be rewarded with tokens such as bitcoins. PoW is a novel consensus and has been exploited by a large number of blockchains. However, since Bitcoin has the risk to suffer from forks, transaction confirmation time is set to around one hour (after 6 blocks being mined). Even worse, the calculation in PoW has led to too much resource dissipation.

Therefore, some other studies [23, 33, 53] were dedicated to improving the original PoW mechanism. For example, Bitcoin-NG [23] is a blockchain protocol based on Nakamoto consensus [5]. It divides time into epochs, and each epoch has a single leader responsible for transaction serialization. In order to support this mechanism, Bitcoin-NG introduces two types of blocks: key block and microblock. The key block, generated by the miners through the PoW mechanism, does not contain transaction data and is only used for the election of the leader. And, the leader is allowed to generate the microblock which contains the packaged transaction data. Thus, transactions can be processed continually until the next leader is elected that significantly reduces transaction confirmation time and improves the scalability. GHOST [53] also builds upon PoW and re-organizes the data structure of Bitcoin to eliminate the security concern of double-spending [54] attacks, spending the same asset more than once, caused by network delay. SPECTRE [33] is a PoW-based protocol that utilizes the structure called direct acyclic graph (DAG) to improve the transaction throughput and reduce the confirmation time of Bitcoin.

PoS (Proof of Stake) PoS is an alternative mechanism that avoids the computational overhead of PoW. Instead of consuming computational resources to get involved in generating blocks, participants in PoS vote leaders by their investment in a blockchain system and thus reduce the confirmation time of transactions. The basic idea of PoS is that nodes with more currencies in the system are less likely to do harm to the system. However, because of the elimination of computational verification, to ensure the security of a PoS protocol is a challenging task. Many secure PoS protocols have been proposed. For example, Ouroboros [26] uses a coin-flipping protocol to elect leaders for the current epoch and seed for the next epoch. Participants in Ouroboros Praos [27] utilize a verifiable random function to generate a random number, which will be used to determine whether a participant can be elected as a leader. Snow-white [25] exploits a random oracle to elect a leader. Furthermore, Ethereum Casper [55] is planned to release in 2020, which is equipped with a PoS protocol and is expected to improve the scalability of Ethereum.

DPoS (Delegated Proof of Stake) DPoS [56] is a new consensus protocol for blockchain and its principle is different from PoS. In DPoS, stakeholders elect a small group of delegates to be responsible for producing as well as validating blocks. DPoS has been adopted as the consensus algorithm for Bitshare [57] and EOS [58] to solve the problem of scalability. This algorithm is divided into two stages. The first stage is the staked voting, in which the nodes holding tokens can vote for the potential block producers, and finally, 21 producers with most votes are selected to create the next block. The idea is to let the token holders in the network vote for producers who can provide great computing power and indirectly vote the malicious nodes. A block is broadcast to other producers to be verified and if more than 15 block producers verify and sign, the block is confirmed. Such voting is continually performed throughout the system to select the producers, but if a selected block producer does not produce a block within 24 hours, it will be replaced by a spare producer. At the same time, the probability of this producer to be selected in the future will be reduced as well because of its previous failures.

In EOS, a block is generated by one producer every three seconds on average, and the average confirmation time for each transaction is about 1.5 seconds. Compared with other mainstream blockchain platforms, EOS can reach an overwhelming million-level TPS. However, its decentralization has been questioned. It is believed that more than 50% of the coins in EOS are occupied by only ten addresses, and less than 1% of EOS addresses hold more than 86% tokens of EOS [59]. The DPoS applied by EOS actually chooses the super node that holds the most resources, resulting in the rights are in the hands of a small number of nodes, which is essentially viewed as a centralized mode.

PBFT (Practical Byzantine Fault Tolerance) PBFT [60] is a replication algorithm that is able to tolerate the Byzantine faults [61], consistency problems caused by unreliable components or nodes in the system, in asynchronous systems and performs more efficiently than early approaches [62–64] . In every view of PBFT, a primary server is selected to be responsible to order messages. When primary receives a client request, a three-phase protocol begins working, including *pre-prepare, prepare, commit* phases. In the *pre-prepare* phase, primary broadcasts the *pre-prepare* messages in an ordered sequence to other replicas. In the *prepare* phase, each server makes a choice to accept the *pre-prepare* message or not. If accepted, the server broadcasts a *prepare* message to all other replicas. When it successfully collect $2f+1$ feedback messages (f indicates the number of faulty nodes), it starts the *commit* phase. Similar to the *prepare* phase, each server broadcasts *commit* messages to others and waits for $2f+1$ feedback messages from other replicas which indicates that a majority of servers agree to accept the client's request and send a reply to the client.

In contrast to PoW, PBFT works without computational tasks. It thus reduces the complexity of consensus to the polynomial level but requires more communication overhead. Some follow-up works build their consensus protocols based on PBFT and make some modifications. For example, Tendermint [65] uses validators with voting power to vote for each round and reach consensus finally. Elastico [28] is a sharding protocol that chooses PBFT as the consensus for each committee of Elastico to agree on a single set of transactions.)

Hybrid Consensus Hybrid Consensus is a protocol that combines some classical consensus protocols. ByzCoin [4] proposes a two-phase protocol based on the idea of Bitcoin-NG [23]. However, it is able to ensure strong consistency by combining PoW and PBFT. In addition, ByzCoin uses a collective signing protocol called Cosi [66] to reduce the cost of the *prepare* and *commit* phases of PBFT and scale it to large consensus groups. Later works such as Hybrid consensus [67], Solidus [68] also propose to combine different protocols with PoW aiming to improve on the throughput and security.

Algorand [24] is a cryptocurrency based on a Byzantine Agreement (BA) protocol. By combining with Verifiable Random Functions [69], users are chosen to become a committee member to participate in the BA and reach consensus on the next set of transactions. To mitigate targeted attacks, the participant will be replaced after sending a message in BA. With all these approaches, Algorand scales to 500,000 users in experiments and achieves high throughput.

Other Consensus Some other new consensus algorithms have been proposed in recent years, including PoA (proof-of-authority) [70], PoC (proof of capacity) [71] and PoP (proof-of-Participation) [72], which make some modifications of the previous consensus to improve the scalability of blockchain.

PoP (Proof of Participation) is a new protocol that implements PoS through the mining mechanism of PoW. PoP selects a list of stakeholders to work out a computational task, which is simpler than that in PoW, to generate a new block. Other stakeholders who did not participate in the mining validate the block and propagate it. Unlike PoS, transaction fees in PoP are only distributed to stakeholders participating in validation and propagation, which thus encourages stakeholders to maintain an online node and sustain the system. PoP includes two layers of security, proof-of-work, and proof-of-stake, that protect the system from security problems (e.g. double-spending) and also consume less energy than the traditional PoW mechanism.

PoC (Proof of Capacity) is a consensus algorithm that utilizes the storage resource (disk space) to mine. Miners in PoC based system stores a list of possible answers before mining. Larger space indicates a higher possibility of generating the next block and getting the reward. PoC is similar to PoW but reduces energy consumption by complex computational tasks.

PoA (Proof of Authority) is a modified form of PoS where a block validator's identity plays the role of stake and relies on a set of selected validators to reach consensus. Since a new block is validated by authorized nodes, a small part of nodes in the network, the speed of validating processes is highly increased. PoA is suitable for permissioned blockchain where nodes' identities are authorized and increases the performance in terms of the TPS.

2.3.1.3   Sharding

Sharding [73] is a traditional technology first proposed in the database field mainly for the optimization of large commercial databases. This method is to divide the data of a large database into a number of fragments, and then store them in separate servers to reduce the pressure of a centralized server, thereby improving the search performance and enlarging the storage capacity of the entire database system.

The basic idea of sharding technology is *divide-and-conquer*. Therefore, applying sharding technology to blockchain is to divide a blockchain network into several smaller networks, each contains a part of nodes, which is called a "shard". Transactions in the network will be processed in different shards, so that each node only needs to process a small part of arriving transactions. Different shards can process transactions in parallel, which can boost the concurrency of transaction processing and verification, thus increasing the throughput of the entire network. While partitioning the whole system into different shards, it is critical to protect the decentralization and security of the system. Several aspects required to particularly take into account: (a) How to reach a consensus in each shard and prevent each shard from suffering some common risks such as 51% vulnerability and Double-spending. (b) How to handle cross-shard transactions quickly while ensuring the consistency of these transactions.

Figure 2.4 shows an example of sharding architecture, where the blockchain network is divided into 3 shards, including three procedures:

- At first, peers in the network are assigned to different shards. In order to reduce the storage overhead of each node, *State sharding* enables nodes in each shard only need to store the state of their own shard.
- *Transaction sharding* distributes transactions to different shards and allow transactions to be processed in parallel. Apart from transactions executed within a single shard, cross-shard transactions are very common in a large system. Therefore, the system should be equipped with some protocols to deal with cross-shard transactions carefully and efficiently.

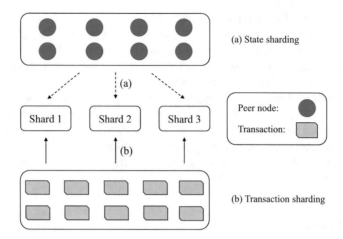

Fig. 2.4 Illustration of sharding. The initial network contains eight nodes (blue circle). After (**a**), nodes are assigned to different shards. (**b**) Transactions are distributed to different shards and be processed in parallel

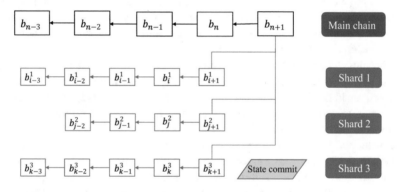

Fig. 2.5 Architecture of the sharding protocol with a main chain

As cross-shard transactions require more communication costs and also increase the confirmation latency, transactions in a sharding-based system should be placed into shards more carefully based on some partitioning rules. This process should consider different factors including the balance among different shards, the possible number of cross-shard transactions and the total amount of data that would be reallocated when rescheduling shards [74]. Some classical graph partitioning algorithms can be adopted, such as Kernighan-Lin algorithm [75] and METIS [76]. Hashing is another straightforward approach that uses the hash result of the unique id of each account as the id of the selected shard.

Some other solutions proposed a new structure consisting of a main chain and multiple shard chains. Each shard maintains a shard chain and commits its state to the main chain periodically. From the architecture shown in Fig. 2.5, we can see that each shard has a dedicated chain. Under this kind of architecture, cross-shard transactions are processed through the main chain by admitting the *receipts* of cross-shard transactions committed by different shards, which can be validated by all shards to ensure the correctness of cross-shard transactions. However, when the scale of cross-shard transactions increases in a blockchain system, the main chain will become the bottleneck of the holistic system since the large volume of transactions brings great pressure of both storage and communications.

We also find that several existing works [28–31] have exploited various methods to optimize their systems based on the sharding technology. Each of those representative works is reviewed as follows.

Elastico Elastico [28] is the first sharding protocol for the permission-less blockchain. In each consensus epoch of Elatico, participants need to solve a PoW puzzle, which will be used to determine the consensus committee. Every committee works as a shard and runs PBFT [60] to reach the consensus and the result will be committed to a leader committee, which is responsible for generating the final decisions on the consensus results of other shards. Finally, the final value will be sent back to update other shards. However, there are several drawbacks of Elastico:

- Elastico generates identities and committees in each epoch. Such frequent operation potentially degrades the efficiency of transaction execution.
- Although each node only needs to verify transactions within its own shard, each node is still required to store all data of the entire network.
- Elastico requires a small size to limit the overhead of running PBFT in each committee, leading to a high failure probability while only tolerating up to a 1/4 fraction faulty nodes.
- Elastico fails to ensure the cross-shard transaction atomicity.

OmniLedger OmniLedger [29], a more recent distributed ledger based on Sharding technique, builds closely on Elastico [28] and tries to solve the problems of Elastico. It uses a bias-resistant public-randomness protocol for shard assignment, which combines RandHound [77] with Algorand [24]. To guarantee the atomicity of cross-shard transactions, OmniLedger introduces a two-phase client-driven "lock/unlock" protocol called Atomix. OmniLedger also adopts the data structure *blockDAG* [32] to make block commitment parallelly and increase transaction throughput via *Trust-but-Verify Validation*. However, the following issues still remain unsolved in OmniLedger:

- Similar to Elastico, OmniLedger is also resilient to Byzantine faults only up to a 1/4 fraction.
- Users in OmniLedger are required to participate actively in cross-shard transactions, which is very difficult to satisfy light-weight users [78]

RapidChain RapidChain [30] is a sharding-based public blockchain protocol that is resilient to Byzantine faults up to a 1/3 fraction of the participants, which is better than the 1/4 fraction of OmniLedger [29]. RapidChain reveals that the communication overhead per transaction is a major bottleneck to the transaction throughput and latency in previous sharding-based protocols [28, 29]. Therefore, Rapidchain reduces the amount of data exchange per transaction and does not need to gossip transactions to the entire network because of the usage of a fast cross-shard verification technique. Additionally, RapidChain utilizes block pipelining to reach a further improvement of throughput and ensures robustness via a reconfiguration mechanism.

Monoxide Monoxide [31] is a scale-out blockchain that proposes *Asynchronous Consensus Zones* and scales the blockchain linearly while considerably maintaining decentralization and security of the system.

The entire network of Monoxide is divided into different parallel zones, each of which only needs to be responsible for itself since blocks and transactions are zone-specific and are only stored in their own zone. Handling transactions across shards (i.e., zones) is an essential issue in sharding-based blockchain systems. In Monoxide, *eventual atomicity* is proposed to ensure the correctness of cross-zone transactions. At the same time, Monoxide proposed an innovative *Chu-ko-nu Mining* that magnifies the mining power, enabling miners to create blocks in different zones via solving one PoW puzzle. Therefore, the difficulty of attacking a single zone is as difficult as attacking the entire network. This characteristic ensures the security of a single zone.

Some other public blockchain projects, including Zilliqa [79] and Harmony [80], also employed sharding technology to solve the scalability of their systems. Zilliqa is the first sharding-based public blockchain with PoW as the consensus algorithm. Zilliqa improves the TPS via processing transactions in different shards, but each node in Zilliqa still needs to store the data of the whole network, which will hinder the system to scale. Later, Harmony also adopts sharding to build a scalable and provably secure public blockchain. Harmony applies a structure with multiple Shard Chains, which processes transactions and store data within the shard, and a Beacon Chain that includes the block header from each Shard Chain and generates random numbers needed in the consensus. Besides, different from Zilliqa, Harmony divides the storage of blockchain data into different shards and a node in a shard only needs to store the data of its own shard.

At present, there are very few efficient sharding protocols that highly guarantee decentralization, scalability, and security. Thus, there remains a large research space for sharding technology.

2.3.1.4 DAG (Directed Acyclic Graph)

The traditional blockchain stores transactions in blocks that are organized in a single chain structure. With this kind of structure, blocks cannot be generated concurrently and thus limits the transaction throughput. In order to solve this problem, an idea dedicated to revising the structure of blockchain called DAG [81] is proposed.

DAG is a finite directed graph with no directed cycles commonly used in the computer science field. An obvious way to transform blockchain into DAG is to let a block act as a vertex in DAG and connect to some previous vertices. However, different from blockchain, DAG allows several vertices to connect to a previous vertex which means concurrent block generation and thus enables more transactions to be included in the system.

Some representative proposals are briefly reviewed as follows. Lewenberg et al. [32] utilize Directed Acyclic Graph of blocks (blockDAG) in their protocol. Different from the traditional structure of blockchain, in this protocol, a new block references multiple former blocks. An inclusive rule is proposed to select a main chain of the formed DAG. Moreover, the contents of off-chain blocks that do not conflict with previous blocks can also be included in the ledger. With the proposed protocol, the system achieves higher throughput.

Later, another DAG-based blockchain called SPECTRE [33] applies the DAG structure to represent an abstract vote to specify the partial order between each pair of blocks, which cannot be extended to a total order over all transactions.

PHANTOM [34] also applies blockDAG to achieve faster block generation and higher transaction throughput. Moreover, PHANTOM proposes a greedy algorithm to order transactions embedded in blockDAG and is able to support smart contract.

Conflux [35] is a fast and scalable blockchain system based on DAG. In Conflux, they proposed two different kinds of edges between blocks (i.e. parent edges and reference edges). A pivot chain formed by parent edges is selected via a selection algorithm. Therefore, the consensus problem of conflux is transformed to reach the consensus of a single chain, which they adopt GHOST [53] to solve.

In industry, there are also several DAG-based projects. A DAG-based cryptocurrency called Dagcoin [36] treats each transaction as a block and focuses on faster security confirmations and greater throughput. Similar to Dagcoin, another branch of studies aim to build DAG-based distributed ledgers, such as IOTA [37], Byteball [38] and Nano [39].

Fantom [82] proposed the *OPERA chain*, a DAG constructed by event blocks, and a Main-chain to determine the ordering between every block. *Lachesis Consensus* is also provided to reach faster consensus via more efficient broadcast.

In Table 2.3, we make a comparison of selected properties (specific structure, consensus, whether ensuring total block order) among some DAG-based protocols. As the table shows, some of them aim at scaling the proof-of-work based system using DAG. And, the specific structure of them also has some differences between each other. Tx DAG stands for a DAG structure that is formed by many independent transactions that are not required to be packed into blocks. Total block order is an essential property that determines the order between every two blocks in the network and thus acts as an important role for protecting the system from several attacks (e.g. double-spending).

Tangle [83] is a DAG network under the basic idea of IOTA. As Fig. 2.6 shows, Tangle is extended by adding directed edges between two transactions. Each edge represents that a new transaction has approved a previous transaction. In IOTA, there is no block, miner and transaction fee involved. Every node can

Table 2.3 Comparsion between different DAG-based solutions

Project	Structure	Consensus	Block total order
Inclusive [32]	Block DAG	PoW	No
SPECTRE [33]	Block DAG	PoW	No
PHANTOM [34]	Block DAG	PoW	Yes
Conflux [35]	Block DAG (with pivot chain)	PoW (GHOST [28]) on a pivot chain	Yes
IOTA [37]	Tx DAG	Cumulative weight of transactions	No
Byteball [38]	Tx DAG	Relying on a reputable group called Witnesses	Yes
Nano [32]	Block-lattice	Balance-weighted votes on conflicting transactions	Yes

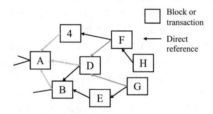

Fig. 2.6 An overview of DAG: each rectangle in the graph represents a block (or a transaction). Multiple blocks (or transactions) can be generated concurrently by linking to previous blocks (or transactions) in DAG (i.e. three orange arrows pointing to A and two blue arrows pointing to D)

create transactions freely after solving a specific computational task and choose two previous transactions to validate and approve them if valid. Later analysis [84, 85] also proves all these properties of Tangle. Besides, algorithms have been proposed to mitigate a kind of double-spending attack in Tangle called parasite chain attacks [108].

With such impressive merits, some other DAG cryptocurrency techniques have been proposed, like new randomized gossip protocol for consensus of Hashgraph [86] and the addition of DAG in Avalanche [87] to extend their consensus protocols, continuously improving the development of DAG.

Compared with blockchain, DAG-based platforms adopt a different ledger-structure and different transaction-confirming methods. However, some questions about IOTA are raised [88], focusing on the claimed great characteristics that IOTA do not need transaction fees and maintains high scalability. Meanwhile, treating each transaction as a block requires more metadata (e.g. reference to other vertices in

DAG) and thus cannot be applied as an efficient method for constructing a scalable system.

And, because of the consensus protocol utilized in some of the current DAG-based ledgers, security issues (e.g. double-spending [89]) and decentralization of these systems are controversial, which will probably limit the further development of DAG.

2.3.2 Layer2: Non On-Chain Solutions

We then classify the Layer-2 approaches into the following categories: *Payment Channel, Sidechain, off-chain computation*, and the *cross-chain*.

2.3.2.1 Payment Channel

The payment channel is a temporary off-chain trading channel, transferring some transactions to this channel to achieve the effect of reducing the transaction volume of the main chain while improving the transaction throughput of the entire system. The representative payment channel solutions include Lightning network [6] adopted by Bitcoin, as well as the Ethereum-based Raiden network [8].

Lightning Network [6] In recent years, the number of Bitcoin transactions has increased drastically, and its shortcomings have exposed, including high transaction delays and expensive transaction fees. To alleviate those drawbacks of the Bitcoin network, developers have proposed a new method—*lightning network*.

To explain briefly, the basic idea of Lightning Network is that two nodes in Bitcoin establish an off-chain trading channel, in which they can carry out multiple low-latency transactions. As shown in Fig. 2.7, this solution includes three

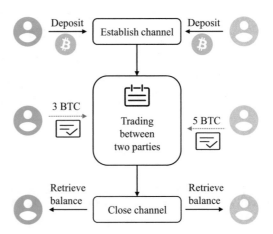

Fig. 2.7 Procedures of lightning network

phases, establishing the channel, trading, and closing the channel. Before launching transactions, the two parties first have saved a certain amount of tokens in the channel as a deposit (greater than the total amount involved in the subsequent transaction), which is the first transaction to open the channel and is recorded on the Bitcoin main chain.

Both parties can then trade with each other in the channel and if one of them cheats, all funds in this channel will be sent to a counterparty as penalty. When closing the channel, the amount of tokens on both sides is submitted to the block of the main chain. Therefore, multiple transactions are completed off-chain and the whole process produces only two transaction records submitted to the main chain. This approach greatly increases the number of transactions when the block size is a constant.

Furthermore, it is not necessary to establish a payment channel between every two parties who intend to exchange tokens. A Payment Channel Network (PCN) is introduced to conduct off-chain transactions between two parties that have no direct payment channel established between them. One participant to route to another via the path between them and make indirect transactions. Figure 2.8 shows the routing schematic diagram of the Lightning network. Node *0* and Node *9* establish a payment channel and carry out transactions directly. Node *1* is able to send transactions to Node *3* via the two channels (i.e. Node *1* to Node *2* and Node *2* to Node *3*). Similarly, Node *4* and Node *8* can trade with each other indirectly. Since transactions can only be sent through a route connected by different payment channels, a proper routing mechanism is needed to ensure the availability of Lightning Network, which has not been developed perfectly. Companies like Lightning Labs [90] implement protocols to build Lightning Network and help users make transactions freely.

Lightning Network provides instant and low-cost payment. However, the flaws of the lightning network are also very obvious. First, the off-chain channel requires

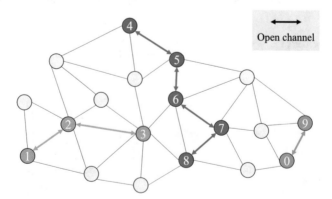

Fig. 2.8 Lightning network topology: a circle represents a user in the lightning network and a left-right arrow indicates a trading channel established between both sides of the arrow

both parties to be online at the same time. Second, it has been reported that the lightning network's large transaction success rate is low [91], indicating that current Lightning Network is not suitable for handling high-value transactions. These two disadvantages listed above greatly limit the wide-adoption of lightning networks.

Raiden Network Raiden Network is a payment-channel for Ethereum. Its implementation is very similar to the Lightning Network. The main difference is that the Raiden Network supports all ERC20 [92] tokens, while the Lightning Network is limited to Bitcoin transactions.

Payment channels have been widely researched in recent years, releasing several implementations of the Lightning Network [93–95]. Besides, there are many other solutions of off-chain payment channel from academia, including Bitcoin Duplex Micropayment Channels [7], Sprites [9], AMHLs [96]. Sprites develops constant locktimes to improve transaction throughput in Payment channel networks and support incremental deposits and withdrawals without interrupting the payment channel. AMHLS utilizes anonymous multi-hop locks to preserve privacy in the Payment channel and also reduce the communication overhead. There remains a large space for research to provide a more effective and secure payment channel.

2.3.2.2 Sidechain

Pegged Sidechain [10] is the first sidechain that enables assets in blockchains like Bitcoin to be transferred between different blockchains while preventing the assets from malicious attackers and also ensuring the atomicity of the transfers.

Figure 2.9 shows an example of transferring assets from parent chain to side chain by the *Two-way peg* protocol proposed in Pegged Sidechains [10]. First, the parent chain sends coins to a special output that cannot be unlocked without a Simplified Payment Verification (SPV) [97] proof on the pegged sidechain. After sending coins is a waiting period called *confirmation period*, which intends to protect the transferring from a denial of service attack and trades latency for security. Unlocking action is followed by the *contest period*, in which the newly-transferred

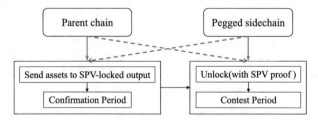

Fig. 2.9 Two-way peg protocol of pegged sidechain [10]: two red dotted lines indicate the procedure of transferring assets from the parent chain to the pegged sidechain. The blue dotted lines show the reverse procedure

assets cannot be spent on the sidechain, aims to prevent double-spending of the previously-locked assets.

Transferring assets from the Pegged sidechain back to the Parent chain is the same procedure as above, so the protocol is also called *Symmetric Two-Way Peg*.

Plasma Plasma [11] is a framework of sidechain attached to the Ethereum main chain. Its root is a smart contract running on the main chain, which records the rules and the state hash of the sidechain. Multiple child chains can be generated from the root, which is continuously expanding and finally become a tree structure. Users can create a ledger on the Plasma chain and achieve asset-transfer between the Plasma chain and the Ethereum main chain via the root. Users can also withdraw their funds from the chain any time.

Transactions can be carried out between different users on the child chains, similar to the situation under Bitcoin's Lightning Network. However, Plasma allows multiple participants to interact without requiring all participants to be online at the same time to update the transaction status.

Furthermore, Plasma can reduce the pressure of the Ethereum main chain by minimizing transaction status so that a simple hash can represent the update of multiple statuses. In this way, Plasma is capable to extend the transactions volume of the side chain.

While improving scalability, Plasma also provides some measures to ensure security avoid security hazards (e.g. double-spending) in sidechains. The Plasma chain submits the hash of the header of its block to the Ethereum main chain periodically. Thus, the main chain can verify the validity of transactions included in Plasma chains. If fraud is found in an invalid block, it will be rolled back with a slashed penalty.

Based on the framework aforementioned, many versions of Plasma have been designed. Minimal Viable Plasma (Plasma MVP) [98] is a simplified version based on the Unspent Transaction Outputs (UTXO) model and shows the fundamental properties of Plasma. Plasma Cash [99], a later improved version of Minimal Viable Plasma, proposes a mechanism in which each deposit operation corresponds to a unique coin ID and uses a data structure called Sparse Merkle Tree [100] to store the transaction history. Plasma Debit [101] is another implementation of Plasma framework and also an extension of Plasma Cash. Plasma is still under development and will be a potential solution to substantially scale out the blockchain systems.

Liquidity Network (Nocust) The previous *state-channel* solutions [6] require at least one transaction on the parent-chain when a channel is established, and also have the drawback that the transaction funds need to be saved in the trading channel as a deposit and the transaction channel relies on complex routing topologies.

The Liquidity. Network [12] team proposed the securely scalable commit-chain named Nocust [102], which has the following excellent properties:

- A new kind of data structure called Merkleized Interval Tree is a multi-layered tree. Individual user account balances are stored in exclusive non-crossing interval space, but the structure ensures that the balances of different users can be summed very quickly to verify whether the amount is the same as that recorded in the smart contract on the parent-chain.

- Nocust is non-custodial, that is, there is no need to limit the funds of the users on the chain, unlike the lightning network which requires participants to deposit in prior for the channel.
- Users do not need to interact with the parent-chain to join the commit-chain. They are free to trade with each other, including transferring funds and receiving funds.
- Nocust can guarantee real-time transactions and reduce transaction delays without additional fees and mortgages.

The experimental results in the work [102] show that Nocust can maintain a very low transaction fee and achieve a high transaction throughput when scaling to one billion users. These merits imply the practicality of its scalability solution.

2.3.2.3   Off-Chain Computation

Miners in Ethereum need to emulate the execution of all contracts to verify their states. The process is costly and limits the scalability of Ethereum. Thus, some solutions have been proposed to build scalable smart contracts.

Truebit   Truebit [15] is a system for verifiable computation that outsources complex computing tasks to an off-chain market. Such the off-chain market executes the tasks and verifies the results and finally submits them back to the main chain. It was originally designed to break the gas restrictions of the Smart Contracts in Ethereum platform. For instance, a DApp needs to perform a very complicated and expensive calculation task which is costly and inefficient in Ethereum. Then, the Truebit protocol is a good option for this DApp. Overall, Truebit is divided into three layers including the *Incentives Layer*, the *Dispute Resolution Layer*, and the *Computational Layer*. Each layer is elaborated as follows.

- *Computational Layer:* In this layer, users submit the computing task code and incentives to publish a task. There is an off-chain computing market, in which the miners listen to tasks and run the code after paying deposits. Each participant who solves a task is called a Solver, and each Verifier is responsible for verifying that a task is completed correctly.
- *Dispute Resolution Layer:* As the name suggests, Dispute Resolution layer is responsible for resolving disputes. When a computation is completed, the verifiers verify the result. If one of the verifiers finds that the result is incorrect, it can call into question about the result, and then both parties will be involved in a verification game. They can use interactive verification to find the specific steps they have in conflict.

    In the verification game, the party who is wrong will be punished, to prevent from deliberately cheating for both parties.

- *Incentives Layer:* Solvers get rewards by solving tasks and verifiers get rewards by detecting errors from the results computed by solvers. However, verifiers can't get a reward if no error found for a long time. If incentives for verifiers are not enough, the number of verifiers in the market will keep losing, resulting in the imbalance of the whole system. To solve this problem, Truebit adds a *forced error* mechanism that enforces the solvers to provide erroneous calculations periodically and add tags in the hash. In this way, when a verifier finds an error, both the solver and verifier can be rewarded, making verifiers profitable.

Arbitrum   Arbitrum [16] introduces a new protocol that improves the scalability of smart contracts by moving the computation of verifying smart contracts off-chain. In Arbitrum, Verifier is a global role that validates transactions, e.g., Miners in Bitcoin. Arbitrum utilizes a Virtual Machine to implement a contract that owns a fund, which cannot be overspent by any execution of the contract. And, every party can create a VM and select a set of VM managers to force the VM to work correctly according to the VM's code. If all managers of a VM agree with the new state of VM, they sign a *Unanimous assertion*. On the other hand, VM managers sign a *Disputable assertion* to challenge the VM's state change and be engaged in the *bisection protocol*. The bisection protocol performs similarly with Dispute Resolution in Truebit, intending to determine if the VM's state change is correct. In this way, only hashes of contract states need to be verified by the Verifier. This releases the pressure of verifiers and also allows contracts to execute privately.

With the support of verifiable computation, large scale computation tasks can be solved off-chain, which provides great improvement in the scalability of blockchain systems.

2.3.2.4   Cross-Chain Techniques

Nowadays, cross-chain projects are also fashionable and viewed as potential solutions to scale out blockchain systems.

Relay technique [13, 14] is another obvious idea of connecting different blockchains together, expecting to build a big network of blockchains and ensuring interoperability between different blockchains. Figure 2.10 shows a model of current inter chain architecture called Relay, the components of which includes *independent blockchains* built atop similar consensus and *relay chain* connecting all independent blockchains. In addition, the *Pegged chain* (e.g. Peg Zone in Cosmos and Parachain bridge in Polkadot) is also provided to bridge existing blockchains with the cross-chain system.

Relay chain in Fig. 2.10 serves the role as a router, enabling new independent blockchains to join in the cross-chain system and adopting cross-chain protocols to process cross-chain transactions more efficiently and also to ensure the consistency.

We then review several representative cross-chain projects as follows.

Fig. 2.10 Architecture for relay [13, 14]

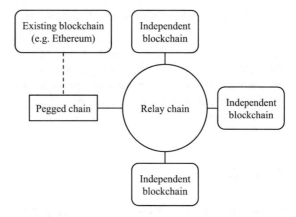

Cosmos Cosmos [13] is an ecosystem of connected blockchains. The network is comprised of many independent blockchains, each of which is called a zone. Powered by consensus algorithms like Tendermint consensus, those zones can communicate with each other via their Inter-Blockchain Communication (IBC) protocol, allowing heterogeneous chains to exchange values (i.e. tokens) or data with each other. Hub (a framework like Relay-chain shown in Fig. 2.10) is the first zone on Cosmos, and any other zones can connect to it. Therefore, Cosmos achieves inter-operability where zones can send to or receive from other zones securely and quickly via Hub, instead of creating connections between every two zones.

Cosmos also provides Tendermint core and Cosmos SDK (Software Development Kit) [103]) for developers to build Blockchains based on Tendermint consensus conveniently such that more blockchains can join the system and gradually extend the scalability of a network. With multiple parallel chains running in the network, Cosmos can achieve a horizontal scalability.

Unfortunately, the popular PoW-featured blockchain such as Bitcoin and Ethereum, cannot connect to Cosmos Hub directly. An alternative solution is to create a customized Peg-zone (like Pegged chain shown in Fig. 2.10) as a bridge to exchange data.

Polkadot Polkadot [14] also outlined a multi-chain protocol that provides a *relay-chain* to connect heterogeneous blockchains. As mentioned already, relay-chain enables an independent blockchain, an example which is called *parachain* in Polkadot, to exchange information and trust-free inter-chain transactability. In addition, parachain bridge can link to already running blockchains such as Ethereum.

All these proposals employed are able to achieve interoperability and scalability.

2.4   Future Directions and Open Issues

Section 2.3 introduces many solutions proposed in recent years dedicated to solving the scalability of blockchain. However, there is still no method that can be applied to existing well-known blockchain systems and solve this problem perfectly. To this end, we should continue to explore and improve existing solutions to achieve a better effect. Here are a few possible directions.

2.4.1   Layer-1

Layer-1 solutions have been studied widely, but it still requires more explorations for scalability solutions. We envision open issues in the directions of *block data* and *sharding techniques*.

2.4.1.1   Block Data

Despite other methods concerning scalability, the individual nodes' limited capability of storage and bandwidth will be the performance bottleneck of blockchain systems. Firstly, increasing TPS indicates that much more block data need to be propagated within the system, which may aggravate the congestion problems. Besides, as the blockchain grows, more blockchain data should be stored by individual nodes. It will increase the pressure of storage and promote the tendency to centralization. Many discussions about chain pruning [104–106] have been proposed. Blockchain pruning approaches aim to remove some historical data that is not critical from the blockchain while preserving the security. The reduction of data releases the storage pressure of full nodes in the blockchain. Therefore, to keep developing blockchain, solutions related to block compression and blockchain data pruning require more optimization and should be applied to real blockchain systems.

2.4.1.2   Sharding Techniques

The sharding technique is a popular and effective solution. A sharding-based blockchain is divided into different shards with proper mechanisms to manage each shard as well as transactions and scales horizontally with the number of nodes. However, the following two issues are still open for further investigations:

1. How to place transactions into different shards. Ninety five percent transactions in OmniLedger [29] are cross-shard transactions, leading to much bandwidth pressure because of the communication cost of cross-shard transactions and thus decrease the performance of the whole sharding-based system. Besides the

communication cost, reconfiguring shards also cause the exchange of a great amount of data. Therefore, better algorithms should be provided to solve the problem.
2. How to improve the efficiency of cross-shard transactions. The existing solutions have achieved several good results by their cross-shard submission protocols. However, since cross-shard transactions involve multiple shards and lead to more bandwidth consumption and longer confirmation time, a more efficient protocol is needed to reduce the confirmation latency. This direction still has a large room to explore.

2.4.2   Layer-2

Regarding the Layer-2 solutions, some of them are still in their work-in-progress stages. In particular, Lightning Network is under the spotlight. Many teams have developed the Lightning Network clients and have achieved a high user-of-experience through a series of improvements in the routing mechanism. When the Ethereum's Plasma framework was proposed, many follow-up teams implemented it to varying degrees, proving the high recognition of sidechain technology. According to the prototypes outlined in this chapter, the subsequent studies should focus on the relationship between the sidechain and the main chain, and how to scale out the blockchain and achieve substantial improvement on overall performance while ensuring its fundamental properties. Cross-chain solutions, like Cosmos and Polkadot, have devised their dedicated protocols in order to build a network of heterogeneous blockchain.

2.4.3   Layer-0

We particularly review some new solutions proposed recently and classify them into the category of *Layer-0*. This type of solutions concern the optimizations of the dissemination protocol for information (transaction or block) in the blockchain network. Nodes in the blockchain network broadcast blocks and transactions to the network, but the broadcast is not efficient enough, leading to latency and high bandwidth usage. Some solutions related to block compression discussed above like *Compact Blocks* [19], also focus on the optimization of block propagation, and thus can be viewed as a Layer-0 solution. As mentioned before, faster block propagation leads to larger blocks and shorter block intervals, thereby increasing transaction throughput. Thus, the protocols aiming at optimizing the data propagation in blockchains are desired in future scalable blockchain systems.

Several approaches intending to improve the propagation protocol have been proposed. For instance, Erlay [40] optimizes Bitcoin's transaction relay protocol to reduce the overall bandwidth consumption while increasing the propagation latency. Velocity [42] also brings some improvement in block propagation by utilizing Fountain code, a kind of erasure code, to reduce the amount of data be propagated. Kadcast [41] proposes an efficient block propagation approach based on overlay structure of Kademlia [107]. bloXroute [43] is a Blockchain Distribution Network (BDN) that helps individual nodes to propagate transactions and blocks more quickly. Besides these solutions, there remains a lot of room for optimizations of propagation protocols of current blockchain systems, such as better routing mechanisms, that will contribute to the improvement of the scalability of blockchain.

2.5 Conclusion

Blockchain technologies have grown rapidly in the past few years and will be applied to more applications in different fields in the foreseeable near future. With the increasing adoption of blockchain technology, the number of users has steadily increased. However, the network congestion problem that has occurred many times and enforced people to carefully think about how to solve the scalability issue of blockchains. To this end, a number of new solutions have been proposed. In this chapter, we describe the blockchain performance problem mainly paying attention to scalability, and then classify the existing mainstream solutions into several representative layers. Besides, we elaborate some popular solutions such as Sharding, Sidechain, and cross-chain, intending to give a comprehensive explanation. Furthermore, we also summarize several potential research directions and open issues based on the drawback found, such as the huge amount of blockchain data that need to be compressed or pruned, the inefficient cross-shard transaction and unfinished protocols to bridge the existing blockchain to cross-chain platforms, aiming at addressing the scalability of blockchain systems.

We expect our classification and the analysis over the current solutions can inspire further booming studies dedicated to improving the scalability of blockchains.

Acknowledgments The work described in this chapter was supported by the National Key Research and Development Program (2016YFB1000101), the National Natural Science Foundation of China (61902445, 61722214) and the Guangdong Province Universities and Colleges Pearl River Scholar Funded Scheme (2016).

References

1. Zheng Z, Xie S, Dai HN, Chen X, Wang H (2018) Blockchain challenges and opportunities: a survey. Int J Web Grid Serv 14(4):352–375
2. Croman K, Decker C, Eyal I, Gencer AE, Juels A, Kosba A, Miller A, Saxena P, Shi E, Sirer EG, et al (2016) On scaling decentralized blockchains. In: International conference on financial cryptography and data security. Springer, Berlin, pp 106–125

3. Scalability of bitcoin. https://en.bitcoin.it/wiki/Scalability
4. Kogias EK, Jovanovic P, Gailly N, Khoffi I, Gasser L, Ford B (2016) Enhancing bitcoin security and performance with strong consistency via collective signing. In: 25th USENIX security symposium USENIX security), vol 16, pp 279–296
5. Nakamoto S, et al (2008) Bitcoin: a peer-to-peer electronic cash system. *Decentralized business review*, 21260.
6. Poon J, Dryja T (2016) The bitcoin lightning network: scalable off-chain instant payments. https://lightning.network/lightning-network-paper.pdf
7. Decker C, Wattenhofer R (2015) A fast and scalable payment network with bitcoin duplex micropayment channels. In: Symposium on self-stabilizing systems. Springer, Berlin, pp 3–18
8. Raiden network. https://raiden.network/
9. Miller A, Bentov I, Bakshi S, Kumaresan R, McCorry P (2019) Sprites and state channels: payment networks that go faster than lightning. In: International conference on financial cryptography and data security. Springer, Berlin, pp 508–526
10. Back A, Corallo M, Dashjr L, Friedenbach M, Maxwell G, Miller A, Poelstra A, Timón J, Wuille P (2014) Enabling blockchain innovations with pegged sidechains, p 72. http://wwwopensciencereviewcom/papers/123/enablingblockchain-innovations-with-pegged-sidechains
11. Poon J, Buterin V (2017) Plasma: scalable autonomous smart contracts. White paper, pp 1–47
12. Liquidity.network. https://liquidity.network/
13. Cosmos. https://cosmos.network/whitepaper
14. Wood G (2016) Polkadot: vision for a heterogeneous multi-chain framework. White Paper
15. Teutsch J, Reitwiessner C (2018) Truebit–a scalable verification solution for blockchains. White Papers. https://people.cs.uchicago.edu/~teutsch/papers/truebit.pdf
16. Kalodner H, Goldfeder S, Chen X, Weinberg SM, Felten EW (2018) Arbitrum: scalable, private smart contracts. In: 27th {USENIX} security symposium ({USENIX} security 18), pp 1353–1370
17. Lombrozo E, Lau J, Wuille P (2015) Segregated witness (consensus layer). *Bitcoin Core Develop. Team, Tech. Rep. BIP, 141.*
18. Bitcoin cash. https://www.bitcoincash.org/
19. Bip152. https://github.com/bitcoin/bips/blob/master/bip-0152.mediawiki
20. Ding D, Jiang X, Wang J, Wang H, Zhang X, Sun Y (2019) Txilm: lossy block compression with salted short hashing. arXiv:190606500
21. Xu Z, Han S, Chen L (2018) Cub, a consensus unit-based storage scheme for blockchain system. In: 2018 IEEE 34th international conference on data engineering (ICDE). IEEE, Piscataway, pp 173–184
22. Dai X, Xiao J, Yang W, Wang C, Jin H (2019) Jidar: a jigsaw-like data reduction approach without trust assumptions for bitcoin system. In: 2019 IEEE 39th international conference on distributed computing systems (ICDCS). IEEE, Piscataway, pp 1317–1326
23. Eyal I, Gencer AE, Sirer EG, Van Renesse R (2016) Bitcoin-NG: a scalable blockchain protocol. In: 13th USENIX symposium on networked systems design and implementation (NSDI'16), pp 45–59
24. Gilad Y, Hemo R, Micali S, Vlachos G, Zeldovich N (2017) Algorand: scaling byzantine agreements for cryptocurrencies. In: Proceedings of the 26th symposium on operating systems principles. ACM, New York, pp 51–68
25. Bentov I, Pass R, Shi E (2016) Snow white: provably secure proofs of stake. IACR Cryptology ePrint Archive 2016:919
26. Kiayias A, Russell A, David B, Oliynykov R (2017) Ouroboros: a provably secure proof-of-stake blockchain protocol. In: Annual international cryptology conference. Springer, Berlin, pp 357–388
27. David B, Gaži P, Kiayias A, Russell A (2018) Ouroboros praos: an adaptively-secure, semi-synchronous proof-of-stake blockchain. In: Annual international conference on the theory and applications of cryptographic techniques. Springer, Berlin, pp 66–98

28. Luu L, Narayanan V, Zheng C, Baweja K, Gilbert S, Saxena P (2016) A secure sharding protocol for open blockchains. In: Proceedings of the 2016 ACM SIGSAC conference on computer and communications security. ACM, New York, pp 17–30
29. Kokoris-Kogias E, Jovanovic P, Gasser L, Gailly N, Syta E, Ford B (2018) Omniledger: a secure, scale-out, decentralized ledger via sharding. In: 2018 IEEE symposium on security and privacy (SP). IEEE, Piscataway, pp 583–598
30. Zamani M, Movahedi M, Raykova M (2018) Rapidchain: scaling blockchain via full sharding. In: Proceedings of the 2018 ACM SIGSAC conference on computer and communications security. ACM, New York, pp 931–948
31. Wang J, Wang H (2019) Monoxide: scale out blockchains with asynchronous consensus zones. In: 16th USENIX symposium on networked systems design and implementation (NSDI'19), pp 95–112
32. Lewenberg Y, Sompolinsky Y, Zohar A (2015) Inclusive block chain protocols. In: International conference on financial cryptography and data security. Springer, Berlin, pp 528–547
33. Sompolinsky Y, Lewenberg Y, Zohar A (2016) Spectre: a fast and scalable cryptocurrency protocol. IACR Cryptology. ePrint Archive 2016:1159
34. Sompolinsky Y, Zohar A (2018) Phantom: a scalable blockdag protocol. IACR Cryptology. ePrint Archive 2018:104
35. Li C, Li P, Zhou D, Xu W, Long F, Yao A (2018) Scaling nakamoto consensus to thousands of transactions per second. arXiv:180503870
36. Lerner SD (2015) Dagcoin: a cryptocurrency without blocks. https://bitslog.com/2015/09/11/dagcoin/
37. IOTA. https://www.iota.org/
38. Churyumov A (2016) Byteball: a decentralized system for storage and transfer of value. https://byteballorg/Byteballpdf
39. LeMahieu C (2018) Nano: a feeless distributed cryptocurrency network. Nano. https://nanoorg/en/whitepaper. Accessed 24 March 2018
40. Naumenko G, Maxwell G, Wuille P, Fedorova S, Beschastnikh I (2019) Bandwidth-efficient transaction relay for bitcoin. arXiv:190510518
41. Rohrer E, Tschorsch F (2019) Kadcast: a structured approach to broadcast in blockchain networks. In: Proceedings of the 1st ACM conference on advances in financial technologies. ACM, New York, pp 199–213
42. Chawla N, Behrens HW, Tapp D, Boscovic D, Candan KS (2019) Velocity: scalability improvements in block propagation through rateless erasure coding. In: 2019 IEEE international conference on blockchain and cryptocurrency (ICBC). IEEE, Piscataway, pp 447–454
43. Klarman U, Basu S, Kuzmanovic A, Sirer EG, Bloxroute: a scalable trustless blockchain distribution network whitepaper
44. Weber I, Gramoli V, Ponomarev A, Staples M, Holz R, Tran AB, Rimba P (2017) On availability for blockchain-based systems. In: 2017 IEEE 36th symposium on reliable distributed systems (SRDS). IEEE, Piscataway, pp 64–73
45. Decentralized application. https://en.wikipedia.org/wiki/Decentralized_application/
46. Vranken H (2017) Sustainability of bitcoin and blockchains. Curr Opin Environ Sustain 28:1–9
47. Decentralized application. https://github.com/bitcoin/bips/blob/master/bip-0141.mediawiki
48. First bitcoin cash block mined. https://news.bitcoin.com/fork-watch-first-bitcoin-cash-block-mined/
49. Block size limit controversy. https://en.bitcoin.it/wiki/Block_size_limit_controversy
50. Block size increase. https://bitfury.com/content/downloads/block-size-1.1.1.pdf
51. Elmohamed S, Towards massive on-chain scaling: block propagation results with xthin. https://medium.com/@peter_r/towards-massive-on-chain-scaling-block-propagation-results-with-xthin-a0f1e3c23919
52. Lumino transaction compression protocol (LTCP). https://docs.rsk.co/LuminoTransactionCompressionProtocolLTCP.pdf

53. Sompolinsky Y, Zohar A (2015) Secure high-rate transaction processing in bitcoin. In: International conference on financial cryptography and data security. Springer, Berlin, pp 507–527
54. Li X, Jiang P, Chen T, Luo X, Wen Q (2017) A survey on the security of blockchain systems. Future Gen Comput Syst 107:841–853
55. Casper-proof-of-stake-compendium. https://github.com/ethereum/wiki/wiki/Casper-Proof-of-Stake-compendium
56. Larimer D (2014) Delegated proof-of-stake (DPoS). Bitshare Whitepaper
57. Bitshares blockchain. https://bitshares.org/
58. "eosio, the most powerful infrastructure for decentralized applications". https://eos.io/
59. Eos:less than 1% of eos addresses hold 86% of the tokens! https://medium.com/@freetokencryptobounty/eos-less-than-1-of-eos-addresses-hold-86-of-the-tokens-5ad4b2eac403
60. Castro M, Liskov B, et al (1999) Practical byzantine fault tolerance. In: Proceedings of the third symposium on operating systems design and implementation (OSDI), vol 99, pp 173–186
61. Byzantine fault. https://en.wikipedia.org/wiki/Byzantine_fault
62. Canetti R, Rabin T (1993) Fast asynchronous byzantine agreement with optimal resilience. In: STOC, Citeseer, vol 93, pp 42–51
63. Malkhi D, Reiter M (1997) Unreliable intrusion detection in distributed computations. In: Proceedings 10th computer security foundations workshop. IEEE, Piscataway, pp 116–124
64. Garay JA, Moses Y (1998) Fully polynomial byzantine agreement for processors in rounds. SIAM J Comput 27(1):247–290
65. Buchman E (2016) Tendermint: byzantine fault tolerance in the age of blockchains. Ph.D. Thesis
66. Syta E, Tamas I, Visher D, Wolinsky DI, Jovanovic P, Gasser L, Gailly N, Khoffi I, Ford B (2016) Keeping authorities "honest or bust" with decentralized witness cosigning. In: 2016 IEEE symposium on security and privacy (SP). IEEE, Piscataway, pp 526–545
67. Pass R, Shi E (2017) Hybrid consensus: efficient consensus in the permissionless model. In: 31st international symposium on distributed computing (DISC 2017), Schloss Dagstuhl-Leibniz-Zentrum fuer Informatik
68. Abraham I, Malkhi D, Nayak K, Ren L, Spiegelman A (2016) Solidus: an incentive-compatible cryptocurrency based on permissionless byzantine consensus. arXiv:161202916
69. Micali S, Rabin M, Vadhan S (1999) Verifiable random functions. In: 40th annual symposium on foundations of computer science (Cat. No. 99CB37039). IEEE, Piscataway, pp 120–130
70. Proof of authority - wikipedia. https://en.wikipedia.org/wiki/Proof_of_authority
71. Proof-of-capacity. https://burstwiki.org/en/proof-of-capacity/
72. Nandwani A, Gupta M, Thakur N (2019) Proof-of-participation: implementation of proof-of-stake through proof-of-work. In: International conference on innovative computing and communications. Springer, Berlin, pp 17–24
73. Shard wiki. https://en.wikipedia.org/wiki/Shard_(database_architecture)
74. Fynn E, Pedone F (2018) Challenges and pitfalls of partitioning blockchains. In: 2018 48th annual IEEE/IFIP international conference on dependable systems and networks workshops (DSN-W). IEEE, Piscataway, pp 128–133
75. Kernighan BW, Lin S (1970) An efficient heuristic procedure for partitioning graphs. Bell Syst Tech J 49(2):291–307
76. Karypis G, Kumar V (1998) A fast and high quality multilevel scheme for partitioning irregular graphs. SIAM J. Sci Comput 20(1):359–392
77. Syta E, Jovanovic P, Kogias EK, Gailly N, Gasser L, Khoffi I, Fischer MJ, Ford B (2017) Scalable bias-resistant distributed randomness. In: 2017 IEEE symposium on security and privacy (SP). IEEE, Piscataway, pp 444–460
78. Light-weight user. https://en.bitcoin.it/wiki/Lightweight_node
79. Team Z, et al (2017) The zilliqa technical whitepaper. Accessed 16 Sept. 2019. https://www.allcryptowhitepapers.com/zilliqa-whitepaper/

80. The harmony team. Open consensus for 10 billion people. https://harmony.one/
81. Dag (directed acyclic graph). https://en.wikipedia.org/wiki/Directed_acyclic_graph
82. Fantom. https://fantom.foundation/
83. Popov S (2016) The tangle. White Paper. https://assets.ctfassets.net/r1dr6vzfxhev/2t4uxvsIqk0EUau6g2sw0g/45eae33637ca92f85dd9f4a3a218e1ec/iota1_4_3.pdf.
84. Kusmierz B (2017) The first glance at the simulation of the tangle: discrete model. IOTA Found. WhitePaper, 1-10. https://www.iota.org/
85. Kusmierz B, Staupe P, Gal A (2018) Extracting tangle properties in continuous time via large-scale simulations. Tech. Rep., Working paper
86. Baird L, Harmon M, Madsen P (2018) Hedera: a governing council & public hashgraph network. The trust layer of the internet, whitepaper 1
87. Rocket T (2018) Snowflake to avalanche: a novel metastable consensus protocol family for cryptocurrencies. https://theblockchaintest.com/uploads/resources/Team%20Rocket%20-%20Snowflake%20to%20Avalanche-A%20Novel%20Metastable%20Consensus%20Protocol%20Family%20for%20Cryptocurrencies%20-%202018%20-%20May%20-%20Paper.pdf. Accessed 4 December 2018
88. Complaints about iOTA. https://juejin.im/post/5c6e0f0bf265da2de66103dd
89. Wikipedia item. Double-spending. https://en.wikipedia.org/wiki/Double-spending
90. Lightning labs. https://lightning.engineering/
91. Bitmex-the lightning network. https://blog.bitmex.com/the-lightning-network/
92. Erc20 token standard. Erc20tokenstandard
93. Lightning network daemon. https://github.com/lightningnetwork/lnd
94. c-lightning—a lightning network implementation in c. https://github.com/ElementsProject/lightning
95. A scala implementation of the lightning network. https://github.com/ACINQ/eclair
96. Malavolta G, Moreno-Sanchez P, Schneidewind C, Kate A, Maffei M (2019) Anonymous multi-hop locks for blockchain scalability and interoperability. In: Network and distributed system security (NDSS) symposium (NDSS)
97. Simplified payment verification. https://en.bitcoinwiki.org/wiki/Simplified_Payment_Verification
98. Minimal viable plasma. https://ethresear.ch/t/minimal-viable-plasma/426
99. Minimal viable plasma. https://ethresear.ch/t/plasma-cash-plasma-with-much-less-per-user-data-checking/1298
100. Sparse merkle trees. https://ethresear.ch/t/optimizing-sparse-merkle-trees/3751
101. Plasma debit: arbitrary-denomination payments in plasma cash. https://ethresear.ch/t/plasma-debit-arbitrary-denomination-payments-in-plasma-cash/2198
102. Khalil R, Gervais A (2018) Nocust–a non-custodial 2nd-layer financial intermediary. Tech. Rep., Cryptology ePrint Archive, Report 2018/642. https://eprint.iacr.org/2018/642
103. Tendermint. https://tendermint.com/
104. Politou E, Casino F, Alepis E, Patsakis C (2019) Blockchain mutability: challenges and proposed solutions. arXiv:190707099
105. Florian M, Henningsen S, Beaucamp S, Scheuermann B (2019) Erasing data from blockchain nodes. In: 2019 IEEE european symposium on security and privacy workshops (EuroS&PW). IEEE, Piscataway, pp 367–376
106. Ethereum chain pruning for long term 1.0 scalability and viability. https://ethereum-magicians.org/t/ethereum-chain-pruning-for-long-term-1-0-scalability-and-viability/2074
107. Maymounkov P, Mazieres D (2002) Kademlia: a peer-to-peer information system based on the XOR metric. In: International workshop on peer-to-peer systems. Springer, Berlin, pp 53–65
108. Cullen A, Ferraro P, King C, Shorten R (2019) Distributed ledger technology for IoT: parasite chain attacks. arXiv:190400996

Chapter 3
On-Chain and Off-Chain Scalability Techniques

Ting Cai, Wuhui Chen, Kostas E. Psannis, Sotirios K. Goudos, Yang Yu, Zibin Zheng, and Shaohua Wan

3.1 Overview

Recently, the Global Alliance of Sharing Economy (GLASE) has present the strategic vision of "double 50% reduction 2030 initiative", i.e., the reduction of global new resource consumption and labor hours by 50%, respectively [1]. Such endeavors emphasize the promotion of sharing and efficient utilization of global resources. Correspondingly, it will trigger an increase of applications of the Internet

1536-1284/22/ $25.00 © 2022 IEEE https://doi.org/10.1109/MWC.004.2100616

T. Cai · Y. Yu
School of Computer Science and Engineering, Sun Yat-Sen University, Guangzhou, China
e-mail: cait9@mail2.sysu.edu.cn; yuy@mail.sysu.edu.cn

W. Chen (✉) · Z. Zheng
GuangDong Engineering Technology Research Center of Blockchain, Sun Yat-Sen University, Guangdong, China
e-mail: chenwuh@mail.sysu.edu.cn; zhzibin@mail.sysu.edu.cn

K. E. Psannis
Department of Applied Informatics, School of Information Sciences, University of Macedonia, Thessaloniki, Greece
e-mail: kpsannis@uom.edu.gr

S. K. Goudos
Department of Physics, Aristotle University of Thessaloniki, Thessaloniki, Greece
e-mail: sgoudo@physics.auth.gr

S. Wan (✉)
Shenzhen Institute for Advanced Study, University of Electronic Science and Technology of China, Shenzhen, China
e-mail: shaohua.wan@ieee.org

© The Author(s), under exclusive license to Springer Nature Singapore Pte Ltd. 2023
W. Chen et al. (eds.), *Blockchain Scalability*,
https://doi.org/10.1007/978-981-99-1059-5_3

of Things (IoT), such as bicycle-sharing, self-service supermarkets, intelligent garbage recycling stations, and supply chains with automatic payments [2].

For most smart wearables and Machine-to-Machine (M2M) devices in IoT networks, data are delivered via wireless communications. Due to the lack of trust and data integrity assurance from untrusted terminals, message broadcast in the IoT wireless network is not always reliable. Therefore, how to ensure reliability and security becomes a significant challenge. Blockchain technology has been exploited as a promising solution to protect data integrity, provenance, and consistency for various IoT networks [3, 4]. Undoubtedly, promotions of sharing economy in the near future will give rise to an extremely large quantity of blockchain nodes communicating through wireless IoT links. Nevertheless, the scalability is an inherent limitation of blockchain, which has been widely accepted as a major barrier to large-scale blockchain applications. Taking Bitcoin as an example, the maximum throughput of blockchain is about 7 Transactions Per Second (TPS); thus, the client requires at least 10 minutes on average for a launched transaction to be included in the blockchain. By contrast, the mainstream of payment technologies, like Paypal or Visa, perform about 200 TPS or more than 5000 TPS, respectively. On the other hand, massive storage, used for duplicating distributed ledgers and storing large raw data derived from numerous IoT terminals, can potentially enhance the urgency of scaling the blockchain.

Many researchers have concentrated on the improvement of scalability that powered the performance of blockchain [5, 6]. To summarize, there are two types of advancements in their explorations. On one hand, some prefer employing *on-chain scaling* to provide high performance for large-scale wireless networks [5]. The core idea is partitioning the blockchain nodes into multiple independent groups, called shards, where each shard processes and maintains related sub-transactions in parallel. Such on-chain scaling thoughts promise to achieve real-time communications in large-scale wireless networks by largely reducing the overheads of communication, computation, and storage.

On the other hand, some pieces of literature explore *off-chain scaling* to address scalability issues [6]. For example, payment channels have been proposed to enable blockchain as a settlement network, allowing the system to process a nearly unlimited number of payment transactions off the blockchain. Thanks to such a design, high-volume transactions could be processed without committing to the blockchain; consequently, instant M2M payments become possible for the blockchain applied in large-scale wireless networks. However, off-chain scaling cannot record comprehensive transaction details, such that encounters the disadvantage of imperfect supports for some transaction scenarios, e.g., large transactions that are highly guaranteed in terms of providing rigorous security.

The large-scale wireless networks inevitably bring complexity and diversity to sharing economy, like ultra-dense small cells, massive IoT devices, diverse demands, and varied transactions. Therefore, a good scaling solution should have capacities of supporting all types of transactions, that is, being supportive in handling fine-grained transactions, which include *macro* and *micro* transactions. As illustrated in Fig. 3.1, *micro-transactions* refer to transactions of a small amount

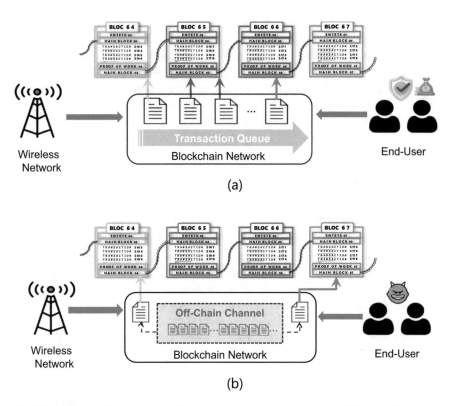

Fig. 3.1 Motivation: in large-scale wireless networks, single on-chain or off-chain scaling cannot support fine-grained sharing economy transactions. Here are illustrations of fine-grained transactions, which include (**a**) *macro-transactions* and (**b**) *micro-transactions*

payment but executed frequently in a real-time manner, expecting to create on-demand and profitable business models [6], e.g., hotspots sharing of WiFi connections, or M2M payments in the IoT. While *macro-transactions* indicate transactions of large values, requiring to record all transactional details on an important business deal in which the security is highly concerned. Concrete examples are sharing transactions of highly valuable resources, wherein secure tracking, monitoring, and intelligent control are preferred [7].

To provide fine-grained transaction support as aforementioned, we exploit combinations of on-chain and off-chain scaling. Nevertheless, a direct combination will bring about new challenges, e.g., atomically processing transactions across shards are high costs with slow processing speed. As such, more sophisticated approaches that are capable of performing the verification of cross-shard transactions efficiently under a joint architecture of on-chain and off-chain are required.

In this chapter, we employ blockchain as the backbone architecture, and propose a *two-layer* scaling sharing framework combining on-chain and off-chain for fine-grained transaction support in large-scale wireless networks. *Layer-one* on-chain layer, designed as sharing-oriented sharding, handles macro-transactions on the chain with security guarantees. *Layer-two* off-chain layer, built up cross-zone channels, allows micro-transactions to be executed in real-time off the chain. With combinatorial designs, we further present protocols of automated transaction workflows on efficient validations of cross-zone transactions. Finally, a proof-of-concept prototype is implemented in a case study about data-shared electric vehicles to demonstrate the effectiveness of our work.

3.2   Related Work

This section briefly discusses the related work as follows.

1. *Large-scale wireless networks:* Recent applications of large-scale wireless networks have redefined many research problems toward computing offloading [8], edge caching [9], resource allocation [10], security and privacy protection [11]. Particularly, we leverage Mobile Edge Computing (MEC) and caching technologies to enhance computing ability and processing power for large-scale wireless networks; therefore, expanding sharing economy.
2. *Blockchain-empowered sharing transactions:* Traditional centralized servers have been heavily debated since they suffer from communication overhead and single points of failure. Blockchain, as a decentralized technology, has provided direct solutions to centralized sharing architecture. Guo et al. [4] utilized blockchain to implement a trusted access system, achieving authenticated and collaborative sharing among multiple IoT terminals. Aloqaily et al. [12] deployed smart contracts on a blockchain-based energy trade framework, such that transactions could be verified and handled in real-time by using encoded logics. However, existing studies single apply the blockchain directly without adjusting its structure.
3. *Scalable designs on blockchain:* Multiple solutions to scalability have been proposed to deal with such an inherent limitation of blockchain, for example, Directed Acyclic Graph (DAG) [13], off-chain channels [6, 14], and sharding [5]. Generally, the transactions in the DAG are no longer organized as a chain structure. Sharding mainly modifies the blockchain designs to support efficient transactions processing. Whereas off-chain channels can make agreements without all participants but with security guarantees; thus, allowing users to handle small but high-frequency transactions off the chain via private communications. Nonetheless, there lack of combinations of on-chain and off-chain. To this end, we apply cross-shard off-chain channels to address the low-efficiency issues of cross-shard transaction verification in sharding, aiming to support all types of transactions for sharing economy in large-scale wireless networks.

3.3   Two-Layer Scaling Sharing Framework Based on Large-Scale Wireless Networks

3.3.1   Framework Overview

Figure 3.2 illustrates the proposed general three-part framework, including sharing economy applications running on the top layer, on-chain & off-chain blockchain system running in the middle, and IoT wireless networks running at the bottom.

IoT Wireless networks introduce the MEC architecture to constitute a cloud-edge-terminal collaborative system, which is capable of providing powerful computing and processing capacities for large-scale wireless networks. On-chain & Off-chain blockchain system serves as the core part, enabling high TPS and low-latency processing on different types of sharing transactions. Assisted by the above-mentioned two parts, the top application layer can be scalable to create novel sharing economy models, such as sustainable energy, spectrum sharing, mobile crowdsensing (MCS) market, and data trading.

More importantly, the middle-part blockchain system contributes to the scalable framework because of a two-layer design combining on-chain and off-chain. *Layer-one* is formed by multiple zones in which consensus is reached by the nodes within each zone in parallel, instead of agreeing across the whole network. It increases transaction TPS and reduces latency, thereby scaling to support macro-transactions. *Layer-two* exploits off-chain channels and repositories to handle high-frequency micro-transactions and enlarge storage. The protocols for such two-layer designs are presented in subsequent Section 3.3.2.

Besides, the framework provides three essential modules to offer sharing-oriented transaction services. That is, Authenticator Module generates identities for registered IoT devices, thereby allowing them to join the blockchain system; On-Chain Management Module assigns the devices to zones corresponding to their geographic coordinates; and Off-Chain Management Module is responsible for determining how a sharing transaction will be proceeded, on or off the blockchain. More details are discussed in Section 3.3.3.

3.3.2   Two-Layer Scaling Protocol

To formalize the detail of two-layer designs, we propose a two-layer scaling protocol. The following explains our protocol in two layers respectively.

Layer-One (*Sharing-Oriented On-Chain Sharding*). Most wireless networks include fixed IoT devices, e.g., base stations, payment machines, or MEC servers, which usually have the larger computing power and behave more reliable than mobile terminals. Thus, we divide zones based on the Global Positioning System (GPS) for fixed IoT devices. Partitioning zones make on-chain transactions to

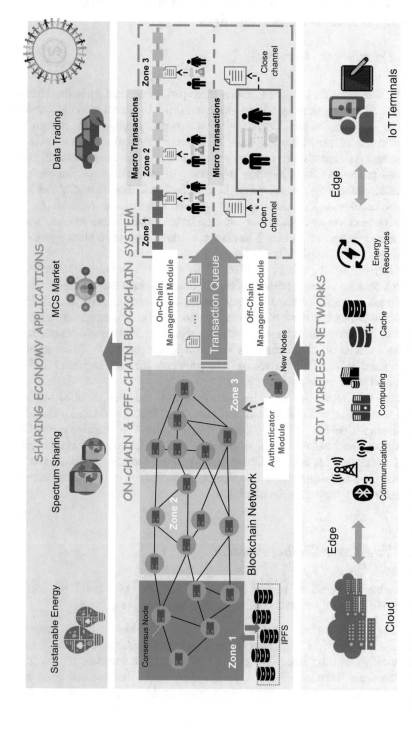

Fig. 3.2 Overview of the two-layer scaling sharing framework in the context of large-scale wireless networks

be processed efficiently due to parallelization. We next discuss the key steps of **Layer-One**.

System Initialization IoT devices are classified into two types of roles, i.e., endorser and client. Endorsers are the fixed IoT devices in charge of making consensus and maintaining global consistency, whereas clients refer to dynamic participating devices that only propose sharing transactions. At each epoch t, the initial blockchain system is $\mathbb{S} = \{s_1, s_2, \ldots, s_m\}$, where m denotes the total number of zones. Each zone is initialized according to the assigned endorser's GPS coordinates. Once $\mathbb{S}$ forms, endorsers will verify and keep identities of others within the local zone.

Device Participation and Zone Assignment Before joining epoch t, IoT device i registers to obtain an identity, i.e., a public key sk_i. Thereafter, according to i's geographic coordinates, it is assigned to the corresponding zone s_i, and works as a client engaging sharing and proposing transactions to nearby endorsers. Considering the actual mobility of IoT devices in the wireless networks, we assume that i can join and leave the blockchain network freely during an epoch reconfiguration [5].

Intra-Zone Consensus The proposed protocol uses **plug-in** pattern to enable the selection of different consensus mechanisms. In a consensus round, the leader of endorsers puts sharing transactions in order and forwards them to others. Once received, all endorsers use the selected consensus protocol to make agreements together. Finally, endorsers send **reply** to the requesting client. Notably, client can be elected as a new endorser by performing authentication and a location check on particular areas. If the old endorsers behave abnormally, e.g., missing blocks or forking, they can be deleted from the endorser list at the next epoch $t + 1$.

Layer-Two (*Cross-Zone Off-Chain Channel*). On-chain sharding inevitably brings a huge challenge, i.e., how to guarantee the atomicity of cross-zone transactions. To atomically process transactions across shards, most existing sharding solutions transform cross-shard transaction into many sub-transactions, then process them on the blockchain. Such solutions could lead to high costs with a slow processing speed. To handle the cross-zone transactions efficiently, we present cross-zone off-chain channels.

Specifically, we devise a synchronous strategy to maintain updating of the state of a channel between two zones. When performing the **Layer-Two** protocol, some sub-transactions are generated and then sent to the **target** zones where they can be verified; the state updates are also completed. Afterward, the state of the **local** zone can be updated.

To illustrate, let a and b denote two IoT devices of zones s_1 and s_2, respectively. We assume that a locks a certain amount of money in a public account of a and b by calling a channel creation function. Next, we detail how to establish the *cross-zone off-chain channel* in **Layer-Two**.

1. a creates a transaction tx to request for establishing a cross-zone off-chain channel, then publishes it in s_1.

2. s_1's endorsers use tx to generate its corresponding sub-transactions tx_i, and send them to the target zone s_2.
3. s_2's endorsers verify tx_i and send an ack message to s_1 after adding tx_i to their own ledger.
4. Once receiving the ack, s_1's endorsers add tx to the ledger. After that, the channel is open.

By balancing channels, a and b can perform multiple cross-zone transactions off the blockchain. To *close the channel*, a proposes a close transaction, and waits the generated sub-transactions to be confirmed by zone s_2. If s_2 confirms and updates its state, an ack message will be sent to zone s_1. After adding the close transaction to the ledger of s_1, the channel can be closed.

3.3.3 Automated Sharing Transaction Workflows

Generally, the proposed framework processes transactions by running four phases, as shown in Fig. 3.3. Wherein Phase #1, depicts the participation of IoT devices.

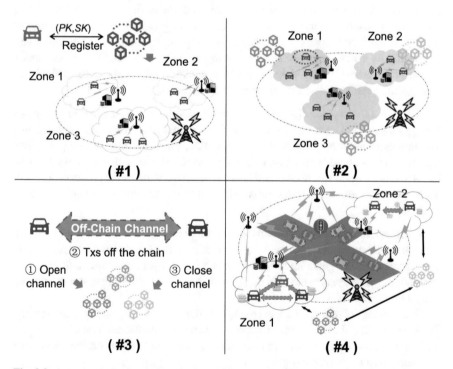

Fig. 3.3 Automated sharing transaction workflows include four phases, i.e., (#1) IoT device participation, (#2) on-chain sharding formation, (#3) cross-zone off-chain channel establishment, and (#4) payment and exchange

According to **Layer-One**, Phase #1 uses Authenticator Module to input IoT device's ID, generate a public/private key pair, and register for the device. Phase #2 employs On-Chain Management Module to assign each registered IoT device into the corresponding zone based on current GPS coordinates.

Next is selecting transaction modes. Notably, sharing economy users can select different scaling patterns for transactions, i.e., on-chain or off-chain, which entirely depends on their demands for specific sharing applications, using macro or micro transactions. Phase #3 assumes that adopting the off-chain transaction mode to handle micro-transactions with high efficiency. According to **Layer-Two**, Phase #3 utilizes Off-Chain Management Module to establish a cross-zone off-chain channel. Afterward, as illustrated in Phase #4, a scalable sharing-oriented IoT wireless system is formed, well preparing for economic payment and exchange. Thanks to smart contracts, the aforementioned phases can be executed automatically as regulatory workflows.

3.3.4   Advantages of Framework

The proposed framework is expected to bring promising benefits summarized as follows.

3.3.4.1   Real-Time

Sharing economy applied in large-scale wireless networks requires high-throughput and low-latency data processing capacities. This framework provides a combinatorial scaling solution to improve performance. Wherein on-chain sharding can partly delegate consensus to a group of zones, each of which processes different transactions independently; thus, maintaining multiple chains in parallel. The other is creating efficient cross-zone off-chain channels for shared devices to make consensus on transactions off the blockchain.

3.3.4.2   Trusted Data Interaction

Due to the upsurge of wireless traffic and connection density, there is a lack of trust among different data holders in large-scale wireless networks. Blockchain technology, as the cornerstone of building trust, has provided the proposed framework with functions to support secure data interactions, e.g., authenticator-based credible IDs, verifiable transmitted data, and smart-contract-enabled transaction workflows.

3.3.4.3 Fine-Grained Transaction Support

Integrating with the two-layer scaling protocol, this framework can scale to support all types of transactions, enabling fine-grained transaction support for multi-device sharing for large-scale wireless networks. Specifically, **Layer-One** guarantees secure and efficient macro-transactions by performing on the chain, whereas **Layer-Two** allows high frequent micro-transactions to be efficiently processed off the chain.

3.4 Case Study: ITS-Data-Sharing Economy

Data generated by advanced Intelligent Transport Systems (ITS) are undergoing exponential growth, which holds great potential to expand opportunities of the sharing economy. As a case study, we consider an ITS data trading scenario about wireless Electric Vehicles (EVs) to implement the proposed framework. As depicted in Fig. 3.3, this scenario considers a set of fixed IoT devices such as macro-base-station, roadside units, 5G small cells, and MEC servers; meanwhile, there exist multiple dynamic participating EVs. The fixed IoT devices initially divide zones and constitute the whole blockchain network, then they role as endorsers that participate in consensus and maintain blockchains. Under these assumptions, we subsequently present a proof-of-concept implementation for our proposals, using a concrete case: a red EV A wants to get shared data $\mathcal{D}$ from the blue EV B by paying x dollars.

3.4.1 Proof of Concept Implementation

To simulate fine-grained sharing transactions, we assume data $\mathcal{D}$ can be split into n chunks, i.e., $\{\mathcal{D}_0, \mathcal{D}_1, \ldots, \mathcal{D}_{n-1}\}$, each with valuable and independent meanings. Figure 3.4 illustrates the procedure details.

EV Participation and Sharding A and B first register to join the blockchain, where an authenticator module will generate their key pairs, i.e., (SK_A, PK_A) and (SK_B, PK_B), using an efficient Elliptic Curve Cryptography algorithm. Thereafter, they can be assigned as clients to corresponding zones, e.g., A belongs to *Zone A* and B belongs to *Zone B*.

Cross-Zone Channel Establishment In order to enable high-frequency data trading, opening up a cross-zone off-chain channel for A and B is necessary. The details are as follows.

- Step 1: A signs and publishes a funding transaction tx_3, sending x dollars via two cross-zone transactions, i.e., tx_3' and tx_3'', to a 2-of-2 multisig address of *Zone B* as deposit funds in the channel.

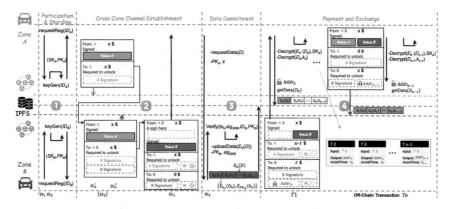

Fig. 3.4 Case study implementation of ITS-data-sharing economy, wherein, a transaction processing consists of four procedures: EVs paticipation and sharding, cross-zone channel establishment, data commitment, and the payment and exchange

- Step 2: B creates a subsequent refund transaction tx_4 to commit that the locked x dollars can be unlocked by A after M nLockTime; B signs the half of tx_4 then sends it to A.
- Step 3: If both A and B agree on the transactions and make sure tx_3'' has been recorded on the ledger of *Zone B*, tx_3' can be added to the ledger of *Zone A*. Thereafter, the off-chain channel across *Zone A* and *Zone B* is open.

Data Commitment To purchase data from B, A needs to commit a request message, indicating wanted data $\mathcal{D}$, public key PK_A, and offered price x. Then, B prepares the data by encrypting data chunks $\{\mathcal{D}_0, \mathcal{D}_1, \ldots, \mathcal{D}_{n-1}\}$ with digital envelope [15]. Herein, the ciphertext pair $\{E_{k_i}(\mathcal{D}_i), E_{PK_A}(k_i)\}$, denoted by $E_k(\mathcal{D}_i)$, stands for the well-prepared data $\mathcal{D}_i$. The split data chunks, $\{\mathcal{D}_0, \mathcal{D}_1, \ldots, \mathcal{D}_{n-1}\}$ are individually encrypted by using randomly generated symmetric keys like $\{k_0, k_1, \ldots, k_{n-1}\}$. Afterward, the well-encrypted datasets $\{E_k(\mathcal{D}_0), E_k(\mathcal{D}_1), \ldots, E_k(\mathcal{D}_{n-1})\}$ are prepared to be uploaded to the off-chain repositories, e.g., Interplanetary File System (IPFS).

For upload, B needs to create a transaction tx_5, making a data commitment signed by sig_{SK_B} and waiting for the blockchain's verification from *Zone B*. Once tx_5 is confirmed, $E_k(\mathcal{D})$ can be uploaded to the IPFS.

Payment and Exchange Next implementation offers the exchange of data storage addresses and paid dollars between A and B. Taking the payment and exchange of chunk $\mathcal{D}_0$ for an example.

- Step 1: First of all, B creates an update transaction $T1$, where the price is t ($t = \frac{x}{n}$) and the nLockTime sets $N_1(N_1 < M)$. Then, B adds on the data address $Addr_0$, signs it with SK_B, and sends $T1$ to A.
- Step 2: Once received, A confirms $T1$ and sends it back to B after signing it.

- Step 3: A obtains $\mathcal{D}_0$'s storage address $Addr_0$, thereby downloading the encrypted data $E_k(\mathcal{D}_0)$ from the IPFS.
- Step 4: To decrypt $E_k(\mathcal{D}_0)$, A uses the private key SK_A to decrypt and get k_0. After that, utilizing k_0 to decrypt $E_{k_0}(\mathcal{D}_0)$ and finally obtain $\mathcal{D}_0$ in plaintext.

That way, leveraging the update transactions, like $T1$, can effectively enable the exchange of transferring t dollars to B, thereby allowing A to obtain its wanted data addresses. To perform the update transactions more faster, the nLockTime in subsequent transactions should set smaller, i.e., $N_n < N_{n-1}$. Finally, A specifies storage hash values to download corresponding data from the IPFS, then retrieves the data via two decrypts, i.e., $Decrypt(E_k(\mathcal{D}), SK_A)$ and $Decrypt(\mathcal{D}, K)$.

The cross-zone off-chain transactions between A and B can last until the exchange of last data chunk $E_k(\mathcal{D}_{n-1})$. The settlement transaction Tn comes into effect as soon as it is signed by both A and B, which can be recorded in the ledger of *Zone B*. Thereafter, the channel will be closed.

3.4.2 Performance Evaluation

To evaluate the efficiency and effectiveness of the proposed framework, we implement a proof-of-concept prototype in Go 1.13. We employ Mininet 2.3.0d6 to build a corresponding physical network to simulate the topology, the bandwidth and delay of links, and the CPU usage of hosts. We run the Mininet on Ubuntu 16.06 on a Dell PowerEdge T630 server to emulate different EVs-data-trading in sharing economic scenarios. Table 3.1 displays the results of multiple experiments about running 100 data sharing transactions under all possible combinations of the bandwidth (10, 20, 30 Mbps), delay (50, 100, 200 ms), and the CPU (0.3, 0.5, 0.8).

In Table 3.1, Procedure 4 shows as the largest time-consuming process mainly due to the step of updating channel, where each round costs an average of 2.65 s on an off-chain update transaction. It seems a little high because such a time overhead contains the consumption of uploading a 100 KB data chunk to the IPFS involved in Procedure 3. Moreover, Procedure 1 uses Curve 25519 to implement signatures, which only needs approximately 0.22 ms to generate new public-private key pairs for each registered EV. In Procedure 2, opening up a cross-zone off-chain channel between two hosts shows a time approximately up to 1.28 s; however, once the channel has been established, it can be used multiple times until the channel is closed. In the experiment, the delay displays a huge amount of influence over overhead costs, whereas the bandwidth under real-world settings of 10 Mbps, 20 Mbps, and 30 Mbps may influence a little. Overall, the communication overhead in this experimental study on ITS-data-sharing economy can demonstrate the feasibility of our framework on the millisecond time scale.

We further conduct a series of experiments to make a performance comparison for three-type transaction processing approaches, as illustrated in Fig. 3.5. Specifically, we use the Mininet to simulate a three-tier network topology, where network

Table 3.1 Performance of the proposed framework in running 100 data sharing transactions by varying the bandwidth (10, 20, 30 Mbps), the delay (50, 100, 200 ms), and the CPU (0.3, 0.5, 0.8)

Settings		Procedure 1 (ms)		Procedure 2 (ms)	Procedure 3 (ms)	Procedure 4 (ms)	
		keyGen(A)	keyGen(B)	Create channel	Encrypt and upload	Update channel	Download and decrypt
Bandwidth, delay (20, 100)	CPU: 0.5	0.14	0.16	1207.67	1722.50 ± 40.88	2527.65 ± 40.98	1732.85 ± 10.75
	CPU: 0.3	0.22	0.16	1209.17	1764.39 ± 43.06	2569.57 ± 43.15	1618.98 ± 2.92
	CPU: 0.8	0.14	0.16	1209.27	1697.38 ± 122.15	2502.69 ± 122.31	1611.22 ± 54.28
Delay, CPU (100, 0.5)	Bandwidth: 10	0.14	0.16	1208.28	1697.08 ± 121.43	2502.37 ± 121.33	1610.49 ± 54.04
	Bandwidth: 30	0.26	0.49	1214.75	1727.17 ± 145.86	2535.06 ± 145.87	1622.26 ± 54.34
CPU, bandwidth (0.5, 20)	Delay: 50	0.26	0.47	614.76	914.64 ± 73.22	1321.59 ± 73.52	824.52 ± 33.42
	Delay: 200	0.26	0.30	2414.72	3273.44 ± 236.65	4880.54 ± 236.37	3210.29 ± 109.38

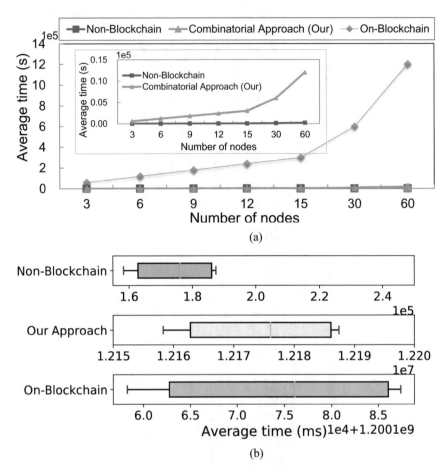

Fig. 3.5 Comparison of three-type transaction supportable approaches, i.e., on-blockchain: on-chain processing with security guarantees; non-blockchain: off-chain processing without security guarantees; our approach: on-chain and off-chain combinations. (**a**) Average time vs scales of networks. (**b**) The latency of three-type networks under a fixed number of nodes (i.e., 60)

switches and links are fixed while different hosts (i.e., A, B, and IPFS nodes) are randomly connected via the switches. As we expected, the results in Fig. 3.5a indicate that the time cost of Non-Blockchain in total shows the best; however, it is considered to be unsafe without the guarantee of blockchains. The average time overhead for On-Blockchain performs high, since it has a confirmation delay of 100 transactions in the experimental test. By contrast, our approach with combinations of on-chain sharding and off-chain channel shows superior performance in that it is as efficient as Non-Blockchain, and meanwhile, it also inherits security properties from the blockchain. Thanks to opening up cross-zone channels, our approach can efficiently perform the verification of massive cross-zone transactions off the blockchain; Fig. 3.5b shows such advantages in terms of latency. Moreover, our combinatorial approach delivers a linear growth and scales well as the number of nodes increases, which is suitable for implementing shared economy services in large-scale wireless networks.

3.5   Conclusion and Open Issues

In this chapter, we have presented a sophisticated combinatorial blockchain architecture to enable scalable sharing economy systems, which can provide real-time, trusted data interactive, and fine-grained sharing transactions for the large-scale wireless networks, allowing high throughput, low latency, and massive storage. Nonetheless, there remain some open issues envisioned as follows.

- **Contract-Based Complete Business Logic:** In reality, a contract-based programmable framework performing complete business logic actions is needed. Then, zone-based smart contracts can be developed to realize efficient sharding settings, e.g., automatically determining the zone assignment of registered IoT devices. Finally, state channels should be applied to allow the mutually distrustful wireless terminals to execute off-chain sharing-defined programs amongst themselves.
- **Multi-Blockchain Driven Platform for Heterogeneous Wireless Sharing Applications:** There exist limitations on empowering a platform that supports heterogeneous functions for diverse wireless sharing applications, e.g., cross-platform identity authentication and security assumptions. Extending sharding to multi-blockchain is an effective solution. However, since parameters vary greatly in different blockchains, making communication across multiple blockchains could be difficult as well as arising some security issues, which requires in-depth study.

Acknowledgments   The work was supported by the National Key Research and Development Plan (2021YFB2700302), the National Natural Science Foundation of China (62172453, 62032025, 62172438), the Program for Guangdong Introducing Innovative and Entrepreneurial Teams (2017ZT07X355), the Pearl River Talent Recruitment Program (2019QN01X130), and the Science and Technology Research Program of Chongqing Municipal Education Commission (KJZD-K201802401).

References

1. Barbosa, NM, Sun, E, Antin, J, Parigi P (2020) Designing for trust: a behavioral framework for sharing economy platforms. In: Proceedings of the web conference 2020, pp 2133–2143
2. Papavassiliou S, Tsiropoulou EE, Promponas P, Vamvakas P (2020) A paradigm shift toward satisfaction, realism and efficiency in wireless networks resource sharing. IEEE Netw 35(1):348–355

3. Hu S, Liang YC, Xiong Z, Niyato D (2021) Blockchain and artificial intelligence for dynamic resource sharing in 6G and beyond. IEEE Wireless Commun 28:145–151
4. Guo S, Hu X, Guo S, Qiu X, Qi F (2019) Blockchain meets edge computing: a distributed and trusted authentication system. IEEE Trans Ind Inf 16(3):1972–1983
5. Wang G, Shi ZJ, Nixon M, Han S (2019) Sok: sharding on blockchain. In: Proceedings of the 1st ACM conference on advances in financial technologies, pp 41–61
6. Gudgeon L, Moreno-Sanchez P, Roos S, McCorry P, Gervais A (2019) Sok: off the chain transactions. IACR Cryptol. ePrint Arch. 2019:360
7. Li P, Miyazaki T, Zhou W (2020) Secure balance planning of off-blockchain payment channel networks. In: IEEE INFOCOM 2020-IEEE conference on computer communications. IEEE, Piscataway, pp 1728–1737
8. Guo H, Liu J, Ren J, Zhang Y (2020) Intelligent task offloading in vehicular edge computing networks. IEEE Wireless Commun 27(4):126–132
9. Huang H, Guo S, Gui G, Yang Z, Zhang J, Sari H, Adachi F (2019) Deep learning for physical-layer 5G wireless techniques: opportunities, challenges and solutions. IEEE Wireless Commun 27(1):214–222
10. Lin K, Li C, Rodrigues JJPC, Pace P, Fortino G (2020) Data-driven joint resource allocation in large-scale heterogeneous wireless networks. IEEE Netw 34(3):163–169
11. Elgabli A, Park J, Issaid CB, Bennis M (2021) Harnessing wireless channels for scalable and privacy-preserving federated learning. IEEE Trans Commun 69(8):5194–5208
12. Aloqaily M, Boukerche A, Bouachir O, Khalid F, Jangsher S (2020) An energy trade framework using smart contracts: overview and challenges. IEEE Netw 34(4):119–125
13. Popov S (2018) The tangle. White Paper, 1(3)
14. Poon J, Dryja T (2016) The bitcoin lightning network: scalable off-chain instant payments. https://www.bitcoinlightning.com/wp-content/uploads/2018/03/lightning-network-paper.pdf.
15. Ganesan R, Gobi M, Vivekanandan K (2010) A novel digital envelope approach for a secure e-commerce channel. Int J Netw Secur 11(3):121–127

Chapter 4
Layered Sharding on Open Blockchain

Zicong Hong, Song Guo, Peng Li, and Wuhui Chen

4.1 Overview

Blockchain draws tremendous attention from academia and industry [1, 2], since it can provide distributed ledgers with data transparency, integrity, and immutability to untrusted parties for pseudonymous online payment, cheap remittance, and various decentralized applications, such as auction houses [3] and marketplaces [4]. However, existing blockchain systems have poor scalability because their consensus protocols involve all nodes [5, 6]. Every node needs to verify and store all transactions and every consensus message needs to be broadcast in the whole blockchain network.

Sharding is one of the most promising technologies that can significantly improve the scalability of blockchain [7–12]. Its main idea is to divide nodes into small groups called *shards*, which can handle transactions in parallel. A comparison between non-sharding blockchain and sharding one is shown in Fig. 4.1a, b. In

IEEE INFOCOM 2021 - IEEE Conference on Computer Communications | 978-1-6654-0325-2/21/ $31.00 © 2021 IEEE https://doi.org/10.1109/INFOCOM42981.2021.9488747

Z. Hong · S. Guo
Department of Computing, The Hong Kong Polytechnic University, Hung Hom, Hong Kong, China
e-mail: zicong.hong@connect.polyu.hk; song.guo@polyu.edu.hk

P. Li
School of Computer Science and Engineering, The University of Aizu, Aizuwakamatsu, Japan
e-mail: pengli@u-aizu.ac.jp

W. Chen (✉)
GuangDong Engineering Technology Research Center of Blockchain, Sun Yat-Sen University, Guangdong, China
e-mail: chenwuh@mail.sysu.edu.cn

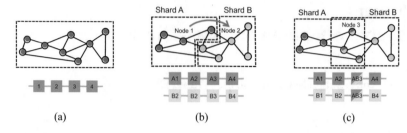

Fig. 4.1 Illustration for different blockchain systems. (**a**) Non-sharding. (**b**) Complete sharding. (**c**) Layered sharding

the non-sharding system, all nodes maintain only one blockchain. In the sharding system, each shard can maintain a blockchain and run its own consensus protocol independently. Elastico [7] is the first sharding system that achieves sharding for transaction computation, but it still needs to broadcast each block to all shards and requires all nodes to store the entire ledger. Afterwards, Omniledger [8] and RapidChain [9] have been developed to further achieve sharding for computation, storage, and communication. Besides, recent research efforts include the sharding for smart contracts [11, 13], security improvement for sharding [10], and sharding for permissioned blockchain systems [12].

The sharding scheme adopted by existing work is considered as *complete sharding* as shown in Fig. 4.1b, where shards are isolated completely and each node belongs to a single shard. The nodes in a shard are responsible for the consensus of this shard, including verification, storage, and communication. Although complete sharding can improve blockchain scalability, it raises additional challenges for cross-shard transactions, which account for a large portion of total transactions in the blockchain. According to statistics, more than 96% transactions are cross-shard in a sharding-based system [9]. Figure 4.1b illustrates a cross-shard transaction sent by Node 1 in Shard A and received by Node 2 in Shard B. Existing sharding systems, e.g., RapidChain [9] and Monoxide [10], divide each cross-shard transaction into several sub-transactions that let associated shards handle them individually to guarantee the atomicity and consistency. Therefore, the system needs to process several sub-transactions per cross-shard transaction, which seriously degrades the sharding performance in terms of throughput and confirmation latency.

In this chapter, we propose Pyramid, a novel *layered sharding* system, whose basic idea is to allow shards to overlap, rather than isolating them completely, so that some nodes can locate in more than one shard as illustrated in Fig. 4.1c. For cross-shard transactions involving the different numbers of shards, nodes located in the overlap of these shards can verify and process them directly and efficiently, rather than splitting them into a number of sub-transactions like the complete sharding. For example, in Fig. 4.1c, Node 3 can verify the cross-shard transaction given in Fig. 4.1b and propose a block including it directly because Node 3 stores the records of both shards.

Although Pyramid is promising to increase system throughput by offering an efficient way to handle cross-shard transactions, its design faces several critical challenges. The first challenge is about consensus protocol design, which specifies how to generate a block and how to verify a block. Existing sharding systems adopt either Proof-of-Work (PoW) or Byzantine-based schemes for block proposal in each shard. Due to the complete sharing, the shards can verify their blocks independently. However, some shards in Pyramid are responsible for generating blocks of cross-shard transactions. The generated blocks need to be sent to corresponding shards for commitment, which makes the consensus protocol design more challenging. The second challenge is about shard construction, i.e., how many shards are needed and which nodes should be assigned to which shards. Different from traditional sharding schemes that all shards have the identical role, shards in Pyramid play different roles. Some shards are responsible for internal transactions, while others should handle cross-shard transactions. It is critical to study shard assignment for Pyramid, which determines system throughput and security level. The main contributions of this chapter are summarized as follows:

- **Layered Sharding Architecture:** We present the formation process of layered sharding. Based on the characteristics of cross-shard transactions, we investigate the verification rules for cross-shard transactions and design a cross-shard structure for blocks. With our cross-shard block design, cross-shard transactions can be included into one single block for the consensus.
- **Layered Sharding Consensus:** We propose a layered sharding consensus protocol to commit cross-shard blocks in each shard depending on the collaboration among nodes in different shards. Compared with complete sharding in which cross-shard transactions are split into multiple sub-transactions and processed in multiple consensus rounds, our layered sharding consensus can commit each cross-shard transaction in one round thus improve the sharding performance.
- **Theoretical Analysis:** We give a theoretical analysis for Pyramid with different sharding structure in the aspect of security, scalability and performance and compare it with the non-sharding and complete sharding system considering the distribution of multi-step transactions.
- **System Implementation:** We develop a prototype for Pyramid and evaluate its performance by comparing it with two state-of-the-art complete sharding systems. The result illustrates that compared with complete sharding, Pyramid improves the transaction throughput up to 2.95 times in a system with 17 shards and 3500 nodes.

4.2 System and Threat Model

4.2.1 System Model

In Pyramid, there are N nodes and S shards in the system. The shards can be divided into two kinds. One includes nodes responsible for handling only internal transactions. They are referred to as *i-shards*. Similar with the shards in complete

Fig. 4.2 Illustration for a
layered sharding system for
i-shard A, B and b-shard C

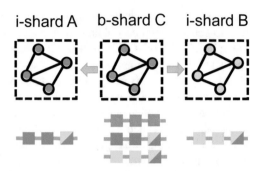

sharding schemes, each i-shard independently verifies internal transactions of the shard. The other one includes nodes bridging multiple i-shards by dealing with cross-shard transactions related to the i-shard. They are referred to as *b-shards*. Note that b-shards can handle internal transactions like i-shards, but they also take the job of processing cross-shard transactions. For example in Fig. 4.2, there are three shards in the system, i.e., i-shard A, i-shard B, and b-shard C. The b-shard C takes the job for cross-shard transactions among i-shard A and B.

Pyramid adopts the account/balance model to represent the ledger state in which each node has a pair of account and balance. The nodes in Pyramid are connected by a partially synchronous peer-to-peer network [14], and messages sent by a node can reach any other nodes with optimistic, exponentially-increasing time-outs.

4.2.2 Threat Model

There are two kinds of nodes in Pyramid: *honest* and *malicious*. The honest nodes abide by all protocols in Pyramid while malicious nodes may collude with each other and violate the protocols in arbitrary manners, such as denial of service, or tampering, forgery and interception of messages. The fraction of malicious nodes is denoted as f in the system. In other words, fN nodes are controlled by a Byzantine adversary. Furthermore, similar to other sharding systems [7–9], we assume that the Byzantine adversary is slowly-adaptive, i.e., the set of malicious nodes and honest nodes are fixed during each epoch and can be changed only between epochs.

4.3 System Design

4.3.1 Layered Sharding Formation

1. Randomness Generation The running of Pyramid proceeds in fixed time periods named *epochs*. At the beginning of each epoch, a randomness is generated via a public-verifiable, bias-resistant, unpredictable and available randomness generation method [15], e.g., the verifiable random function [16], verifable delay function [17], and trusted execution environment [12], similar to that of other sharding systems [8, 9]. It can be considered as a separated module in a sharding system and is orthogonal with our work, thus we do not discuss in detail.

2. Participation For each node, before joining an epoch, a fresh Proof-of-Work (PoW) puzzle is generated based on its public key and the randomness of the epoch. To participate in an epoch, a node needs to solve its exclusive puzzle generated in the epoch. After solving the puzzle successfully, a node needs to append its solution into an identity blockchain to register its identity. The identity blockchain is a PoW-based blockchain which is specialized to record identities of nodes, the same as the identity blockchain in [6, 8, 9]. The difficulty of PoW puzzle in each epoch can be adjusted according to the number of identities in the previous epoch to keep the number of nodes stable. If there are more than N identities in the previous epoch, the difficulty will be increased in this epoch, otherwise it will be reduced.

3. Assignment Each admitted node is assigned a shard ID randomly based on the identity of the node and the randomness generated in the epoch. The shard IDs are divided into two types, i.e., i-shard ID and b-shard ID, and each b-shard ID is corresponding to a number of i-shard IDs. The setting for shard IDs will be discussed in Sect. 4.4 that shows the setting bears on the security, scalability and performance of layered sharding. The nodes with i-shard IDs belong to the i-shards while the nodes with b-shard IDs belong to the b-shards. Note that the results of assignment for all nodes in the epoch are public and they can be computed based on the randomness in the epoch and the identity chain.

4.3.2   Cross-Shard Block Design

Transaction Definition A transaction is a payment between two accounts, namely *sender* and *receiver*. If the sender and receiver of a transaction are located in different shards, we call it a *cross-shard* transaction. A more general case about transactions involving more than two accounts and supporting smart contract is discussed in Sect. 4.3.4.

Validation Rule The validity of each transaction can be divided into *source validity* and *result validity*. The source validity denotes that the state of the sender satisfies the condition for the transaction, i.e., the sender has sufficient money, and the result validity denotes that the state of the receiver accords with the running result of the transaction, i.e., the receiver receives proper money. Only the transactions with the above two validities are supposed valid. However, the two validities for a cross-shard transaction are separately verified by two shards. In the complete sharding [10], the cross-shard transaction needs to be divided into three sub-transactions, i.e., two internal transactions and one relay transaction, to be processed in the system.

Fig. 4.3 Structure of a
cross-shard block for i-shard
A and B

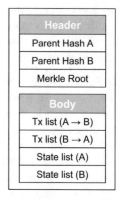

Block Design In Pyramid, each shard has a blockchain. Nodes in each i-shard store one blockchain. For each b-shard, besides its own blockchain, nodes in it store multiple blockchains, the number of which equals the number of i-shards bridged by the b-shard. Different from complete sharding, in Pyramid, nodes in b-shard can verify both the source validity and result validity of cross-shard transactions. Thus, the nodes in a b-shard can propose blocks including valid cross-shard transactions among the related i-shards, for which we propose a new cross-shard block structure as follows.

Each cross-shard block is composed of a *header* and a *body*. The header includes the hashes of parent blocks in the related i-shards and the Merkle tree root of the body. The body includes transactions and states involving with the related shards. Figure 4.3 illustrates a cross-shard block related to i-shard A and B. The body includes the cross-shard transactions between i-shard A and B, i.e., Tx list (A → B) and Tx list (B → A), and the states of accounts in i-shard A and B, i.e., State list (A) and State list (B).

Although a valid cross-shard block can be proposed by any node in a b-shard, to guarantee the consistency of states between the b-shard and its related i-shards, the cross-shard block needs to be agreed by the other nodes in the b-shard and its related i-shards depending on a layered sharding consensus in the next subsection.

4.3.3 Layered Sharding Consensus

In Pyramid, each epoch consists of a number of consensus rounds. In each consensus round, a leader will be randomly elected based on the randomness of the epoch. For each i-shard, its leader can propose a block including its internal transactions and the corresponding consensus process is similar with traditional complete sharding systems. For each b-shard, its leader can propose a block including its internal transactions or a cross-shard block associated with multiple i-shards. If the leader

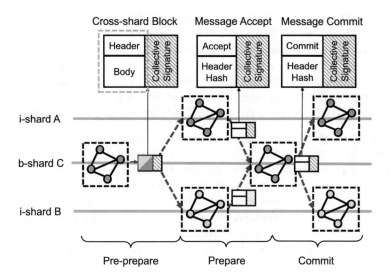

Fig. 4.4 Layered sharding consensus

of a b-shard proposes a cross-shard block, the cross-shard block is committed via a layered sharding consensus as follows.

Figure 4.4 illustrates an example of committing a cross-shard block proposed by the leader in the b-shard. The procedure of committing the cross-shard block includes three phases:

1. Block Pre-prepare As shown in Fig. 4.4, in this round, the leader of the b-shard proposes a cross-shard block related to i-shards A and B. According to Sect. 4.3.2, the nodes in the b-shard store blocks of both i-shards A and B, thus they can validate the transactions related to accounts in i-shard A and B. Therefore, the b-shard can treat the cross-shard transactions as its internal transactions.

The nodes in the b-shard achieve a consensus of the cross-shard block via a BFT protocol. For scalability, we adopt CoSi [18], a collective signing protocol that can efficiently scale to thousands of nodes, similar to the ByzCoinX in Omniledger [8]. This protocol can generate a multisignature co-signed by a decentralized group of nodes. A cross-shard block with a collective signature of a two-third super-majority of nodes attests that the b-shard agrees on it under a Byzantine environment. Besides, the collective proof constructed by echoes message using BFT in RapidChain [9] also works.

However, the cross-shard block cannot been committed yet, because the nodes in associated i-shards do not know the block and have not updated their local states according to the cross-shard transactions. Thus, the cross-shard block with the collective proof of the b-shard will be sent to the nodes of associated i-shards, i.e., i-shard A and B.

2. Block Prepare After receiving the cross-shard block with the collective proof from the b-shard, nodes in each i-shard can verify the collective signature based on public keys recorded in the identity blockchain. Then, each related i-shard can achieve a consensus for the block via the collective signing too. After the consensus is successfully reached, the i-shard sends a message of *Accept*, including the hash of header and a collective signature to the b-shard. Note that the condition for message of *Reject* is about the conflict among blocks, which will be given in the Sect. 4.3.4.

3. Block Commit After the pre-prepare phase, nodes in the b-shard initialize a counter with the number of its related i-shards. When a node in the b-shard receives a valid message of *Accept* from an associated i-shard, it will decrease its local counter and broadcast the message to other nodes in the b-shard. When the counter equals to 0, nodes in the b-shard can ensure that the cross-shard block can be committed in this round. As in PBFT, block prepare phase is insufficient to ensure that the block will be committed [6], thus an additional collective signing is needed to guarantee that the cross-shard block will be committed and a message of *Commit* including the hash of header and a collective signature will be also sent to the related i-shards.

4.3.4   Design Refinements

General Cases The above description is based on a payment between two accounts, i.e., a transaction with single step. However, the multi-step transactions, i.e., transactions involving many interactions among accounts, are common in current systems. (The figures are provided in Sect. 4.6.3.) A multi-step transaction is a sequence of interactions among accounts. Each interaction involves two accounts and its function can be the money transfer, creation and function-call of smart contracts, etc [2]. The multi-step transaction can be a cross-shard transaction involving several i-shards and be committed by the b-shard bridging these related i-shards using the layered sharding consensus in the same way as described above.

Parallel Commitment In the above design, a cross-shard block occupies the consensus round of the b-shard and its related i-shards, which hinders the commitment of internal transactions. However, internal transactions that do not conflict with the cross-shard block, i.e., involving different accounts, can be committed in each shard at the same round safely.

Therefore, we do a little improvement for Pyramid to identify conflicting blocks and commit non-conflicting blocks in each i-shard in parallel. In the prepare phase, based on the transaction list in the received blocks, each i-shard can identify the conflicting blocks. Next, based on the randomness of the epoch, each i-shard accepts one from all conflicting blocks randomly and rejects the other blocks. Thus, among all conflicting blocks, only one block can have message *Accept* and the other blocks only have message *Reject*, which stops the conflicting blocks to be committed and commits the non-conflicting blocks at the same round.

Storage Optimization According to Sect. 4.3.2, a cross-shard block includes the account states of all its associated i-shards. After the cross-shard block is committed via the layered sharding consensus, each related i-shard needs to store the block, leading to storage redundancy of account states. To reduce the storage overhead, nodes in each related i-shard can ignore the state list of other i-shards in cross-shard blocks. For example, for nodes in i-shard A, the State list (B) in the cross-shard block is redundant thus they can ignore the State list (B).

Relay Mechanism In the above design, each leader can propose cross-shard blocks related to at most its related i-shards. It raises the problem that to process all cross-shard transactions, every possible b-shard should exist, which is impossible because there are a limited number of nodes in the system. Thus, we develop Pyramid based on a relay mechanism for cross-shard transactions originating in [10].

The main idea of the mechanism is that it can divide a cross-shard transaction into a number of internal transactions. Similarly, in Pyramid, if each cross-shard transaction can be divided into several cross-shard transactions, each of which involves parts of related i-shards, the above problem can be solved. To adopt it in Pyramid, we take some minor modifications compatible with our above design. First, after a block is committed successfully, both its header and the collective signature will be broadcast to and stored in all nodes in the system. The body includes an additional list named *outbound transaction list*. The list consists of transactions whose senders belong to the related i-shard of the body but receivers do not belong to any related i-shards of the block. Thus, these outbound transaction can pass the source validity in this round. For example, the outbound transaction list of the block of Fig. 4.3 can include transaction whose senders are in i-shard A and receivers are in any i-shard except i-shard A and B, and these transaction cannot pass the result validity in this round because of the limitation of the leader. Although they are not completely committed in this round, the leader or any other nodes can send them and their corresponding Merkle tree path to the next step i-shards. Then, in the following consensus rounds, other leaders in i-shards or b-shards can use the Merkle tree path and the block header as a proof to continue the verification for these transactions.

4.4 Analysis

In this section, we give a theoretical analysis for a layered sharding system with S shards and compare it with a complete sharding system with S shards and a non-sharding system in the aspect of security, scalability and performance.

First of all, we define the layer distribution as $\mathbf{d} = \{d_1, d_2, \cdots, d_{S-1}\}$, where d_1 denotes the number of i-shards, other d_i denotes the number of b-shards bridging i shards and $\sum_{1 \le i \le S-1} d_i = S$. The layer distribution denotes the sharding structure for Pyramid. Note that a b-shard in the layered sharding can bridge $S-1$ shards at most. The complete sharding can be considered as a particular case for the layered sharding where all nodes are located in the i-shards, $d_1 = S$.

4.4.1 Security Analysis

For the security, we prove the *safety* and *liveness* property of layered sharding consensus. Similar to other consensus protocols [9, 12, 14], the safety indicates honest nodes agree on the same valid block in each round and the liveness indicates the block finality, i.e., every block proposed by the leader in each round will eventually be committed or aborted.

Theorem 4.1 *The layered sharding consensus achieves safety if there are no more than $v < \frac{1}{3}$ fraction of malicious nodes in each shard.*

Proof Given no more than $v < \frac{1}{3}$ malicious nodes in each shard, the intra-shard consensus can guarantee the cross-shard block proposed by the b-shard is valid. Then, a message along with a collective signature is honest because honest nodes are the super-majority, i.e., more than two-thirds, of the shard. Meanwhile, the message cannot be modified and forged because the collective signature can be used to detect forgery and tampering. Therefore, the communication among shards can safely proceed if there are no more than $v < \frac{1}{3}$ fraction of malicious nodes in the involved shards, which can guarantee that all related shards can receive the valid cross-shard block. The prepare phase and commit phase in the consensus similar to the two-phase commit protocol in other distributed systems [11, 12]. The prepare phase aims to reach the tentative agreement of commitment for cross-shard transactions and the commit phase aims to perform the actual commit of the transactions among the related shards. Thus, honest nodes in all related shards including i-shards and b-shards agree on the same valid cross-shard block in each round, i.e., the consensus achieves safety.

Theorem 4.2 *The layered sharding consensus achieves liveness if there are no more than $v < \frac{1}{3}$ fraction of malicious nodes in each shard.*

Proof According to the system model in Sect. 4.2.1, because the nodes are connected by a partially synchronous network and each shard has no more than $v < \frac{1}{3}$ malicious nodes, the BFT protocol adopted as the intra-shard consensus of each shard can achieve liveness. According to Theorem 4.1, each shard agrees on the same block in each round. Therefore, no malicious nodes can block the consensus indefinitely and each block will be eventually be committed or aborted, i.e., the protocol achieves liveness.

Therefore, the system failure can be defined as the event that there exists a shard with no less than 1/3 fraction of malicious nodes in the system. In Pyramid, the number of nodes in each shard is $n = N/S$. According to the cumulative hypergeometric distribution function same as [9, 12], the upper bound of the probability for the system failure in each epoch $Pr[Failure]$ can be computed by

$$Pr[Failure] < S \sum_{i=\lfloor n/3 \rfloor}^{n} \frac{\binom{fN}{i}\binom{N-fN}{n-i}}{\binom{N}{n}}. \tag{4.1}$$

By adjusting the number of nodes N and number of shards S according to (4.1), i.e., to satisfy that the system fails in each epoch with low probability, i.e., $Pr[Failure] \leq 2^{-\lambda}$ where λ is the security parameter in our system, Theorem 4.1 and 4.2 can be achieved, i.e., the layered sharding consensus achieves safety and liveness.

4.4.2 Scalability Analysis

For the scalability of a blockchain system, we define scalability parameter ω as the average complexity for the bandwidth, storage, and computation in one node in the system. For example, a b-shard bridging i i-shards needs to receive, store, and validate the blocks of i i-shards besides its own task, thus its bandwidth, storage, and computation complexity is $\frac{i+1}{S}$. Therefore, the scalability parameter of a layered sharding system can be defined as

$$\omega = \frac{1}{S} \cdot \frac{d_1}{S} + \frac{3}{S} \cdot \frac{d_2}{S} + \cdots + \frac{d_{S-1}}{S} = \frac{d_1 + \sum_{2 \leq i \leq S-1}(i+1)d_i}{S^2}. \tag{4.2}$$

According to (4.2), the scalability parameter of complete sharding is $\omega^{complete} = \frac{1}{S}$ and that of non-sharding is $\omega^{non} = 1$. The scalability parameter of layered sharding is between that of complete sharding and non-sharing blockchain and increases as the b-shards bridging more i-shards increase. In other words, when there are more b-shards bridging more i-shards in the system, the average complexity for the bandwidth, storage, and computation will increase.

4.4.3 Performance Analysis

For the performance of a blockchain system, we analyze the transaction throughput and confirmation latency of the system. The transaction throughput denotes the number of transactions processed by the system per second and the confirmation latency denotes the delay between the time that a transaction starts to be processed until the transaction is committed.

The performance of a sharding system can be affected by cross-shard transactions, thus we need to consider the distribution of cross-shard transactions in the system when evaluating its performance. We first define the distribution of transaction step $\boldsymbol{\alpha} = \{\alpha_1, \alpha_2, \cdots, \alpha_A\}$ in which α_k is the percentage of transactions involving k accounts and A is the largest possible number of accounts involving by a transaction. The distribution $\boldsymbol{\alpha}$ can be collected from a real blockchain system. Next, the distribution $\boldsymbol{\alpha}$ can be converted into another distribution $\boldsymbol{\beta} = \{\beta_1, \beta_2, \cdots, \beta_S\}$ in which β_1 is the percentage of internal transactions and other β_k is the percentage of cross-shard transactions involving k shards via a simple sampling simulation.

For each shard, because of the communication complexity of the intra-shard consensus, the latency of a consensus round will be influenced by the number of nodes in the shard. Thus, we define the latency of a consensus round in a shard with n nodes as a decreasing function $f(n)$ [19], the specific form of which depends on the type of intra-shard consensus and the propagation method in the network. We define the maximum number of transactions processed in a shard in each consensus round as K.

In a complete sharding system, each cross-shard transaction involving k shards needs to be divided into k sub-transactions at least. Thus, the maximum transaction throughput of the complete sharding system with S shards is $TPS^{complete} = \frac{SK}{f(\frac{N}{S})}(\beta_1 + \frac{\beta_2}{2} + \cdots + \frac{\beta_S}{S})$. In a non-shard system, there do not exist cross-shard transactions thus the transaction throughput of a non-sharding system is $TPS^{non} = \frac{K}{f(N)}$. It is obvious that if there are more cross-shard transactions involving more shards in the system, the transaction throughput of complete sharding systems deteriorates while that of non-sharding systems remains unchanged.

According to Sect. 4.3, the nodes in a b-shard bridging i shards can process cross-shard transactions involving i shards at most. Furthermore, for a cross-shard transaction involving more than i shards, the nodes in the b-shard can process i sub-transactions using the relay mechanism. Therefore, the maximum transaction throughput of a layered sharding system is $TPS^{layer} = \frac{SK}{f(\frac{N}{S})} \sum_{1 \le i \le S} \frac{d_i}{S}(\sum_{1 \le j \le i} \beta_j + \sum_{i+1 \le j \le S} \frac{i\beta_j}{j})$. When there are more b-shards bridging more i-shards in the layered sharding system, the transaction throughput of the system will increase.

In the complete sharding system, each of the sub-transactions for a cross-shard transaction needs to be committed in a round one by one, thus the expected confirmation latency is $CONF^{complete} = f(\frac{N}{S}) \sum_{1 \le i \le S} i\beta_i$. In the non-sharding system, the expected confirmation latency is $CONF^{non} = f(N)$. In the layered sharding system, the cross-shard transaction can be committed in a round if it is committed by a b-shard bridging its related shards, thus the expected confirmation latency is $CONF^{layer} = f(\frac{N}{S})$.

4.5   Evaluation

4.5.1   Implementation

We implement a prototype of Pyramid in Go[1] for performance evaluation. For comparison, we also implement two complete sharding prototypes. According to Sect. 4.3.3, since the intra-shard consensus in the layered sharding can be substituted by any other BFT consensus, to ensure the result will not be affected by the difference in intra-shard consensus, we adopt the ByzCoinX proposed in Omniledger [8] for the intra-shard consensus for these two complete sharding prototypes. The difference between two prototypes is the cross-shard transaction processing. The first one uses the relay mechanism in Monoxide [10] and the second one uses the transfer mechanism in RapidChain [9].

4.5.2   Setup

Similar to most running blockchain testbeds, the bandwidth of all connections between nodes are set to 20 Mbps and the links are with a latency of 100 ms in our testbed. In a consensus round, each node can verify up to 4096 transactions, each of which is 512 bytes. We generate a transaction data set in which the average step of transactions is set as 6. Furthermore, based on the data provided by XBlock [20], we can collect a historical transaction set of Ethereum. The security parameter λ is set as 17, which means the failure probability needs to smaller than $2^{-17} \approx 7.6 \cdot 10^{-6}$, i.e., one failure in about 359 years for one-day epochs.

4.5.3   Throughput

We measure the transaction throughput in transactions per second (TPS) for complete sharding and layered sharding with varying shard number S and scalability parameter ω and the result is illustrated in Fig. 4.5. The shard number S is set to 5, 7, 9, 11, 13, 15, 17, 20 and the scalability parameter ω is set to 0.2, 0.3, 0.4, 0.5. The layer distribution **d** is set based on the scalability parameter. The fraction of malicious nodes f is set as 12.5%. To guarantee the safety and liveness with high probability, according to (4.1), we adjust the number of shards when the number of nodes changes. As shown in Table 4.1, all cases of the experiment in Fig. 4.5 satisfy $Pr[Failure] < 2^{-17}$. Figure 4.5 illustrates that the TPS of layered sharding increases $1.5 \sim 2$ times when doubling the shard number, and the TPS increases by

---

[1] https://golang.org/.

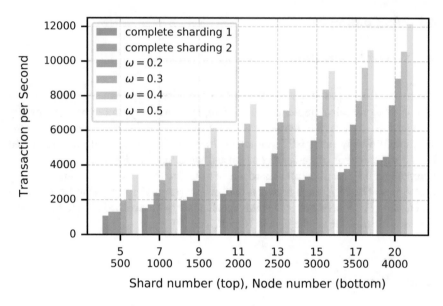

Fig. 4.5 Transaction throughput for layered sharding with varying shard number S and scalability parameter ω

Table 4.1 Failure probability for varying shard number and node number when percentage of malicious node $f = 12.5\%$

Shard number S, node number N			
Failure probability $Pr[Failure]$			
5, 500	7, 1000	9, 1500	11, 2000
$1.5 \cdot 10^{-9}$	$8.4 \cdot 10^{-12}$	$5.1 \cdot 10^{-13}$	$1.4 \cdot 10^{-13}$
13, 2500	15, 3000	17, 3500	20, 4000
$2.8 \cdot 10^{-14}$	$3.9 \cdot 10^{-14}$	$1.7 \cdot 10^{-14}$	$1.1 \cdot 10^{-13}$

about 50% compared with two complete sharding prototypes for every 0.1 growth of scalability parameter ω.

We also evaluate the transaction throughput and failure probability influenced by the varying fraction of malicious nodes in Pyramid with shard number $S = 17$ and the scalability parameter $\omega = 0.3$. In our implementation, a malicious node can work when it is elected as a leader, and it generates and broadcasts the wrong block to interfere with the normal running of consensus. Figure 4.6 illustrates that as the fraction of malicious nodes increases, the TPS of Pyramid decreases in the approximate proportion. It is because the layered sharding consensus can guarantee that the blocks proposed by malicious nodes will be detected and aborted. Furthermore, as shown in the figure, the failure probability increases when there are more malicious nodes in the system and the percentage of the malicious node needs to be less than 19% to satisfy $Pr[Failure] < 2^{-17}$.

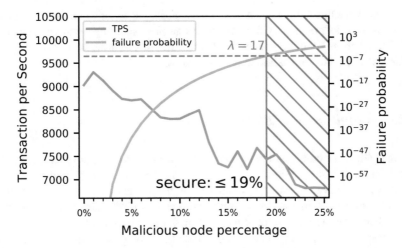

Fig. 4.6 Transaction throughput and failure probability for varying malicious node fraction with shard number $S = 17$ and scalability parameter $\omega = 0.3$

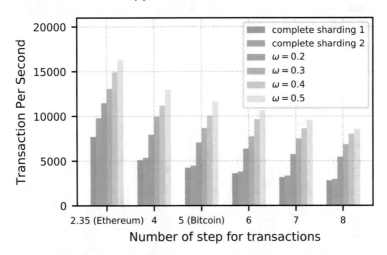

Fig. 4.7 Transaction throughput for transactions with different number of steps with shard number $S = 17$

The above experiments are based on the transaction set in which the average step of transactions is 6. However, in different systems, the average step of transactions is different. Furthermore, the proportion of multi-step transactions is increasing over time because of the popularity of smart contracts which can produce transactions with more complex logic. We evaluate the performance of layered sharding when there are different numbers of steps for transactions in the system with 17 shards and 12.5% malicious nodes and the result is illustrated in Fig. 4.7. As shown in Fig. 4.7, the TPS decreases with the increase of the number of steps. Furthermore, the effect of the throughput boost of layered sharding is better when the transactions have more number of steps. Compared with complete sharding prototype 1, layered sharding with $\omega = 0.5$ achieves 2.12 times for transactions with 2.35 step and achieves 3.03 times for transactions with 8 steps.

4.5.4 Confirmation Latency

We then study the confirmation latency of transactions in complete sharding system and layered sharding system. As shown in Fig. 4.8, the latency increases as the number of shards increases and decreases as the scalability parameter increases. For the number of shards, it is because more shards in the system result in more cross-shard transactions. According to Sect. 4.4.3, cross-shard transactions need more consensus round to be committed, thus the average confirmation latency of transactions increases. For the scalability parameter, it is because a higher scalability parameter denotes more b-shards in the system and a b-shard can commit cross-shard transactions related to the shards it bridges in one consensus round, which greatly shorten the confirmation latency.

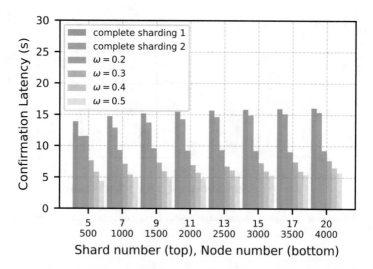

Fig. 4.8 Confirmation latency for layered sharding with varying shard number S and scalability parameter ω

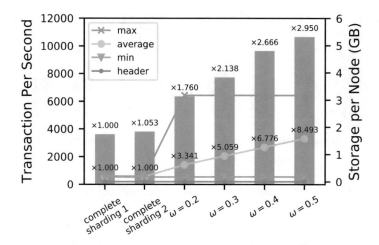

Fig. 4.9 Storage overhead per node after processing 1 million transactions for layered sharding with varying scalability parameter ω

4.5.5   Storage Overhead

We evaluate the storage overhead per node after processing 1 million transactions for different scalability parameter ω when there are 17 shards and 3500 nodes and show the evaluation result in Fig. 4.9. First, we can observe that as the scalability parameter ω increases, both the transaction throughput and average storage overhead increase. In particular, compared with complete sharding prototype 1, layered sharding with $\omega = 0.5$ can improve the transaction throughput to 2.95 times when introducing 8.49 times average storage overhead. Note that the main bottleneck in most sharding-based blockchain systems is the transaction throughput rather than storage overhead currently because the storage overhead can be solved by state-compaction process such as checkpoint mechanism [8, 21]. Second, we can observe that the maximum storage per node is unchanged in layered sharding, which is because the maximum storage mainly depends on the maximum number of i-shards bridged by a b-shard in the system. Finally, compared with the entire block, the storage of headers can be ignored.

4.5.6   Commit Ratio

According to Sect. 4.3.4, in each round, there may exist conflicting blocks that are proposed by different leaders but involve the state of the same accounts. Only one block can be committed among the conflict blocks. To study the block conflict in layered sharding, we measure the commit ratio for varying shard numbers and scalability parameters in Pyramid. The commit ratio denotes the proportion of

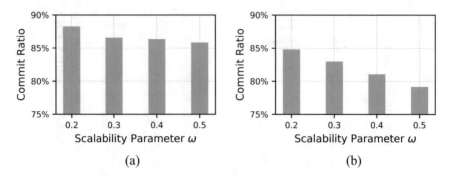

Fig. 4.10 Commit ratio for varying shard number and scalability parameter ω. (**a**) Shard number $S = 5$. (**b**) Shard number $S = 20$

committed blocks. Figure 4.10 illustrates that as the scalability parameter increases, the commit ratio in the system decreases. It is because there are more b-shards in the system, which causes conflict probability higher and more blocks to be aborted. Furthermore, we can see that the decrease in the commit ratio for shard number $S = 5$ is less than that for shard number $S = 20$. It is because there are fewer accounts in a shard when the shard number increases, which causes a higher conflict probability.

4.6 Discussion

4.6.1 Comparison with Shard Overlapping in Complete Sharding

In the sharding formation of RapidChain [9], shards can be sampled with or without replacement from the total population of nodes. If the complete sharding samples shards with replacement, nodes can be located in multiple shards, however, which is different from the layered sharding. In the complete sharding, although the nodes in multiple shards also store blocks of multiple shards, they only propose blocks involving one single shard in each consensus round, which will not improve the performance.

4.6.2 Heterogeneous Blockchain Node

In most sharding systems, the blockchain nodes are assumed to be homogeneous for computation, storage, and communication, which keeps a major bottleneck to the performance of sharding and violates the practice. Sharding complicates the structure of the blockchain system and makes it hierarchical. The computation, storage, and communication capacity of a node can influence its ability to process transactions, store historical data and relay message in the consensus of a sharding system. Therefore, it is important to consider the heterogeneity of blockchain nodes for improving the scalability of a sharding system. Furthermore, in practice, the nodes can be kinds of IoT devices or edge/cloud servers [22]. For example, in a blockchain smart grid, vehicles, roadside units, and gas/washing stations can be the blockchain nodes [23]. In a blockchain smart home, smartphones, personal computers, and other smart devices can be blockchain nodes [24]. Heterogeneous blockchain nodes with different capacity can be assigned to different layers in the layered sharding. For example, nodes with higher capacity of computation, storage, and communication can be assigned to the higher layer in our layered sharding system with higher probability, which will be considered in our future work.

4.6.3 Multi-Step Transactions

For the account/balance model, there are a number of operations raising the interactions among smart contracts, including the creation of new contracts, function-call of and data-return from other existing contracts [2, 25]. According to the data provided by XBlock [20], we conduct an analysis for Ethereum from July 30th, 2015 to July 6th, 2019 and find more than 15% smart contract related transactions are composed by more than 1 steps and the average number of accounts in a transaction is 3.35. Furthermore, because of the popularity of more complex smart contracts, the proportion of multi-step transactions will be increasing over time. For the UTXO model, the Pay-to-Script-Hash popularizes multi-step transactions [26]. Based on Bitcoin data, the average number of inputs and outputs in a transaction is 2 and 3, respectively [27]. According to Sect. 4.5.3, the layered sharding can boost the transaction throughput more effectively when transactions have more steps, therefore we believe the layered sharding can make more sense in the future.

4.7 Conclusion

We present Pyramid, the first layered sharding blockchain system. At its core, Pyramid allows some shards storing the state of multiple other shards to form layered sharding structure thus handles cross-shard transactions efficiently. It exploits shards to work as a bridge among other shards to verify and process cross-shard transactions so that their atomicity and consistency can be guaranteed with lower overhead. In order to commit the cross-shard transactions safely and efficiently in the layered sharding, Pyramid propose a new structure of cross-shard blocks, and accordingly provides a layered sharding consensus that can scale well as the number of related shards for cross-shard blocks. Finally, the evaluation result illustrates that layered sharding provides improvements in many aspects. In particular, compared with complete sharding, layered sharding can improve the transaction throughput up to 2.95 times in a system with 17 shards and 3500 nodes. In the future work, we plan to study the dynamic layered sharding and the transactions placement method for layered sharding.

Acknowledgments The work described in this chapter was supported by the National Key Research and Development Plan (2018YFB1003800), the National Natural Science Foundation of China (61872310, 61802450), JSPS Grants-in-Aid for Scientific Research grant number JP19K20258, Hong Kong RGC Research Impact Fund (RIF) with the Project No. R5060-19 and R5034-18, General Research Fund (GRF) with the Project No. 152221/19E, Collaborative Research Fund (CRF) with the Project No. C5026-18G, the Natural Science Foundation of Guangdong (2018A030313005), the Program for Guangdong Introducing Innovative and Entrepreneurial Teams (2017ZT07X355), and the Pearl River Talent Recruitment Program (No. 2019QN01X130).

References

1. Nakamoto S (2008) Bitcoin: A peer-to-peer electronic cash system. Decentralized Business Review 21260
2. Wood G (2014) Ethereum: asecure decentralised generalised transaction ledger. Ethereum Project Yellow Paper
3. Auctionity, The world's largest blockchain auction house for crypto collectibles. https://www.auctionity.com/
4. OpenSea, A peer-to-peer marketplace for rare digital items and crypto collectibles. https://opensea.io/
5. Eyal I, Gencer AE, Sirer EG, Renesse RV (2016) Bitcoin-NG: a scalable blockchain protocol. In: 13th USENIX symposium on networked systems design and implementation (NSDI 16). USENIX Association
6. Kogias EK, Jovanovic P, Gailly N, Khoffi I, Gasser L, Ford B (2016) Enhancing bitcoin security and performance with strong consistency via collective signing. In: 25th USENIX security symposium (USENIX security), Austin, TX, August 2016, vol 16, pp 279–296. USENIX Association
7. Luu L, Narayanan V, Zheng C, Baweja K, Gilbert S, Saxena P (2016) A secure sharding protocol for open blockchains. In: Proceedings of the 2016 ACM SIGSAC conference on computer and communications security (CCS 16). ACM, New York
8. E Kokoris-Kogias, P Jovanovic, L Gasser, N Gailly, E Syta, B Ford (2018) Omniledger: a secure, scale-out, decentralized ledger via sharding. In: 2018 IEEE symposium on security and privacy (SP)
9. Zamani M, Movahedi M, Raykova M (2018) Rapidchain: scaling blockchain via full sharding. In: Proceedings of the 2018 ACM SIGSAC conference on computer and communications security (CCS'18). ACM, New York
10. Wang J, Wang H (2019) Monoxide: scale out blockchains with asynchronous consensus zones. In: 16th USENIX symposium on networked systems design and implementation (NSDI'19). USENIX Association
11. Al-Bassam M, Sonnino A, Bano S, Hrycyszyn D, Danezis G (2017) Chainspace: a sharded smart contracts platform. CoRR, abs/1708.03778
12. Dang H, Dinh TTA, Loghin D, Chang EC, Lin Q, Ooi EC (2019) Towards scaling blockchain systems via sharding. In: Proceedings of the 2019 international conference on management of data, SIGMOD'19. ACM, New York

13. Y Tao, B Li, J Jiang, HC Ng, B Li, C Wang (2020) On sharding open blockchains with smart contracts. In: 2020 IEEE 36th international conference on data engineering (ICDE)
14. Castro M, Liskov B (1999) Practical byzantine fault tolerance. In: Proceedings of the third symposium on operating systems design and implementation (OSDI'99). USENIX Association
15. Wang G, Shi ZJ, Nixon M, Han S (2019) SoK: sharding on blockchain. In: Proceedings of the 1st ACM conference on advances in financial technologies. ACM, New York
16. Micali S, Rabin M, Vadhan S (1999) Verifiable random functions. In: 40th annual symposium on foundations of computer science (Cat. No. 99CB37039), pp 120–130. IEEE, Piscataway
17. Boneh D, Bonneau J, Bünz B, Fisch B (2018) Verifiable delay functions. In: Annual international cryptology conference. Springer, Berlin, pp 757–788
18. E Syta, I Tamas, D Visher, DI Wolinsky, P Jovanovic, L Gasser, N Gailly, I Khoffi, B Ford (2016) Keeping authorities "honest or bust" with decentralized witness cosigning. In: 2016 IEEE symposium on security and privacy (SP), pp 526–545
19. Z Ni, W Wang, DI Kim, P Wang, D Niyato, Evolutionary game for consensus provision in permissionless blockchain networks with shards. In: 2019 IEEE international conference on communications (ICC'19), pp 1–6
20. Zheng P, Zheng Z, Dai HN (2019) XBlock-ETH: extracting and exploring blockchain data from ethereum. Working Report
21. Avarikioti G, Kokoris-Kogias E, Wattenhofer R (2019) Divide and scale: formalization of distributed ledger sharding protocols. Preprint. arXiv:1910.10434
22. Chen W, Zhang Z, Hong Z, Chen C, Wu J, Maharjan S, Zheng Z, Zhang Y (2019) Cooperative and distributed computation offloading for blockchain-empowered industrial internet of things. IEEE Internet Things J 6:8433–8446
23. Jiang T, Fang H, Wang H (2019) Blockchain-based internet of vehicles: distributed network architecture and performance analysis. IEEE Internet Things J 6:4640–4649
24. Dorri A, Kanhere SS, Jurdak R, Gauravaram P (2017) Blockchain for iot security and privacy: the case study of a smart home. In: 2017 IEEE international conference on pervasive computing and communications workshops (PerCom workshops)
25. Chen T, Zhu Y, Li Z, Chen J, Li X, Luo X, Lin X, Zhange X (2018) Understanding ethereum via graph analysis. In: IEEE INFOCOM 2018 - IEEE conference on computer communications
26. Antonopoulos AM (2017) Mastering bitcoin: programming the open blockchain. O'Reilly Media, Newton
27. Visuals B, Average number of inputs and outputs of a transaction in bitcoin. https://https://bitcoinvisuals.com/

Chapter 5
Sharding-Based Scalable Consortium Blockchain

Peilin Zheng, Quanqing Xu, Zibin Zheng, Zhiyuan Zhou, Ying Yan, and Hui Zhang

5.1 Overview

Blockchain and blockchain-based smart contracts have wide applications nowadays [1]. Consortium blockchain systems are maintained by all the consortium members, carrying out business such as cross-border exchange, goods tracing, and so on [1]. However, the performance of consortium blockchain cannot meet the requirement of applications [2]. For example, as well-known, e-commerce shopping festivals require more than 100,000 TPS (Transaction Per Second) at their peaks, which cannot be supported by mainstream consortium blockchain systems currently. Therefore, improving the performance of consortium blockchain is urgent.

In order to improve the blockchain performance, sharding is one of the optional methods. There are lots of studies that focus on blockchain sharding, (e.g., Elastico [3], RapidChain [4], Monoxide [5], AHL+ [6], Tao et al. [7], Huang et al. [8]). The common idea of these studies is to divide the transactions and servers into different shards. Generally, each shard is a blockchain, of which the transactions are validated by several corresponding servers. These shards can communicate with each other

0733-8716 © 2022 IEEE Digital Object Identifier https://doi.org/10.1109/JSAC.2022.3213326

P. Zheng
School of Computer Science and Engineering, Sun Yat-Sen University, Guangzhou, China

Q. Xu · Z. Zhou · Y. Yan · H. Zhang
Blockchain Platform Division, Ant Group, Hangzhou, China

Z. Zheng (✉)
GuangDong Engineering Technology Research Center of Blockchain, Sun Yat-Sen University, Guangdong, China
e-mail: zhzibin@mail.sysu.edu.cn

© The Author(s), under exclusive license to Springer Nature Singapore Pte Ltd. 2023
W. Chen et al. (eds.), *Blockchain Scalability*,
https://doi.org/10.1007/978-981-99-1059-5_5

through cross-shard protocols. Thus the throughput of the entire network is the sum of all shards, which has been improved.

However, the previous sharding studies focus little on consortium blockchain, and they cannot meet the following practical requirements of consortium blockchain: **(1) High cross-shard efficiency:** A transaction that needs to be executed on multiple shards is called a cross-shard transaction. In previous public blockchain sharding research, the cross-shard efficiency is sacrificed for security because of the incompleteness of the ledger. However, consortium blockchain requires a complete ledger in practice and higher cross-shard efficiency than public blockchain. Novel cross-shard approaches need to be designed. **(2) Flexible multiple-shard contract calling:** Previous studies focus on simple payment transactions or simple payment contracts on the blockchain. However, most consortium blockchain applications run on complex smart contracts. One contract on consortium blockchain might call the state in several shards and contracts, which cannot be supported well by previous work. For example, according to our statistics of real-world shopping cases in Taobao.com [9], one user can buy up to 50 items (on different shards) in one transaction. We also prove this challenge by evaluating an e-commerce contract with real-world shopping transactions in Sect. 5.4.2. **(3) Strict transaction atomicity:** The business models on consortium blockchain need strict transaction atomicity [10], and this atomicity should be ensured within one block. Previous sharding studies cannot ensure strict atomicity in such a short time within a block. **(4) Shard availability:** The data on the consortium blockchain is read and written by the members far more frequently than public blockchain, requiring higher availability. Improving the complexity of the system will reduce availability. Thus a new method needs to be designed to enhance availability.

To solve the above problems in consortium blockchain sharding, we propose *Meepo*, as its idea is to use Multiple Execution Environments Per Organization. The topology of servers in Meepo is shown in Fig. 5.1, where each consortium member holds all the shards. In Meepo, we provide four solutions for the above challenges:

Cross-epoch and Cross-call is the main idea of this chapter. It is an internal cross-shard protocol for the consortium member. In Meepo, after the consensus of each block ends, each shard begins to communicate across shards. This process is called cross-epoch. Cross-call is the message from one shard to another. It results

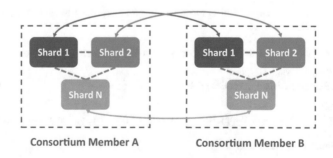

Fig. 5.1 Topology of servers in sharded consortium blockchain

from cross-shard transactions, such as cross-shard payments. Meepo aggregates cross-calls into several cross-epochs in order. In this way, cross-shard communication can be done efficiently and orderly within each consortium member, ensuring the consistency of them.

Partial Cross-call Merging Strategy is used to improve the smart contract flexibility in sharded environments. Meepo allows smart contracts to send the cross-calls that are with partial parameters from different shards, then merges these partial cross-calls into a full one to execute it on one shard, like a callback function. In this way, using only one transaction, the state of different shards can be parallelly operated or passed into one shard for complex smart contracts.

Replay-epoch is designed to ensure the transaction atomicity. Once some transaction exceptions (errors) occur, all the shards will replay the transactions without the errors, namely replay-epoch. Only the successful transactions will be executed, and the wrong ones will be reverted. In this way, Meepo provides atomic guarantees for cross-shard transactions within the duration of one block.

Shadow Shard Based Recovery is proposed to enhance the availability of the consortium member. It is a hot backup method. We equip the shards with several backup servers called shadow shards. Once any shard is down, the consortium member can switch to its corresponding backup to continue the execution of blockchain transactions. Thus it can reduce the impact of a single point of failure on system availability.

Evaluation We evaluate the performance of Meepo through the implementation on OpenEthereum, named Meepo-OpenEthereum,[1] on a test-bed of 128 AliCloud servers. Setting 32 shards and 4 consortium members ($32 \times 4 = 128$ servers), under the workload of more than 100,000,000 transactions among 3,276,800 accounts, Meepo can achieve more than 140,000 cross-shard TPS. The same configuration also shows more than 50,000 TPS under the transactions of real-world shopping behaviors from Taobao.com [9]. All the scripts and logs are also open-source for verification.[2] Detailed evaluation will be given in Sect. 5.4.

In summary, the contributions are as follows:

- We propose Meepo, as a sharded consortium blockchain system, with a cross-epoch based cross-shard protocol designed for consortium blockchain, achieving high cross-shard efficiency.
- We design a partial cross-call merging strategy to enable smart contracts to make flexible calling to multiple shards, meeting the requirement of complex business models on consortium blockchain systems.
- We propose a replay-epoch based method to cancel the operation of error transactions, ensuring strict transaction atomicity in the time of one block.
- We propose a hot backup method for sharded consortium blockchain, namely shadow shard, to improve the robustness of the consortium member.

---

[1] https://github.com/InPlusLab/Meepo/.

[2] https://github.com/tczpl/MeepoBenchmark/.

5.2 System Model

In this section, we will propose an overview of Meepo. First, we will describe the goals and challenges of the sharded consortium blockchain. After that, for each challenge, we will propose our solution in the following sections.

5.2.1 Challenges (Goals)

In most business scenarios in consortium blockchain, each consortium member needs to hold the complete ledger and state, since the complete business data is needed by all the consortium members. In other words, in practice, although the transactions are divided into different shards, the state of shards is best to be possessed by every consortium member to improve the authority and availability of the ledger. In this case, the topology of the sharded consortium blockchain is shown in Fig. 5.1.

Besides the above goal of ledger completeness, there are some other goals that are also challenging, as follows:

C1: High Cross-Shard Efficiency Cross-shard transaction is a transaction executed in more than one shard. In sharded consortium blockchain, the cross-shard transactions might be very frequent. For example, as for a payment application, the payment might be from one shard to another, needing cross-shard communication. And, especially in consortium blockchain, we cannot set up the account distribution to reduce the cross-shard communication either, since users' potential behaviors in the future cannot be predicted. In this case, although we can improve the performance of computing and storage through sharding, the overall performance of the network will still be limited to the performance of cross-shard communication. In other words, the performance of the entire network depends on the performance of cross-shard communication. Therefore, the only way is to improve cross-shard efficiency, which is the key challenge of the sharded consortium blockchain.

C2: Flexible Multiple-Shard Contract Calling Previous blockchain sharding research focuses on a transaction model that is just from one shard to another, such as a payment or a one-hop calling from one account to one contract. However, smart contracts are not always as simple as payment, especially in consortium blockchain. For an e-commerce example, if a customer wants to order several items that are on different shards, his transaction needs to get prices and stocks from different shards. When the transaction wants to operate the state of multiple shards, using the previous methods, it has to go through several shards in serial. Thus that can be a long way in the network of sharded consortium blockchain, leading to inefficiency. In a public blockchain, this phenomenon is not particularly significant. However, in consortium blockchain, smart contracts are more complicated due to the aggregation of more data and more complex business models (will be evaluated in Sect. 5.4.2).

Therefore, it is the key challenge and requirement for consortium blockchain to enable flexible multiple-shard contract calling in the sharded environment.

C3: Strict Transaction Atomicity Transaction atomicity is essential in both public and consortium blockchain. For a specific real-world example, the bank's batch deduction will operate the state of accounts on multiple shards. These operations should succeed or fail together, namely transaction atomicity. Previous studies can be divided into two common methods to enhance cross-shard atomicity. One is the asynchronous method, allowing blockchain transactions across several blocks with a final asynchronous check. The other is a Two-phase Commit method (e.g.lock-commit), which is close to some deterministic concurrency control protocols such as Calvin [11]. Unfortunately, these two methods cannot work very well in sharded consortium blockchain for the following reasons. As an example of a bank, the first method is not acceptable since the delay is high and cannot provide immediate confirmation, while the second method locks all the related accounts, preventing them from other transactions in this duration. Therefore, previous studies cannot be used on sharded consortium blockchain to ensure strict transaction atomicity in an acceptable short time, which is also an important challenge.

C4: Shard Availability In consortium blockchain, availability is vital. As mentioned before, consortium members need to read and write the data of shards. In addition, cross-shard communication of Meepo also needs the shards to be online (will be proposed in the next section), resulting in very high requirements for shard availability, which becomes a problem in sharded consortium blockchain. A simple hot or cold backup of data cannot solve this problem since the shard plays a vital role in the verification and execution of blocks. Moreover, the synchronization and switching of backups need to maintain communication and consistency with other shards. In Meepo, as for a member, the network situation and shards must be in good condition, or it will fall behind other peers. Designing a new mechanism to improve shard availability becomes a challenge.

5.2.2 Our Solution

Facing the above challenges, we provide the corresponding solutions in Meepo, as the overview shown in Fig. 5.2. Once the blocks reach the consensus in different shards, cross-shard communication will begin through these approaches. As Fig. 5.2 shows, **S1** and **S2** are used for cross-shard calling. More specifically, **S1** is designed to attack the problem of **C1**, enabling efficient cross-shard communication based on the cross-epochs and cross-calls. And **S2** is proposed to achieve flexible contract calling, enabling the smart contracts to call the state on different shards and contracts. Moreover, **S3** is designed to revert the operation of error transactions, which is the solution to the challenge in **C3**. Finally, **S4** ensures shard availability when any machine is down, solving **C4**. The relationship of the four solutions is as follows. S1 is the main idea and also the basis of Meepo. It solves the main challenge

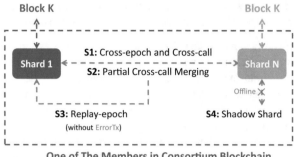

Fig. 5.2 Overview of cross-shard solutions in Meepo

C1. However, S1 leads to three new challenges: flexibility (C2), atomicity (C3), and availability (C4). Therefore, we need S2, S3, and S4 to solve the challenges caused by S1.

5.3 Detailed Cross-Shard Solutions

5.3.1 Cross-Epoch and Cross-Call

Main Idea To achieve high cross-shard efficiency, we propose a cross-shard protocol based on the cross-epochs and cross-calls. The main idea is to import several cross-epochs between the blocks, as shown in Figs. 5.3 and 5.4. After the block propagation and validation are completed, the shard communicates and executes cross-shard transactions. Figure 5.4 shows an example with three shards. As shown in Fig. 5.3, an arrow represents a data package from one shard to another. Each data package consists of a set of messages, which are the cross-calls to the

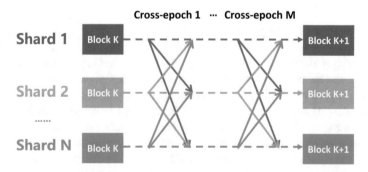

Fig. 5.3 Cross-epochs after blocks as cross-shard communication in Meepo

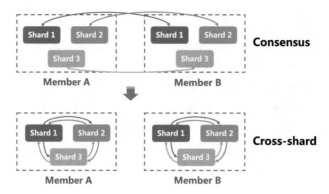

Fig. 5.4 Example of consensus and cross-shard communication in Meepo

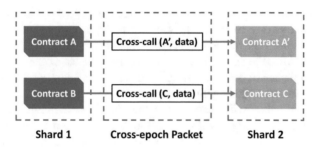

Fig. 5.5 Cross-calls in cross-epoch of Meepo

same shard, executed by the target shard. The execution of one cross-epoch can generate cross-calls, which will be executed in the next cross-epoch. When there are no more cross-calls, the cross-epochs finish. After that, the shards begin to generate or import the next blocks. Note that a "shard" here refers to a server that belongs to a consortium member. And the communication of the above "shards" is in the internal network of the consortium member.

Difficulty The exact problem is how to arrange the cross-calls into the cross-epochs and how to make the cross-epochs be in the same order in such a complex distributed system.

Details At each cross-epoch, Meepo arranges the cross-calls from one shard to another into one packet. The packet is shown in Fig. 5.5. As an example of an EVM-based smart contract, one cross-call can be represented as a tuple of <*ShardID, Contract, Data*>, where *ShardID* is the index of the target shard, *Contract* is the address of the calling contract, and *Data* includes the calling function and the parameters. The calling contract can be any address, including the original contract itself. What should be noted is that, in consortium blockchain, generally, there is no native cryptocurrency like Ethereum [12], and the assets are stored in contracts. Thus we do not design a "Value" filed in the structure of cross-call.

Algorithm 1: Pseudocode of example of asset transferring contract using cross-call in Meepo

---

1 public function transfer (to, value):

2   require(balanceOf[msg.sender]>=value);

3   balanceOf[msg.sender] -= value;

4   **CrossCall**(shardOf[to], this, "add", to, value);

5 cross function add (to, value):

6   balanceOf[to] += value;

To aid understanding, we provide the pseudocode example of an asset transferring smart contract (see footnote 2), as shown in Algorithm 1. This contract uses the public function "transfer" to do the cross-shard transaction, which can be called by the clients. After the smart contract deducts the balance of the sender, it sends a cross-call to the shard of "to", calling itself (the same address on another shard) to execute the function "add" with the parameters "to" and "value". In this call, the "add", "to", and "value" will be encoded as the "data" shown in Fig. 5.5. Finally, on the target shard, the contract will execute the "add" function to add up the asset, finishing the cross-shard transaction. Note that the "add" is a "cross" function, representing that it can only be triggered in the cross-epoch, protecting it from being triggered by malicious users.

In the specific design in Meepo, there are more fields in the structure of cross-call. The structure of cross-call can be represented as the tuple of <From, To, Data, IsPartial, TxHash>. We add up two more fields (*IsPartial* and *TxHash*) to the original blockchain transaction (From, To, Data), in order to prepare for the *Partial Cross-call Merging Strategy* and *Repay-epoch*. In the meanwhile, we omit the *ShardID* filed because it is represented in the cross-epoch packet, as shown in Table 5.1. Table 5.1 shows the detailed structure of a cross-epoch packet in Meepo. Besides a serial of cross-calls, we add up more fields in it. The *ErrorTx* field is designed to broadcast the transaction exceptions for all the shards, in preparation for the *replay-epoch*. Moreover, the *EpochNumber* field is designed to identify different epoch packets when the packets arrive out of order in such a distributed system of the consortium member, as shown in the following steps.

Suppose there are **N** shards and **M** cross-epochs for cross-shard communication, in the duration of the cross-epoch, each shard goes through 3 steps: (1) Sending: Each shard sends totally *N-1* packets to others. (2) Waiting: Each shard waits for the packets from other shards. This step might be mixed with the same step in other cross-epochs, as some shards could be faster than others. For example, if *Shard 1* is faster than *Shard 2* and *Shard 3*, then Shard2 may receive packet of *Cross-epoch 2* from *Shard 1* before *Shard 2* receives packet of *Cross-epoch 1* from *Shard 3*. With the *EpochNumber*, *Shard 2* can identify the packet of *Cross-epoch 2*. Without the

Table 5.1 Detailed structure of cross-epoch packet

Filed	Description
CrossCalls[]	An array of the cross-calls.
Finished	Whether the shard has no cross-calls.
ErrorTx[]	Hash values of the error transactions.
FromShard	The shard where the packet is from.
ToShard	The shard where the packet is to.
EpochNumber	The cumulative number of the epochs.

EpochNumber, the order in *Shard 2* will be wrong. In this step, the shard will not execute the packets until all of them (*N-1* packets from others) are received. (3) Executing: Each shard executes the cross-calls in the order of the index of shards. Once there are any new cross-calls, the shard goes back to the first step. After *M-1* epochs, all the shards finish their jobs, then send the "Finished" messages as the final packets of this block. In this way, no matter how many cross transactions there are, the total packets needed is $N \times (N - 1) \times M = O(N^2)$. Hence the packets can be fast transmitted in the local network of the consortium member. Note that Meepo does not set up an upper bound of M, which might lead to a dead loop. This could be prevented by contract developers or solved in future works.

Advantage This cross-shard protocol handles the cross-shard communication among the consortium member in order to improve the cross-shard efficiency. Since the communication just happens in the local network of the consortium member, the network speed can be fastened than the speed of the previous studies that are in the Internet environment. Moreover, in one member, different shards can trust each other because they belong to the same consortium member. However, in the public blockchain, shards need to sacrifice efficiency to complete some kind of encryption proof. Therefore, by making use of the network condition and trustworthiness within the consortium member, the cross-shard efficiency can be improved. The evaluation will be proposed in Sect. 5.4.

5.3.2 Partial Cross-Call Merging Strategy

Main Idea Facing the challenge of flexible multiple-shard contract calling, we propose a partial cross-call merging strategy. As shown in Fig. 5.6a, Meepo allows the shards to send the cross-call with only partial parameters, namely partial cross-

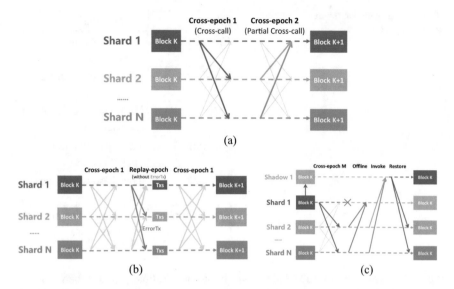

Fig. 5.6 Cross-shard communications of S2, S3, S4 in Meepo. (**a**) Partial cross-calls. (**b**) Replay-epoch. (**c**) Shadow shard

call, then merges them into one full call to execute on the target shard. Given the example of e-commerce, suppose a customer of *Shard 1* wants to buy the items of *Shard 2* and *Shard N*. In *Cross-epoch 1*, *Shard 1* sends the request (contract calling) to reduce the stocks and get the prices of the items. And then, *Shard 2* and *Shard N* respectively return the price in a partial call, without knowing the others' price. Finally, *Shard 1* merges their parameters by the hash value of the original transaction to deduct the customer's balance.

Difficulty The exact problem is how to guarantee the correctness and consistency of complex contracts.

Details In the detailed design, the partial cross-call merging includes the following three steps: (1) Mark: This step is done by the shard that sends the partial cross-call. The shard will mark which cross-calls are with partial parameters. In the actual implementation, the marking step can be done in two optional ways. One is to check the completeness of parameters after generating a cross-call, which has an overhead on the shard. The other is to distinguish the operation of full cross-call and partial cross-call, which is safer but causes a little bit of overhead on the smart contract developers. (2) Stack: When the shard receives the marked partial cross-calls, it will stack them by the hash value of their origin transactions, putting them in memory temporarily. (3) Merge: Once a partial cross-call is stacked, the shard will check whether the parameters in the stack are sufficient. If so, the shard will merge them into a full cross-call, then execute it. In one epoch on one shard, only one full cross-call of the original transaction will be merged and executed, identified

---

Algorithm 2: Pseudocode of example of e-commerce shopping contract using partial cross-call in Meepo

---

1 public function buy (item1, item2):

2   **CrossCall**(shardOf(item1), this, "getPrice1", item1);

3   **CrossCall**(shardOf(item2), this, "getPrice2", item2);

4 cross function getPrice1 (item1):

5   **CrossCall**(origin, this, "settle", priceOf[item1], _);

6 cross function getPrice2 (item2):

7   **CrossCall**(origin, this, "settle", _, priceOf[item2]);

8 cross function settle (price1, price2):

9   balanceOf[tx.origin] -= (price1+price2);

---

by its hash value. Actually, if the developer wants to reduce the time of checking the parameters, this step can be done after all the stacking is finished.

We also provide a pseudocode example of an e-commerce shopping contract (see footnote 2) using the partial cross-call in Meepo, as shown in Algorithm 2. In this example, the customer uses the function "buy" to buy two items, of which the prices (or stocks) are stored on other shards. First, the original shard will send two cross-calls to those shards in Line 2 and 3. And then, both shards will return the prices in the partial cross-call, leaving one parameter to be blank, as shown in Line 6 and 9. Finally, on the original shard of the customer, the parameters of price are merged to settle the transaction, as the function "settle". This contract will also be evaluated with real-world shopping behaviors in Sect. 5.4.2.

Advantage This strategy improves the flexibility of smart contracts, enabling smart contracts to operate the state on different shards, even in parallel calls. Furthermore, it also enhances the cross-shard efficiency of some complex contracts. Suppose a smart contract depends on the state from N shards, without this strategy, it should go through a long way for N epochs. However, using the partial cross-call merging strategy, the number of epochs can be reduced to two, as it just calls the state parallelly and gets the callback. Hence the complexity of time can be transferred from $O(N)$ to $O(1)$. The comparison of performance will be evaluated in Sect. 5.4.2.

5.3.3 Replay-Epoch

Main Idea To ensure the strict transaction atomicity, we import replay-epochs among the cross-epochs to revert the state operation by error transactions. As Fig. 5.6b shows, after the contract execution in one cross-epoch, if there are any errors, the shards will enter the so-called replay-epoch. In this epoch, all the shards will remove the error transaction from the block, then replay the block and the cross-epochs. In order to achieve this, the hash values of the error transactions will be propagated to all the shards. In this way, the final executed blockchain transactions will all be the successful ones, and the error transactions will do nothing to the state of contracts. It means that the state operations of any cross-shard transaction will all succeed or fail.

Difficulty Based on the main idea, the actual difficulty is to make the shards know about the error transactions that should be removed from execution.

Details Suppose there are N shards executing T transactions and E of them are with errors, Meepo divides the replay-epoch into two steps. (1) Throw exceptions: After the execution of a normal cross-epoch, the shard will check whether there are any exceptions during the execution. If so, the shard will enter the relay-epoch, sending the E hash values of the error transactions to the other $N - 1$ shards, in order to ask them to enter the replay-epoch. (2) Replay block: After receiving the hash values of the error transactions, the shards will replay the transactions in their blocks, skipping the error transactions. In other words, the shards need to execute $T - E$ transactions. This step will not cost much as the first time of executing the block. Because in the first time, the shard should validate the signature of the transactions before execution, but only execution is needed during the replay-epoch.

It is also optional to record the index of the original shard in the cross-call all the time so that the hash value of the error transaction is not needed to be propagated. However, it would cause a larger overhead on the network, since there is a great number of cross-calls but only a few of them might throw exceptions. Especially in practical consortium blockchain, the contract code is carefully reviewed by developers to reduce exceptions.

Advantage The most important advantage of the method is that it ensures the transaction atomicity in the duration of one block. This is also benefited from the high efficient cross-shard communication. As mentioned, the public blockchain cannot achieve this since the network delay is too long for the error transactions to be propagated, resulting in the cross-block atomicity or lower availability of the locked state. However, as for consortium blockchain, where each member holds all the state, the error transactions can be propagated in the local network, giving the time for the shards to replay the correct transactions. Suppose there are R replay-epochs, then the total complexity of packets is raised from $O(N^2)$ to $O(R \cdot N^2)$. Our experiment shows that this method costs an acceptable time to replay the block in exchange for the atomicity of the transaction, which will be evaluated in Sect. 5.4.3.

5.3.4 Shadow Shard Based Recovery

Approach Facing the challenge of shard availability in **C4**, Meepo proposes a recovery approach based on the hot backup shard, namely *Shadow Shard Based Recovery*. The architecture is shown in Fig. 5.6c. Meepo equips each shard with a shadow shard as a backup. Each pair of shards is like a master-slave backup architecture. The shadow shard copies the block and state from its master shard. It does not join in the consensus or communication with other shards. In the meanwhile, it is known by other shards. When any shard crashes, the corresponding shadow shards will be invoked by others, restoring the state to prevent the entire consortium member cluster from downtime.

Difficulty The exact problem in shadow shard is that the time and the state for backup switching need to be agreed upon between the shards when any shard crashes.

Details Meepo uses a recovery strategy shown in Fig. 5.6c to solve the problem of consistency, including the following steps: (1) Copy: During the time of the normal execution, the shard will copy the blocks and cross-calls to its shadow shard, as the blue arrow on the upper left in Fig. 5.6c. (2) Offline: The shard crashes and becomes offline. This can be detected by other shards independently via a timeout of a heartbeat packet or timer. (3) Invoke: Once the normal shards detect the offline event, they will send the message to the corresponding shadow shard. These messages are called "invoke" messages since they are used to make the shadow shard join into consensus and cross-shard communication. As for the shadow shard, it will remain silent until it receives enough "invoke" messages. The "invoke" messages must be counted as $N - 1$ in total because the shadow shard needs to ensure that all the normal shards switch the connections to it. (4) Restore: Finally, the shadow shard will send its block height back to the normal shards to restore the state and continue communication after that block. Given the example in Fig. 5.6c, the state might be different on *Shadow 1* and *Shard 1*, since *Shard 1* has executed M cross-epochs but *Shadow 1* has not. Therefore, it is necessary to restore the block height.

In Meepo, the availability (or reliability) of a shard is measured as follows. In a period of time t, if a shard is online and it acts normally in consensus and cross-shard communication for the time t_a, then its availability is $\lambda = \frac{t_a}{t}$. Suppose the availability of one shard is λ ($\lambda < 1$), when the number of shards increases to N, the availability of the consortium member will be reduced to λ^N. Using one shadow shard for each shard, the reliability of each shard is $(1 - \lambda)^2$. Hence, the availability can be kept by $(1 - (1 - \lambda)^2)^N$, which is higher than the previous λ^N. It will be further evaluated in Sect. 5.4.4.

Advantage This hot backup approach helps the consortium member to improve its shard availability. It uses some acceptable redundancy in exchange for the high availability of the system. Moreover, for some applications that require extreme reliability, the shards can be equipped with more than one shadow shard to enhance availability and reliability.

5.4 Implementation and Evaluation

In this section, we will conduct experiments for Meepo to answer the following research questions (RQs): **RQ1:** How is the cross-shard efficiency in different shard scales? **RQ2:** How is the performance of the complex smart contracts that depend on several shards? **RQ3:** How is the consumption of the replay-epoch handling the transaction atomicity? **RQ4:** How is the availability using the shadow shard? Note that these four RQs are corresponding to the four solutions in Meepo.

It is also worth noting that lots of state-of-art sharding studies focus on the public blockchain and do not open the source code. Although AHL+ [6] is open-source, it is implemented on the contract model of Hyperledger Fabric, and its consortium member does not hold all shards. Hence comparing AHL+ to Meepo would be a comparison of "apple to orange", which is unfair. The only thing that we can make quantitative evaluation is the one-hop calling (Sect. 5.2.1 in previous research, which is implemented in our following E-commerce Shopping Contract to be compared with the S2 in Meepo.

Implementation In our previous work [13], we developed Meepo-Go-Ethereum (Meepo-Geth) in Golang, as it is based on the Go-Ethereum [14]. However, as claimed in [13], Meepo-Geth suffers from performance issues from garbage collection and batch submission. After the work is published publicly, another version is provided in Rust, namely Meepo-OpenEthereum (see footnote 1). OpenEthereum [15] (also named Parity before 2021) and Go-Ethereum are the two popular clients in Ethereum [16]. They are both with two default consensus protocols. One is Proof of Work (PoW) which is used for public blockchain, the other is Proof of Authority (PoA) which can be used for consortium blockchain. In this chapter, we do not change the consensus protocol; thus, we use the embedded PoA consensus protocol. In the following benchmark, the PoA period [15] is set to 1 second, which is the minimum time difference between adjacent blocks. Another reason for the choice of OE is that it is developed in Rust, and the Rust program is usually with high performance as well-known. Even though OE is almost abandoned by the Ethereum community, its program and model still work for the current Ethereum blockchain. Section 6.7 provides more discussions on other blockchain systems with other consensus protocols. Other details of Meepo-OpenEthereum (see footnote 1) (Meepo-OE) could be found from Github.

Contracts We use two common cases in consortium blockchain: (1) Asset Transferring Contract: Consortium members use it to transfer assets (e.g., cross-border payment). The accounts in the contract are divided into different shards. The pseudocode is already shown in Algorithm 1. In the following benchmark, we will send transactions that trigger its "transfer" function to evaluate its performance.

Note that all the "transfer" transactions are cross-shard in this contract. The number of accounts is set case by case as a variable in each experiment, as it will affect the performance, which will be later evaluated. (2) E-commerce Shopping Contract: Consortium members use it to record the circulation of items and check bills. The items and customers are recorded on different shards. The pseudocode is shown in Algorithm 2. In the following benchmark, we will send transactions that trigger its "buy" function to evaluate its performance. In addition, we also implement another "buy" as the one-hop calling for comparison. Moreover, we use an user behavior dataset [9], including the real-world shopping behaviors (purchasing items) in Taobao.com from Nov. 25 to Dec. 03 in 2017, to test this contract. Specifically, it includes the shopping behaviors among 672,404 users and 638,962 items.

As for the client that sends transactions to the contracts, we use Web3.js [17] to submit the signed transactions to call the contracts in each shard. The Solidity codes and clients of the two contracts can be found in Github (see footnote 2).

Experimental Setup We run the Meepo-OE on the test-bed of 128 Elastic Cloud Servers (ECS) provided by AliCloud. The ECS type is ecs.i2.xlarge. Each server machine is equipped with 4 vCPU, 32 GiB memory, and 894 GiB NVME disk. Although all the servers are in one data center (region), we will evaluate the size of block, in order to estimate the network consumption where the members are in different data centers in Sect. 5.4.1. We use the test-bed to run the transactions to answer RQ1-3. After that, we conduct a simulation experiment to answer the RQ4.

Common Metrics Two common metrics are measured as follows. (1) Throughput: The throughput is the number of transactions that Meepo-OE can process onto the blockchain within a specified period of time. (2) Latency: The latency of a transaction is measured from the time when the transaction is submitted to the time when the transaction is confirmed by all the members. Moreover, the latency of a block is the average latency of its transactions. The other metrics will be described in each research question. Detailed calculation methods can also be found from the Github (see footnote 2).

5.4.1 RQ1: Cross-Shard Efficiency

To answer this research question, we mainly explore two key factors that affect the performance of Meepo in asset transferring: the number of shards (RQ1-1) and the number of accounts (RQ1-2). Other unexplored factors could be explored in future work.

RQ1-1: How is the cross-shard efficiency in different shard scales?

Approach To evaluate the cross-shard efficiency, we use the *Asset Transferring Contract* in the configuration of the different number of shards and the different number of members. We set 102,400 accounts in each shard. And then, we trigger the cross-shard "transfer" function to send the asset to them in 1 account. After

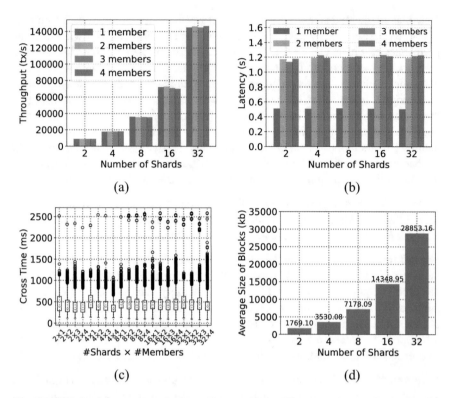

Fig. 5.7 RQ1-1: performance evaluation of Meepo-OE in different number of shards (102,400 accounts per shard, 32x4=128 machines in maximum). (**a**) Throughput. (**b**) Latency. (**c**) Cross time. (**d**) Block size

it processes more than 3,125,000 transactions per shard, we measure the average throughput and latency. We also measure two more metrics for explaining the differences: (1) Block Size: The total size of the blocks of different shards in the same height. This is used to evaluate the network consumption of external communication among the members because the members need to propagate the blocks in the external network. (2) Cross Time: The time used for cross-shard communication and execution in a block. This is used to evaluate the time of internal communication of each consortium member.

Results As shown in Fig. 5.7a, the throughput of Meepo-OE rises as the number of shards increases. In the configuration of 32 shards and 4 consortium members, the throughput is 146714.9472 transactions per second (TPS). In this configuration using $32 \times 4 = 128$ servers, the number of processed cross-shard transactions is more than $32 \times 3,125,000 = 100,000,000$, transferring the assets among $102,400 \times 32 = 3,276,800$ accounts. Hence, under the same configuration, Meepo-OE has about 10% higher throughput than Meepo-Geth [13]. The throughput increases almost linearly with the number of shards. Because the cross time is less than 600 ms for most blocks, as shown in Fig. 5.7c. As shown in Fig. 5.7c, the boxes are at around 500 ms, although a few outliers (the dots) are higher than 1000 ms. Hence the internal communication does not go beyond the PoA period (1 second). Thus the curve can be linear Fig. 5.7b shows the latency of 1 member is shorter than others (2, 3, 4 members) since it does not need to propagate the blocks to other members. We also observe that, given the same number of shards, different numbers of members (2, 3, 4) have similar throughput and latency. This is because the PoA protocol itself does not show a significant difference for the different number of members if there is only one authority [15]. Figure 5.7d shows that the block size is around 29M bytes in 32 shards, indicating that the external network of members should be able to transmit 29M bytes in one second in order to achieve the 140,000+ TPS for 32 shards. In this case, the requirement of minimum bandwidth for the external network of a member is around 29 M byte/s $\times$ 8 bit/byte $= 261$ Mbps. This is just the *minimum* bandwidth requirement because a member can be connected to N ($N \geq 1$) members, where the bandwidth should be larger than $261 \cdot N$ Mbps. In addition, in this experiment, we have not chosen more than 4 consortium members (e.g., 16 shards $\times$8 members) because our quota of servers cannot rent 32 shards with more members. Therefore, we cannot measure the maximum TPS at this number of members ($32 \times 8 = 256$), which can be done in future work.

RQ1-2: How is the cross-shard efficiency in different account scales?

Approach We use a similar approach in RQ1-1. The differences are as follows. Firstly, we set only one consortium member to evaluate the throughput in the different numbers of shards. Secondly, we set 32 shards and 4 members (32x4=128 servers) to see the curves of the 120s throughput (the time window is 120 seconds) in different account scales. For example, if there are 204,800 accounts and 32 shards, then each shard has $\frac{204,800}{32} = 6,400$ accounts.

Results As shown in Fig. 5.8a, the maximum throughput of Meepo-OE is more than 600,000 TPS in 128 shards. We cannot evaluate more shards since we do not have a more quota of servers. We observe that there is a gap between the 204,800 and 3,276,800 accounts. Hence we need to explore different account scales in 32 shards $\times$ 4 members. As Fig. 5.8b shows, when the accounts are fewer than 819,200, the 120s throughput is stable at the level of over 140,000 TPS. However, when the accounts are 1,638,400 or 3,276,800, the curves are stable at a lower level at around 130,000 TPS. Because when there are more accounts, the state of the contract is larger, resulting in more middle nodes in the Merkle Patricia Tree in Ethereum [18], taking longer time as more operations of the middle nodes. Meepo reduces the impact of this bottleneck by sharding the state but does not eliminate it. Note that this is not a conflict with the RQ1-1 since RQ1-1 measures the throughput on average, but RQ1-2 measures the 120s throughput.

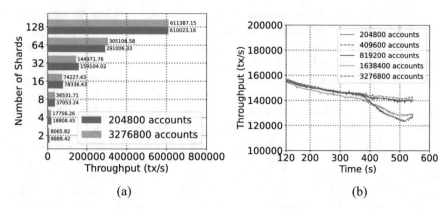

Fig. 5.8 RQ1-2:throughput of Meepo-OE in different shard and account scales. (**a**) One member. (**b**) 32 shards × 4 members

---

Answer to RQ1 Meepo-OE can reach over 140,000 TPS on average with 32 shards and 4 members, using 32 × 4 = 128 servers, and processing over 100,000,000 cross-shard asset transactions. In our experiments, given the same account scale, throughput increases almost linearly with the number of shards, which shows the feasibility of Meepo.

5.4.2 RQ2: Multi-State Dependency

Approach To evaluate the performance of handling multi-state dependency, we use the *E-commerce Shopping Contract* in the configuration of different numbers of shards and 4 members. We trigger the contract through the real-world "buy(user, items)" transactions from Taobao.com [9], in the way of partial cross-call merging strategy (With Partial') and one-hop calling (Without Partial'). After it processes more than 12,500 transactions per shard, we measure the average throughput. We also measure three more metrics for explaining the differences: (1) Block Duration: The processing time of the blocks at the same height, i.e., the time from generating/importing block K-1 to generating/importing block K. (2) Communication Time: The time that used for cross-shard communication in a block, i.e., the time of "Sending" and "Waiting" in Sect. 5.3.1. (3) Epoch Number: The number of all the epochs of the blocks at the same height.

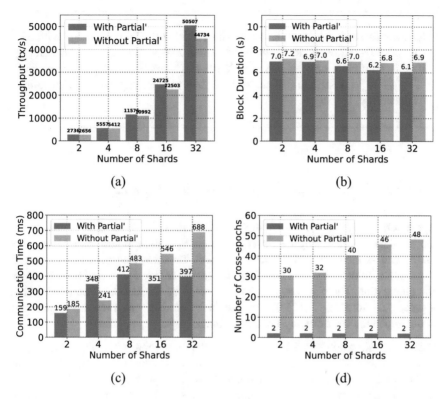

Fig. 5.9 Performance evaluation of Meepo-OE using partial cross-call merging strategy in e-commerce shopping contract. (**a**) Throughput. (**b**) Block duration. (**c**) Communication time. (**d**) Epoch number

Results As Fig. 5.9a shows, the maximum throughput of Meepo-OE is more than 50,000 TPS in 32 shards × 4 members, with the partial cross-call merging strategy. However, when we use the one-hop calling method (Without Partial'), the throughput is only 44,734 TPS. We explore the gap by measuring the other metrics on average. First, as shown in Fig. 5.9b, the block duration of one-hop calling is longer than the partial', and the gap increases from $7.2 - 7.0 = 0.2$ s to $6.9 - 6.1 = 0.8$ s as the number of shards increases. This mainly results from the cross-shard communication time as shown in Fig. 5.9c. Moreover, the communication time is longer because the one-hop calling has far more cross-epochs than partial', as shown in Fig. 5.9d. Because in real-world shopping behaviors, one user could buy up to 50 items, as mentioned. This leads to many cross-epochs since the one-hop calling needs to go through all the items one by one.

Answer to RQ2 Meepo-OE can reach over 50,000 TPS on average with 32 shards and 4 members, under the workload of real-world shopping behaviors. In this configuration, the proposed partial cross-call merging strategy has $\frac{50507-44734}{44734} = 12.9\%$ higher throughput than the one-hop calling, indicating its feasibility.

5.4.3 RQ3: Consumption of Transaction Atomicity

Approach To evaluate the consumption of handling the transaction atomicity, we use the *Asset Transferring Contract* in the configuration of different numbers of shards and 4 members. Moreover, we inject the error transactions in different proportions. In this way, Meepo-OE will enter the replay-epoch during cross-shard communication. The percentage of errors is set to 0, 10, 30, 50, 70, and 90%. After it processes more than 3,125,000 transactions per shard, we measure the average throughput and time of replay-epoch of a block (replay-epoch time).

Results As shown in Fig. 5.10a, comparing the throughput where the error proportion is 0% with 10%, we observe the throughput is reduced by little. The reason is that when there are error transactions, the replay-epoch will make the block be executed again, which costs more time. However, it should be noted that this cost of time is worthy, as it ensures the strict atomicity of the blockchain transactions in the duration of one block. In the asset transferring of consortium blockchain, even though the throughput might be reduced by half, the total throughput of the system is still high. And, the error transaction does not happen all the time. On the contrary,

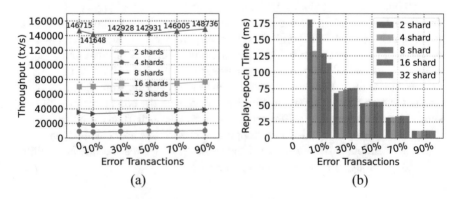

Fig. 5.10 Performance evaluation of Meepo-OE using replay-epoch in account transferring contract. (**a**) Throughput. (**b**) Replay time

it can hardly ever happen in a consortium blockchain because the upper application in a consortium blockchain can check whether the transaction will succeed before sending the transaction to the blockchain. In this case, in a long period of time, the system will only have a very short time to reduce throughput due to error transactions. Thus this reduction can be acceptable. We can also observe that, as the error proportion rises, the throughput increases to the level of all successful transactions, even the throughput of "90%" is higher than "0%" in 32 shards. The replay-epoch time is measured in Fig. 5.10b. When there are 90% error transactions, there are only 10% transactions that need to replay. Only 10% I/O times of disk are needed. In this case, it saves 90% of time [18] for writing the state changes into the disk. The I/O times are always the bottleneck of blockchain state processing. Hence saving the I/O times can achieve higher throughput than the "0%".

Answer to RQ3 As shown in the experiments, the replay-epoch costs more time that might reduce the throughput of Meepo in some cases. But the impact on throughput is lower than 5% for the test cases. Hence the costs are acceptable, showing the feasibility of our proposed method.

5.4.4 RQ4: System Availability

Approach To evaluate the availability of the consortium member, we simulate the availability of the consortium member in Meepo in the different numbers of shards and different configurations of single peer reliability. Each shard is equipped with a shadow shard, and we suppose the switching time in the hot backup method can be ignored. We mark the reliability of the single peer as λ, as mentioned in Sect. 5.3.4. In this evaluation, the configurations are set to $\lambda = 0.95$, $\lambda = 0.99$, and $\lambda = 0.999$, respectively.

Results The results are shown in Fig. 5.11. Although most cloud servers can achieve availability [19] (or reliability) that is higher than 99%, for companies that build their own data centers, the availability of a single server can be 95% or less. As shown in Fig. 5.11a, as the number of shards increases, the availability of the "No Shadow" decreases to less than 20%, which is an unacceptable level. With the shadow shard, the availability can be enhanced by more than 90%, of which the improvement is significant. This situation also happens in Fig. 5.11b, as the availability of the consortium member can be reduced to a level lower than 80%, which is unacceptable in consortium blockchain. However, if we use the shadow shard to enhance the availability, the availability of the consortium member will be added up to more than 99.5%, where $\lambda = 0.99$. In this case, the shadow shard does enhance the availability of the consortium members in the sharded environment.

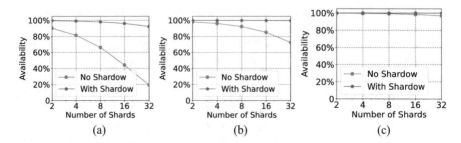

Fig. 5.11 Simulated availability of Meepo consortium member. (**a**) λ=0.95. (**b**) λ=0.99. (**c**) λ=0.999

If the consortium member is using the cloud server with high reliability, it might have no needs to equip the shadow shard. Figure 5.11c shows there is no significant difference between using the shadow shard or not.

Answer to RQ4 As for the servers that the availability is 0.95 or 0.99, or lower, the shadow shards can enhance the availability of members significantly. As for the servers where the availability is 0.999, it also works, although the improvement is not significant. In short, consortium members should decide if they should use shadows as appropriate.

5.5 Conclusion

In this chapter, we propose Meepo, a systematic study on the sharded consortium blockchain systems. It uses a cross-epoch based protocol to achieve high efficient cross-shard communication. Furthermore, we provide a partial cross-call merging strategy to support the multi-state calling of complex smart contracts. We also preserve the strict transaction atomicity as the original blockchain via a replay-epoch based cross-shard protocol. Additionally, we add shadow shards as the backup for the shards to prevent the system from being blocked by a single point of failure. Experimental results on 128 servers show its feasibility that it can achieve more than 140,000 TPS in 32 shards and 4 members.

Acknowledgments The research is supported by the National Key R&D Program of China (2020YFB1006001), the National Natural Science Foundation of China (62032025), Technology Program of Guangzhou, China (202103050004), and the Alibaba Group through the Alibaba Innovative Research (AIR) programme.

References

1. Huang H, Kong W, Zhou S, Zheng Z, Guo S (2021) A survey of state-of-the-art on blockchains: theories, modelings, and tools. ACM Comput Surv 54(2):1–42
2. Dinh TTA, Wang J, Chen G, Liu R, Ooi BC, Tan BC (2017) Blockbench: a framework for analyzing private blockchains. In: Proceedings of the 2017 ACM international conference on management of data SIGMOD'17, pp 1085–1100
3. Luu L, Narayanan V, Zheng C, Baweja K, Gilbert S, Saxena P (2016) A secure sharding protocol for open blockchains. In: Proceedings of the 2016 ACM SIGSAC conference on computer and communications security (CCS'16), pp 17–30
4. Zamani M, Movahedi M, Raykova M (2018) Rapidchain: scaling blockchain via full sharding. In: Proceedings of the 2018 ACM SIGSAC conference on computer and communications security (CCS'18), pp 931–948
5. Wang J, Wang H (2019) Monoxide: scale out blockchains with asynchronous consensus zones. In: USENIX symposium on networked systems design and implementation (NSDI), pp 95–112
6. Dang H, Dinh TTA, Loghin D, Chang EC, Lin Q, Ooi BC (2019) Towards scaling blockchain systems via sharding. In: ACM international conference on management of data, pp 123–140
7. Tao Y, Li B, Jiang J, Ng HC, Wang C, Li B (2020) On sharding open blockchains with smart contracts. In IEEE 36th international conference on data engineering (ICDE), pp 1357–1368
8. Huang H, Peng X, Zhan J, Zhang S, Lin Y, Zheng Z, Guo S (2022) Brokerchain: a cross-shard blockchain protocol for account/balance-based state sharding. In: IEEE conference on computer communications
9. Zhu H, Li X, Zhang P, Li G, He J, Li H, Gai K (2018) Learning tree-based deep model for recommender systems. In: Proceedings of the 24th ACM SIGKDD international conference on knowledge discovery & data mining, pp 1079–1088
10. Mehrotra S, Rastogi R, Breitbart Y, Korth HF, Silberschatz A (1992) Ensuring transaction atomicity in multidatabase systems. In: Proceedings of the eleventh ACM SIGACT-SIGMOD-SIGART symposium on principles of database systems, pp 164–175
11. Thomson A, Diamond T, Weng SC, Ren K, Shao P, Abadi DJ (2012) Calvin: fast distributed transactions for partitioned database systems. In: Proceedings of the 2012 ACM SIGMOD international conference on management of data, pp. 1–12
12. Buterin, V. (2014). A next-generation smart contract and decentralized application platform. white paper, 3(37): 2–1
13. Zheng P, Xu Q, Zheng Z, Zhou Z, Yan Y, Zhang H (2021) Meepo: sharded consortium blockchain. In: IEEE 37th international conference on data engineering (ICDE), pp. 1847–1852
14. Go Ethereum (2017) https://github.com/ethereum/go-ethereum/
15. OpenEthereum (Parity) (2017) https://github.com/openethereum/openethereum/
16. Wood G (2014) Ethereum: a secure decentralised generalised transaction ledger. Ethereum Project Yellow Paper, 151
17. Web3.js (2017) https://github.com/ChainSafe/web3.js/
18. Wood G (2014) Secure decentralised generalised transaction ledger. Ethereum Project Yellow Paper, 151:1–32
19. Zheng Z, Zhou TC, Lyu TC, King I (2012) Component ranking for fault-tolerant cloud applications. IEEE Trans Serv Comput 5(4):540–550

Chapter 6
State Sharding for Permissioned Blockchain

Peilin Zheng, Quanqing Xu, Xiapu Luo, Zibin Zheng, Weilin Zheng, Xu Chen, Zhiyuan Zhou, Ying Yan, and Hui Zhang

6.1 Overview

Blockchain can enhance the interoperability of the industrial IoT devices [1, 2] from different manufacturers. However, the throughput of existing blockchain systems is too low to process the transactions from massive IoT devices. Matured IoT platforms need high throughput. For example, [3] allows millions of devices to communicate with the IoT Platform at the same time. But current blockchain systems cannot handle such a high workload.Improving blockchain performance becomes an urgent research problem, and it is also the key motivation of this chapter.

Recent studies [4] have pointed out that the major bottlenecks of blockchain systems lie in **network delay** and **transaction execution**. Existing blockchain systems can be divided into permissionless blockchain and permissioned blockchain according to the permission of peers. Permissionless blockchain systems (e.g., Bitcoin [5], Ethereum [6]) are usually running on top of unstable networks with

© 2021 IEEE https://doi.org/10.1109/TII.2022.3164433.

P. Zheng · W. Zheng · X. Chen
School of Computer Science and Engineering, Sun Yat-Sen University, Guangzhou, China

Q. Xu · Z. Zhou · Y. Yan · H. Zhang
Blockchain Platform Division, Ant Group, Hangzhou, China

X. Luo
Department of Computing, The Hong Kong Polytechnic University, Hung Hom, Hong Kong, China

Z. Zheng (✉)
GuangDong Engineering Technology Research Center of Blockchain, Sun Yat-Sen University, Guangdong, China
e-mail: zhzibin@mail.sysu.edu.cn

© The Author(s), under exclusive license to Springer Nature Singapore Pte Ltd. 2023
W. Chen et al. (eds.), *Blockchain Scalability*,
https://doi.org/10.1007/978-981-99-1059-5_6

low bandwidth and low throughput due to low entry barriers for validating peers. Hence, network delay is their major bottleneck because the block and transaction propagation are slow. In contrast, permissioned blockchain systems (e.g., Hyperledger Fabric [7]) are usually deployed on the network with less number of peers and good network conditions.Thus their performance bottleneck is the execution of transactions, which is the target bottleneck in this chapter, evaluated in Sect. 6.5.3.

By now, earlier studies have been proposed in sharding to improve blockchain performance, e.g., Elastico [8], Zilliqa [9], OmniLedger [10], Monoxide [11], Rapidchain [12], etc. They divide the network into different shards, where the peer validates only partial transactions. These solutions can be summarized as "network sharding". They break the bottleneck of network delay, especially for the permissionless blockchain. However, they cannot be applied to the permissioned blockchain due to the following reasons: **(1) Low data availability and security:** Permissioned blockchain requires higher data availability and security than permissionless blockchain, because the data is frequently read and written for the business. However, the aforementioned solutions usually let the peer hold partial data of the blockchain, and thus the data availability and security may be jeopardized; **(2) Low cross-shard efficiency:** A transaction in sharded blockchain may depend on more than one shards, then it is called a cross-shard transaction. When processing cross-shard transactions, the blockchain needs to spend more time in cross-shard communication. Generally, the cross-shard efficiency reflects on the throughput and latency. The aforementioned solutions usually sacrifice cross-shard efficiency in exchange for security. However, the permissioned blockchain has better promise for security and needs lower latency of cross-shard transactions.

In summary, existing solutions were designed for the blockchains with low network bandwidth. Exploiting better network conditions (e.g., higher bandwidth, lower delay), a new algorithm is needed to enhance the performance of blockchain systems. In this chapter, we focus on breaking the bottleneck of the transaction execution instead of network delay for permissioned blockchains.

Existing blockchain systems usually execute the transactions on one server, and thus the limited computing resources become the bottleneck of execution [4]. An intuitive approach to accelerate the transaction execution is extending one single server to a cluster, which is the main idea of this chapter. However, towards this main idea, we need to address two challenges. **C1: Transaction Structure:** The transactions relevant to smart contracts, which are autonomous programs running on top of blockchains, cannot be executed in a distributed way. Although some research (e.g., ParBlockchain [13], FISCO-BCOS [14]) tries to achieve parallel execution, the limited disk I/O on a single server still restricts the performance. Hence, a new transaction structure for distributed execution is needed. **C2: State Consistency:** Distributed execution of blockchain transactions makes it hard to deliver messages among servers of one cluster and maintain consistency across different clusters.

Motivated by the above challenges, we propose *Aeolus* (Aeolus symbolizes fast transaction execution), which achieves distributed execution of blockchain transactions through state sharding. Figure 6.1 shows the architecture of Aeolus blockchain network. Different IoT devices connect to a permissioned blockchain

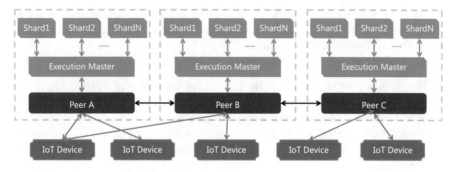

Fig. 6.1 Architecture of aeolus blockchain with IoT devices

peer, which handles the consensus protocol computation with other peers. Each peer uses their equipped cluster to execute (validate) the transactions.

Based on this architecture, Aeolus proposes the following solutions to address the mentioned challenges.

S1: Distributed Blockchain Transaction Structure is a new structure of blockchain transactions. The main idea is to import extra parameters to divide the smart contract execution into different stages according to different shards. The stages on the same shard will be executed sequentially for maintaining the order and consistency of blockchain transactions. Furthermore, the stages of different shards have no conflicts with each other so that they can be executed simultaneously. This solution is different from traditional distributed database transactions. The significant difference is that, blockchain transaction is used for triggering complex smart contracts, but database transaction is used for operating tables.

S2: Distributed State Update Sharding is an algorithm to divide the state into different shards and update them by a "Master-Shards" architecture. The master handles the block validation and then distributes the transactions to different shard servers for execution. Different shard servers deliver the messages through the master for the cross-shard transactions. Finally, the master fetches the execution result (state-root, which is similar to traditional blockchain systems like Ethereum and Fabric), which is compared with other blockchain clusters to keep the consistency.

We emphasize that Aeolus changes the transaction structure but not the block structure. In blockchain systems, many popular consensus protocols (e.g., PoW [5], PoS [15], PoA [16], PBFT [17], etc.) reach the consensus of blocks by verifying the headers. The header verification is related to the block structure rather than the transaction structure, thus it is decoupled with the transaction execution.Therefore, Aeolus can be adapted with existing consensus protocols without changing the security assumptions and fault tolerance of peers.

We implement Aeolus based on Go-Ethereum (Aeolus-Geth) and carefully evaluate its performance as well as compare it with other blockchains. The experimental results show that Aeolus gets the performance improvement. On a test-bed including 132 AliCloud servers, our system can deliver more than 100,000 Transactions Per

Second using 32 shards per peer. Aeolus-Geth runs stably for more than 8 hours, under the benchmark workloads from real-world Ethereum transactions, including more than 190,000,000 ERC20 transactions.

The major contributions of this chapter include:

- We propose Aeolus to accelerate blockchain transaction execution via a distributed architecture, motivated by the evaluated performancebottleneck of transaction execution in the permissioned blockchain.
- We propose a new distributed blockchain transaction structure that enables the transaction to be executed on multiple servers to accelerate the transaction execution.
- We propose a novel distributed state update sharding algorithm as a "Master-Shards" architecture, which makes full use of the resources on shard servers and reaches consensus in the blockchain network.
- We implement the new solutions in Aeolus and conduct extensive experiments to evaluate them. The experimental results show that Aeolus outperforms existing platforms and it can achieve more than 100,000 transactions per second in 32 shards.

6.2 System Overview

This section introduces Aeolus from an overview perspective. The details will be described in Sects. 6.3 and 6.4.

Architecture The architecture of Aeolus is shown in Fig. 6.1. As mentioned in Sect. 6.1, in order to improve the computing resources during transaction execution, Aeolus extends the single blockchain peer into a cluster. The main idea is to make full use of the computing resources in the cluster, and then the time of transaction execution will be shortened. Hence it improves the performance of blockchain. In the following, we will propose the roles in the topology in Fig. 6.1, then give an example of transaction execution flow in Aeolus.

Roles Traditional blockchain systems take one server as a peer. In Aeolus, each *Peer* is equipped with an *Execution Master* and several *Shard Servers*.

As shown in Fig. 6.1, all these roles are servers, but have different functions as follows. **Peer** is still the node as it is in traditional blockchain, which commits the block, validates the block, and joininto the blockchain consensus with other peers in the network. However, the transaction execution environment is not on this server, but on the *Execution Master* and *Shard Servers*. **Execution Master** can be considered as a router for the blockchain transactions among the *Shard Servers* to execute the transactions and return the execution result to the *Peer*. **Shard Server** is the exact executor of blockchain transactions. The state is divided into different shards that are handled by different shard servers. Each shard server executes the transactions that operate the shard state on it. As the green area in Fig. 6.1 shows,

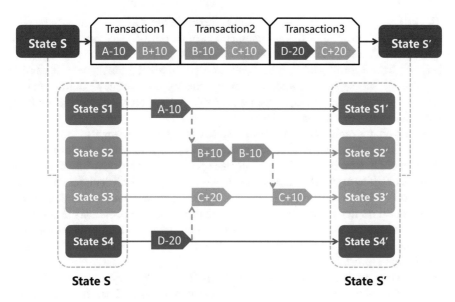

Fig. 6.2 Transaction execution flow in Aeolus

each peer has a local execution environment of blockchain transactions, which is only served to themselves independently. Moreover, the green area is only used for transaction execution (validation), where future work can be done to make it join into the consensus protocol (e.g., computing hash code for proof of work). In this way, each cluster can be regarded as a blockchain peer, and the increased complexity does not break the equivalence of blockchain peers. Each blockchain peer can reach consensus as before.

Transaction Execution Flow   Based on the above architecture, the transactions in one block can be executed. Figure 6.2 shows an example of the transaction execution flow on Aeolus. In this figure, **State S** is changed by several transactions one by one. Areas of different colors represent different stages of the transaction, and different stages operate on different state shards. Taking a specific example in Fig. 6.2, **State S** is divided into 4 state shards. The accounts A,B,C,D are respectively on the state S1,S2,S3,S4. **Transaction1** is a transaction that transfers $10 from A to B, thus it need to deduct the balance of A (A-10) then add it to B (B+10). And so do Transaction2 and Transaction3. In one transaction, different stages should follow the order in the transaction. Nevertheless, in different transactions, different stages (shown indifferent colors) operating different states are mutually exclusive. Thus they can be executed in parallel.

In this example, traditional blockchain will execute 6 state operations one by one, shown as the upper part of the figure. But Aeolus only executes them as follows. First, S1 and S4 execute the (A-10) and (D-20) in parallel. These two operations result in the next step. Second, S2 and S3 execute the (B+10) and

(C+20) in parallel. After that, S2 and S3 execute the (B-10) and (C+10) in serial. In total, despite of the communication time, only 4 steps are needed for 6 operations. Therefore the execution time can be shortened. As for the dependency between Transaction1 and Transaction2, in a permissioned blockchain, it can be handled by the sender (developer) through existing concurrency control studies [18, 19], which is not the major contribution of Aeolus. Future work could be done for handling dependency in the master.

Based on this architecture, there are two key technical challenges:

C1: How to divide the smart contract execution into stages by transaction structure? On permissioned blockchain, the applications are always based on smart contracts. Different from the simple payment transaction, it is difficult for the master to determine which stage and which shard for the smart contract transactions since the master does not execute transactions. The *cross-shard transactions* in previous studies cannot be applied to Aeolus, since they need to change the consensus protocol, discussed in Sect. 6.6. Our solution to this challenge is the *Distributed Blockchain Transaction Structure* (Sect. 6.3).

C2: How to divide the state and keep the consistency among different clusters? Aeolus expands one blockchain peer into a cluster. First, it is a problem to determine how to divide the state into shards. Second, it is important to ensure that the transaction execution sequence is consistent among clusters. However, the network and computing resources in different clusters can be different. Therefore, it is challenging to keep the consistency of state in different clusters with high execution efficiency. Our solution to this challenge is the *Distributed State Update Sharding* (Sect. 6.4).

6.3 Distributed Blockchain Transaction Structure

From Sect. 6.2, we learn that, after dividing the state into different shards, we need to execute the transaction on the corresponding shards. Moreover, the transaction atomicity should also be handled. Thus the structure of blockchain transactions should be improved. In Aeolus, the transaction can be represented as a tuple of *<PubKey(from), Contract(to), Input, Signature, Shard, Stage>*. In this structure, *<PubKey(from), Contract(to), Input, Signature>* is inherited from the traditional blockchain, such as Ethereum and Fabric. Aeolus improves the blockchain transaction structure by additional parameters: **Shard** and **Stage**.

6.3.1 Shard Flag and Stage Flag

In Aeolus, transactions operating different state shards are executed on different shard servers, as shown in Fig. 6.2. **Shard Flag** is used to show which shard the transaction should be executed on. The execution of a transaction is divided into different stages. Each stage is marked by a flag. That is the **Stage Flag**. The flag is used to represent which stage the transaction is in. The operation in one stage is fully executed on one shard server. Hence, one stage consists of the state operation only on one shard server. Moreover, as defined in the smart contract, different stages can be executed on the same shard, if needed. The reason to set *Shard* and *Stage* is that, in this way, the execution master can deliver the transaction to the exact shard server without any execution or complex parsing. From the perspective of users and smart contract developers, the differences between Aeolus and traditional blockchain transactionsare in two folds:

- The smart contract developer should use *Stage Flag* to divide the contract function. The example of Aeolus smart contracts in handling cross-shard function and atomicity will be given in the next subsections.
- The transaction sender is required to indicate the first shard server that the transaction will be delivered by setting the *Shard* field in the transaction. After the execution on the first shard server, the transaction could be delivered to other exact shard servers by a "JUMP" operation, which will be introduced in the next subsection.

We claim that it is easy for the developer to set a correct *Shard Flag* while sending a transaction. In Sect. 6.4.1, an internal shard mapping function will be described. The developer can use the function to generate a *Shard Flag* corresponding to the parameters of the calling contract.

6.3.2 JUMP Operation

JUMP operation is given for the transaction to be executed in different shard servers. As shown in Fig. 6.3, there is a transaction that is divided into three stages. Firstly, the transaction is delivered to *Shard1* to execute the *a* stage. The execution result of *a* will generate a message for the master to forward to *Shard2* to execute *b*. And so do *b* and *c*. Note that Fig. 6.3 shows the sequential manner of stages for only one transaction. Suppose there are more transactions, the stages in different transactions (e.g., the *a* in transaction X and the other *a* in transaction Y) can be executed in parallel. Hence the execution can be accelerated.

Fig. 6.3 Cross-shard message delivery by JUMP operation

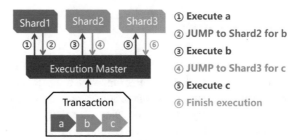

① Execute a
② JUMP to Shard2 for b
③ Execute b
④ JUMP to Shard3 for c
⑤ Execute c
⑥ Finish execution

Algorithm 1: Example of cross-shard contract function

---

1 function Transfer (from, to, value) {
2   Stage 0:
3   if (balanceOf[from]<value) return;
4   balanceOf[from] -= value;
5   JUMP(SHARD_OF(to), 1) ;
6   Stage 1:
7   balanceOf[to] += value;
8 }

The JUMP message can be represented as a tuple of *<OriginTx, Shard, Stage>*, where *OriginTx* is the origin transaction. During the execution of a block, the JUMP messages of different transactions can be packed together. In other words, the execution of a block is divided into different rounds. Each round consists of the stages of different transactions. The cross-shard message delivery is done between the rounds. A cross-shard message includes many JUMP messages so that the internal communication of the cluster is reduced to a minimum. Sincerely, JUMP operation increases the complexity of smart contract development. However, we claim that this increase is acceptable and worthy, as the developer just needs to divide the function into stages and combine them through the JUMP operation.

In Aeolus, the JUMP operation is a built-in function preset in the contract execution environment. It requires two input parameters, the shard index, and the stage. Algorithm 1 shows a typical example of a cross-shard smart contract function. This function is used to transfer assets (or so-called tokens) between accounts (*from* and *to*). Before executing this function, the transaction sender should set the *Shard Flag* as the index of the shard server that handles the state of *from*. This function has two stages, and it defaults to begin at *Stage0*. In this stage, the balance of *from* is checked and reduced by *value*. Then it "jumps" to the shard server, which increases the balance of *to* on it. *SHARD_OF(to)* is another function that returns the corresponding index of the shard server, which will be described in Sect. 6.4. Thus, the cross-shard function of smart contracts can be executed in different shard servers.

6.3.3 Atomicity

In traditional blockchain systems (e.g., Ethereum, Fabric), the transaction only has two statuses: success or failure. Once the transaction is failed for any exceptions of the smart contract, all the operations would be given up that the state will not be changed. This characteristic is called **Atomicity** [20] in database systems. Since the transaction is executed in different shards, it is hard to ensure the atomicity across different shards. In previous blockchain sharding research, Elastico, OmniLedger, RapidChain, and Monoxide use different strategies to ensure the atomicity of blockchain transactions. The limitation is that their strategies have to match their consensus protocol. Moreover, their consensus protocols will cause new security problems (discussed in Sect. 6.6). In Aeolus, the goal is not to change the block structure and consensus protocol to keep the security, so that the atomicity should be ensured by the blockchain transaction itself. To achieve the atomicity of transactions, the key is that the change of the state in different shards should be reverted when the execution fails. In the distributed blockchain transaction structure, one of the possible methods is to set the master to record the change in every shard so that it can revert the change. However, in this way, the master will afford a much larger workload than the shard servers, which results in the performance bottleneck. In this chapter, Aeolus provides two optional methods to revert the state in failed transactions to ensure the transaction atomicity. One is **Rollback Stage**, the other is **Block Atomicity**. The **Rollback Stage** is similar to the exception handling function in the traditional programs. In those stages that might cause the exception, which results in the execution failure, Aeolus requires the contract developer to define the *rollback stage*, which consists of the operation to revert the state.

Ideally, most blockchain transactions should be executed successfully since most exceptions could be avoided by checking the contract state before execution, i.e., using code like "if-else". However, in practical applications, there could be few exceptions that could not be checked before execution. Thus the rollback stage is necessary to keep the atomicity of the blockchain transaction. In practical permissioned blockchain systems, the exceptions are rare. Because the peers and contracts in the permissioned blockchain systems are stable, and all the contract code has been carefully checked and tested. Under this premise, **Block Atomicity** can be considered. The method is that, once the *Execution Master* finds any exception of transactions thrown, the master will revert all the state on the shard server. In other words, any exception in the transactions of a block will make all the transaction execution of the block fail. This is a one-size-fits-all approach. However, there will be few failed blocks if there are few failed transactions.

6.4   Distributed State Update Sharding

This section will propose how Aeolus distributes the state onto different shard servers and keeps the consistency of the blockchain in different clusters. The pseudocode of distributed state update sharding algorithm is shown in Algorithm 2, explained in the following subsections. It accepts the blockchain transactions and shards as an input, then comes out with the world state, which is represented as the "stateRoot".

Algorithm 2: Pseudocode of distributed state update sharding algorithm

---

Input: Blockchain transactions *txs*, Shards *shards*
Output: World State *stateRoot*

```
1  while txs ≠ [] do
2  |    /* Round begins */
3  |    for s in shards do
4  |    |    s ←^{send} txs[s]
5  |    end
6  |    stateRoot = init()
7  |    /* Asynchronous*/
8  |    for s in shards do
9  |    |    packet ←^{get} s
10 |    |    JUMPS[s] ← packet.JUMPS
11 |    |    stateRoot = stateRoot ⊕ packet.stateRoot
12 |    end
13 |    txs ←^{update} JUMPS
14 end
15 return stateRoot
```

6.4.1 Sharding Strategy

In Aeolus, the state is distributed into shards, which are held on different shard servers. The aim of the sharding strategy is to determine which shard should be operated when create or update a state record (e.g., a key-value pair). In Aeolus, we argue that the sharding strategy of the state of blockchain should meet the following requirement. (1) The sharding strategy needs to make the state evenly distributed across all the shard servers. This is related to the load balancing of shard servers. Consider an extreme case, and if the sharding strategy makes the state spread across only a few shard servers, then the transaction will be all executed on those servers, resulting in very low resource utilization. (2) The sharding strategy should be dynamic for different data types of input parameters. For those blockchain systems with a single function that is only conducted for transferring cryptocurrencies (e.g., Bitcoin), the sharding strategy could be static. For example, the strategy could be calculating the first k bits of the sender's address as the index of shard [11]. However, this kind of strategy does not work for the state of the smart contract because the input parameters could be all kinds of data types (e.g., char, string). Therefore, in blockchain-based smart contracts, the sharding strategy of the state should be dynamic for different data types. (3) The sharding strategy should be able to be flexibly controlled by the smart contract developer. In practical blockchain application scenarios, developers need to perform batch state queries based on actual factors, such as business type. If the developer can determine which shard server that data is located in, the query efficiency will be improved since only a few shard servers are needed. In other words, the sharding strategy is not entirely transparent to the smart contract developer. However, it can also be autonomous through simple programming such as using a hash function. With the above concerns, Aeolus leaves the *Shard Flag* in the structure of the transaction and the JUMP operation for the developer to set, so that the requirement (3) could be satisfied. Aeolus provides an internal shard mapping function as Eq. 6.1. In this equation, *arg* is the given parameter, which needs to be mapped to one shard, such as the account. *HASH(arg)* is a hash function (e.g., MD5, SHA256) that could be chosen by the blockchain manager to give the hash value of an argument (arg).*n* is the number of shard servers in the cluster. In this way, Aeolus meets the requirement (1) and (2). Note that, even though the state (e.g., accounts) is distributed evenly, the transactions might not always even to each shard since some accounts would send more transactions than others. This is called a **Hot-spot Account** problem in blockchain sharding. The impact of such unevenness will be evaluated in Sect. 6.5.6.

$$SHARD\_OF(arg) = HASH(arg)\%n \tag{6.1}$$

This sharding strategy is used in line 3 to 5 in Algorithm 2.

6.4.2   Round-Based Distributed State Update

From Sect. 6.3.2, we can learn that the execution of a block is divided into different rounds. Each round consists of the stages of different transactions. The "JUMP" messages are packed and delivered between rounds. In the first round, the transactions are distributed to the corresponding shard servers. After that, the remaining stages of transactions will be delivered back to the master. The delivered messages can be represented as the following equation.

$$JUMPS_r(i, :) = Round_r(i).result \tag{6.2}$$

As shown in Eqs. 6.2 and 6.3, $JUMPS_r(i,j)$ represents the cross-shard message in round r from shard i to shard j. $Round_r(i)$ represents the set of transactions that are executed on Shard i in round r. In this round, the $JUMPS_r(i,j)$ can be considered as the execution result of the transactions in this round. After that, the master needs to determine what to execute in which shard server in the next round. The messages that the master sends to the shard server can be represented as Eq. 6.3.

$$Round_{r+1}(s) = \bigcup_{i=1,2,\ldots n, j=s} JUMPS_r(i, j) \tag{6.3}$$

In this equation, $Round_{r+1}(s)$ represents the set of transactions that are executed on Shard s in round $r+1$. It can be calculated as the union of the JUMP messages that "jump" to Shard s. In this way, the overhead of the network of each round can be reduced to a minimum. After all the execution, the traditional blockchain system uses a string called state-root to represent the status of the whole state. The state-root is recorded in the block in order to check whether the execution result is the same as other blockchain peers. In Aeolus, the state-root is reserved as **multi-state-root**, which can be calculated as the following equation:

$$mulStateRoot = stateRoot_1 \oplus stateRoot_2 \oplus ... \oplus stateRoot_n \qquad (6.4)$$

where *mulStateRoot* represents the multi-state-root of the state that could be calculated as the result of a continuous XOR calculation of all the stateRoot of shard servers. The reason for using XOR instead of continuous hashing or other methods is that XOR is not related to the order of operations. In multi-thread communication within the cluster, the order of messages from the shards to the master can be different. Therefore, by using XOR, the master can process the returned messages as quickly as possible, without waiting for all shards to return. This round-based distributed state strategy is shown in line 8–12 in Algorithm 2.

In summary, with the same sharding strategy and round-based distributed state update approach, different clusters can do the same execution of the block and check the result with other clusters. In this way, the consistency of blockchain can be kept in Aeolus.

6.5 Evaluation

For practical usage and evaluation, we implement Aeolus to answer the following research questions: **RQ1:** Is transaction execution the bottleneck of current blockchain systems in permissioned peers? **RQ2:** How is the scalability of Aeolus in different numbers of shards? **RQ3:** How is the performance of Aeolus compared to other existing blockchain systems? **RQ4:** How is the performance of Aeolus according to the different configurations of transaction workload? These research questions are answered in the corresponding subsections as follows.

6.5.1 Implementation

We develop Aeolus to check the feasibility, called Aeolus-Go-Ethereum (Aeolus-Geth), as it is based on the Go-Ethereum [16], one of the popular Ethereum clients. Based on Go-Ethereum, Aeolus-Geth mainly modifies the modules of EVM (Ethereum Virtual Machine), StateDB, and Worker, with about 3500 LoC above that of Geth's codebase. Although Ethereum is mainly designed as a permissionless blockchain, its client provides both permissioned and permissionless protocols. As for permissioned scenarios, Geth has embedded a Proof-of-Authority consensus protocol called "Clique" for permissioned blockchain, which is also used in Aeolus-Geth.

6.5.2   Experimental Setup and Workloads

We run Aeolus-Geth on AliCloud. Each server is equipped with an Intel Xeon 8269CY CPU, 4 CPU cores, 32GB of RAM, 1.8TB SSD. The number of servers is case by case in the experiment. In maximum, we use 4 permissioned peers, and each of them consists of 32 shards. Thus the test-bed includes $(32 + 1) \times 4 = 132$ servers in maximum. The other blockchain systems are also run on the same configuration machine. Unless otherwise specified, each experiment is conducted in a permissioned blockchain consisting of four peers.

Workloads We use the public Ethereum dataset [21] to extract real-world transactions. It consists of more than 190,000,000 ERC20 transactions among 37,397,908 addresses, extracted from Ethereum #0 to #10,000,000 blocks. The same transactions are organized into two workloads: ERC20-Balanced and ERC20-Unbalanced. The ERC20-Balanced is balanced for each shard that the address distribution is even. The ERC20-Unbalanced is unbalanced that the address distribution is uneven. Monoxide [11] uses the same ERC20 workload to evaluate real-world asset transferring. Aeolus processes the transfer functions in these workloads as fully cross-shard, with the pseudocode shown in previous sections.

6.5.3   RQ1: Bottleneck of Current Blockchain

To verify the motivation of Aeolus, we first evaluate the performance of current blockchain systems. As well-known, the bottleneck of the blockchains lies in the consensus protocol in the permissionless blockchain. However, as for permissioned blockchain, an empirical experiment is needed to show the performance of the transaction execution in existing platforms. We run four famous blockchain systems (Geth [16], Peercoin [15], Binance Smart Chain [22], Solana [23]) with different consensus protocols (Proof-of-Work, Proof-of-Stake, Proof-of-Staked-Authority, Proof-of-History) as a private chain to see their performance in the permissioned blockchain. We instrument the source code of clients to measure the cost distributions of transaction executions and consensus protocol. The cost is measured by the average time of consensus and execution in each block. Note that the threat to the validity of this experiment is that different systems could show different performances under different configurations (e.g. difficulty in PoW, authorities in PoSA) and workloads.

The results are shown in Fig. 6.4. As for Geth and Bsc (Binance Smart Chain), they both run the EVM smart contract and spend more time in execution than consensus. The difference between them is that PoW consumes more computing resources than PoSA thus taking more time in consensus. Peercoin (PoS) processes the Bitcoin-like transactions, which are faster than EVM contracts, but its PoS still shows faster than execution in the permissioned peers. As for Solana, its consensus protocol [24] consists of PoH (Record) and TBFT (Vote) and its execution consists

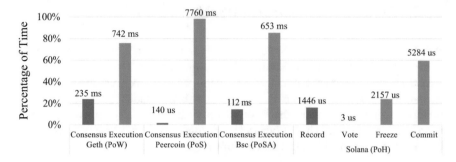

Fig. 6.4 Performance bottleneck of current blockchain with different consensus protocols (Geth, Peercoin, Bsc, and Solana)

of Freeze and Commit. Figure 6.4 shows that the green part is greater than the blue part, indicating that the percentage of time in execution is larger than that in consensus.

In summary, in a permissioned blockchain where is with good network conditions for consensus protocol, the transaction execution is the bottleneck of current systems, as it occupies most of the block time on average.

6.5.4 RQ2: Scalability of Aeolus

The idea of Aeolus is promising to improve the scalability of the blockchain system. Thus we need to find out whether Aeolus is scalable with the increasing number of servers.

Based on the ERC20-balanced workload, we use a smart contract to test the performance in different configurations. The benchmark contract consists of two functions. The function "NewAccount(account)" (hereinafter referred to as "NewAccount") is used to push a new element into the array of accounts, reflecting the performance of the underlying key-value database and the non-cross-shard performance. The function "Transfer(from, to, value)" (hereinafter referred to as "Transfer") is the most called function in real-world blockchain systems as Ethereum [21]. It reduces the balance of an account and transfers the money to another account. In a sharded environment, it can reflect the performance of cross-shard transactions and is also tested by other sharding research [11].

Figure 6.5a shows that the measured throughput (Transactions Per Second) scales out as the number of shards increases. The upward trend is almost linear. At the experiment of 32 shards, Aeolus-Geth achieves 100,915.9 TPS for key-value insertion in "NewAccount", and 95,696.6 TPS for cross-shard transactions in "Transfer". More specifically, in this case, we use $(32 + 1) \times 4 = 132$ servers to conduct a permissioned blockchain with 4 peers, each with 32 shards.

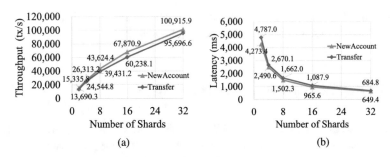

Fig. 6.5 Scalability of Aeolus-Geth in different number of shards (running ERC20-Balanced workload, each peer is with 2, 4, 8, 16, 32 shards, measuring the throughput and latency). (**a**) Throughput. (**b**) Latency

The transactions are confirmed in 1600 blocks, with 65,536 transactions per block, to make the system performance tend to a stable value. We also focus on the latency, observed by the client, from the time the transaction is submitted to the time the block is notified. It includes the time of transaction submission, execution, persistence, and response. The measured latency is shown in Fig. 6.5b. At the experiment of 32 shards, the average latency is 684.8 ms, which is acceptable in the applications of permissioned blockchain systems. As the number of shards grows, the latency decreases. Figure 6.5b shows that the latency reaches the limit at a certain value since the block persistence and transaction submission also take a certain amount of time. As Fig. 6.5 shows, the performance of the workload of "Transfer" is lower than the "NewAccount". Because "Transfer" is a cross-shard transaction, which needs one more round.

To evaluate the robustness of our system on a large scale, we run the ERC20-Balanced workloads for 10 times in 16 shards. It takes 8 hours for our system to deal with the transactions, as shown in Fig. 6.6. At the first run of ERC20-Balanced, since the state and cache expand with the raising accounts, the TPS decreases, and the memory increases. After that, since the number of accounts is constant, the

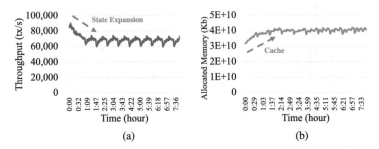

Fig. 6.6 Robustness of Aeolus-Geth in big scales (running 190,000,000 ERC20 transactions for 10 times, spending 8 hours in total, each peer is with 16 shards, measuring the throughput and memory consumption). (**a**) Throughput. (**b**) Memory of shard

fluctuation is caused by the distribution of transaction accounts. The TPS tends to a stable value, which reflects the robustness of Aeolus-Geth.

6.5.5 RQ3: Comparison with Other Systems

Since Aeolus is mainly designed for the permissioned blockchain, we compare the performance of Aeolus with other blockchain systems in the permissioned scenario of four peers in the consortium. We run Aeolus-Geth, original Go-Ethereum 1.9.12 (Geth), FISCO-BCOS v2.0 (FISCO), Hyperledger Fabric v1.4 (Fabric) with the same workload. In a specific implementation, Aeolus-Geth, Geth, and FISCO run the EVM contract, while Fabric runs the contract in docker container [7]. Built-in consensus protocols in these systems are used, as Aeolus-Geth and Geth use the Clique protocol, Fabric uses the Raft protocol, and FISCO uses the PBFT protocol. Since there are four peers in the permissioned blockchain, each system consists of 4 blockchain peers with the same configuration. In addition, Fabric has one more orderer and Aeolus equips each peer with 32 shard servers. We test these blockchain systems with the workload of invoking two benchmark functions. The result of the comparison is shown in Fig. 6.7. As for transferring assets (cross-shard transaction), which is one of the most important scenarios, Aeolus-Geth can reach 95,696.6 TPS, which is 15.6 times that of the original Geth, 16.2 times that of FISCO, and 229.4 times that of Fabric. As Fig. 6.7b shows, Aeolus-Geth shows lower latency than Geth and FISCO, but higher than Hyperledger Fabric.

Then we will discuss the detailed comparison of the experiment. As for Aeolus-Geth and the original Geth, Aeolus-Geth executes the transactions in a distributed way. As for FISCO-BCOS, FISCO also uses EVM contracts. However, in the real-world token transactions, a great number of tokens are transferred to the same account, then FISCO needs to execute them in serial to avoid conflicts. Hence FISCO shows lower throughput. As for Hyperledger Fabric, we use the default configuration and it generates blocks at a fast speed. Each block is with about 10–20 transactions, generated in the duration of 20–30 ms, leading to lower throughput but also lower latency for Fabric.

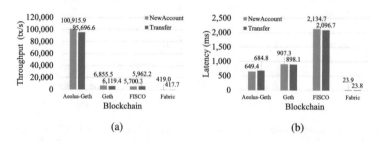

Fig. 6.7 Comparison of Aeolus-Geth, Geth, FISCO-BCOS, and fabric (running ERC20-Balanced workload, using 4 peers, measuring the throughput and latency). (**a**) Throughput. (**b**) Latency

Note Fabric configuration cannot be changed to involve more transactions in a block to improve the throughput. Once we improve this configuration, more conflicts would be in the write set of Fabric, leading to transaction failure.

In short, under the similar ERC20 workload to Monoxide [11], measured by the clients, Aeolus-Geth delivers 15.6x throughput of the original Geth. As for the other blockchain sharding studies, unfortunately, we can only compare with their claimed TPS in Sect. 6.6, although the consensus protocols and test-beds could be very different. The reasons and detailed comparison is also given in Sect. 6.6.

6.5.6   RQ4: Impact of Workload

From Sect. 6.5.4 we have learned that the performance of Aeolus can be affected by the number of shards and the state scales. Moreover, the transaction workloads can also have significant impacts on the performance. There are several critical factors of workload which affect its performance: the size of block and the unevenness of transactions in each shard (aka shard distribution). In this subsection, we will test different workloads to find the impacts.

In blockchain systems, a block needs to propagate in the peer-to-peer network, thus the block size affects the performance. The size of the block depends on the number of transactions per block. In the previous experiment of Aeolus-Geth, the workloads are set with 65,536 transactions per block. Therefore, We use the workloads in different Transactions Per Block (TPB). The results are shown in Fig. 6.8. If TPB is too small, the block costs little time for execution, wasting much time in communication, resulting in lower throughput. However, even using a workload of 1024 TPB, Aeolus-Geth achieves more than 18,000 TPS, which is also higher than the compared blockchain systems in RQ2. Smaller blocks result in lower latency, as shown in Fig. 6.8b. If the block consists of 16,384 transactions, the latency is about 200 ms. Therefore, if the blockchain application requires a latency

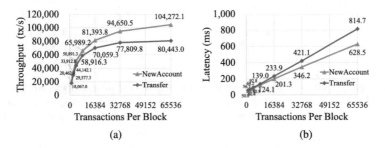

Fig. 6.8 Impact of the number of transactions in A block (running 6,553,600 transactions of ERC20-Balanced workload, packing 2048, 4096, 8192, 16,384, 32,768, 65,536 transactions per block, measuring the throughput and latency, each peer is with 16 shards). (**a**) Throughput. (**b**) Latency

of about 200 ms, Aeolus-Geth can also meet the requirement, with the throughput of 70,000 TPS to 80,000 TPS, equipped with 16 shards.

In the Internet environment, the bandwidth is not unlimited. Thus we need to measure the network consumption in Aeolus-Geth. The size of the block including 65,536 "NewAccount" transactions is about 8987.2 kb. As for "Transfer", the size of the block is 15,334.3 kb on average, as the transaction data includes more parameters for the contract function. Take the "NewAccount" block with 65,536 TPB as an example, the latency is 628.5 ms and the size is 8987.2 kb. This indicates that Aeolus-Geth requires the network speed to be higher than 8987.2 kb/628.5 ms = 14.3 mb/s, to achieve the throughput of 104,272.1 TPS. Nowadays, this network requirement is acceptable in most Internet Service Providers. As for internal communication, the major data packet is the packet of JUMP messages. The size of compressed JUMP messages of each block is only 1750.3 kb on average, which can be propagated very fast through the internal network of the cluster.

Figure 6.9 shows the scatter diagram of performance under different uneven workloads. One dot represents one block, the horizontal axis is the unevenness of its transactions in each shard, and the vertical axis is throughput and latency. In this chapter, we calculate the unevenness by the ratio of the max number of transactions in one shard to the average. For example, in a block with 65,536 transactions in 16 shards, if the maximum number of one shard is 8192, then the unevenness is 8192/(65,536/16) = 2. Figure 6.9 shows that the throughput goes lower in the more uneven block. The reason is that, in each round of Aeolus, the execution master has to wait for all the shards to finish the round before the next round. Therefore, the execution will be blocked, waiting for the last one who has the most transactions. And this waiting in the master is worthy. It is very likely to provide a global clock for each shard, making it easier and safer for the developers to write smart contracts.

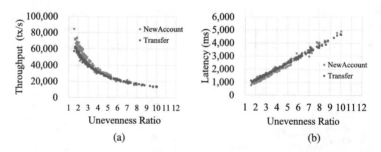

Fig. 6.9 Impact of the evenness of shards (running 6,553,600 transactions of ERC20-Unbalanced workload, measuring the throughput and latency, each peer is with 16 shards, unevenness is the ratio of the max number of transactions in one shard to the average). (**a**) Throughput. (**b**) Latency

6.6   Related Work

Since this chapter proposes the Aeolus as a sharded permissioned blockchain, the related studies will be categorized into sharded permissionless blockchain and permissioned blockchain. After that, we will provide a detailed comparison.

Permissionless Blockchain Sok [25] provides a systematic review on blockchain sharding techniques. Luu et al. [8] propose a secure sharding protocol for the permissionless blockchain. After that, more sharding strategies of blockchain are proposed. Zilliqa [9] blockchain assigns validating peers to each shard in groups of 600. OmniLedger [10] distributes generated verifier identities to different shards through blockchain. RapidChain [12] is proposed to be resilient to Byzantine faults from up to 1/3 malicious peers. RepChain [26] integrates reputation scores with sharding-based blockchain with an incentive mechanism, characterizing the heterogeneity among the validators. Monoxide [11] uses Chu-ko-nu mining to defend 51% malicious peers in the sharded blockchain. As for dynamic sharding, Tao et al. [27] propose an inter-shard merging algorithm for shard merging and an intra-shard transaction selection mechanism select transactions for validation. And Huang et al. [28] propose a cross-shard blockchain protocol that exploits fine-grained state partition. In the cryptocurrency community, Ethereum 2.0 [6] uses shading with a beacon chain to maintain the security and consistency for shard chains.

Permissioned Blockchain AHL+ [29] enhances Hyperledger Fabric with a Two-phase Commit method to process the distributed transactions in the sharded permissioned blockchain. Huang et al. [30] propose a DPP-based algorithm that can alleviate the imbalanced transaction assignment in the PBFT-based sharded permissioned blockchain. ByShard [31] is proposed as a unifying framework for the study of sharded blockchain in the Byzantine environment, with eighteen cross-shard transaction processing protocols. Blockchain also has wide applications in industrial IoT security [32, 33]. Jia et al. [34] design a model of blockchain-enabled federated learning [35] to enhance security in the industrial IoT.

Comparison We compare Aeolus with the related sharding studies that claim to have been actually tested on machines, comparing the parameters of throughput, shards, and machines. Sincerely, the test-beds could be very different, since we cannot obtain the source code from others for a more fair evaluation. Even though AHL+ is open-source, it is based on Fabric where the smart contract model is completely different from Aeolus-Geth. As shown in Table 6.1, Aeolus-Geth shows better cross-shard throughput than the others, as the others are mainly designed for permissionless blockchain. The advantages of Aeolus are as follows. From above, except for Aeolus, the blockchain peer cannot maintain the full ledger. As mentioned before, maintaining a partial ledger will take a longer time for cross-shard communication. Because the peer that holds a partial ledger needs extra cryptographic algorithms or network communication to trust another peer. However, in Aeolus, the ledger is fully maintained by the peer, thus improving the cross-

Table 6.1 Comparison between Aeolus and related blockchain sharding studies (CS' represents cross-shard)

Permission	Blockchain	CS' TPS	# Shards	# Machines
Permissionless	Elastico [8]	40	100	800
	Ominiledger [10]	5860	16	60
	RapidChain [12]	7380	250	32
	Monoxide [11]	11,694	2048	1200
	RepChain [26]	6852	225	900
Permissioned	AHL+ [29]	3000	36	972
	Aeolus-Geth	**95,696**	32	132

shard efficiency. Moreover, this partial ledger is not suitable for some kinds of blockchain applications. Especially in a permissioned blockchain, the peer in the network usually needs to interact with all the data in the ledger. Once the peer does not own the complete ledger by itself, the credibility and availability of the data will decline. In this chapter, the blockchain peer in Aeolus still maintains the ledger completely to enhance the trust-worthy.

6.7 Discussion

Generality As mentioned before, Aeolus only changes the transaction structure rather than the block structure. And, in blockchain, most consensus protocols (e.g., PoW [5], PoS [15], PoA [16], PBFT [17], etc.) reach the consensus of blocks among peers. Hence Aeolus can be adapted to these consensus protocols without tuning. However, PoH [24] needs a further extension to be adapted since PoH sequences the transactions rather than the blocks, where the sequences should be verified.

Elastic Scaling In most blockchain applications, the performance requirements are not always high. To save the fees and reduce operating costs, it is necessary to study the method of automatically expanding and reducing the number of shards.

6.8 Conclusion and Future Work

In this chapter, we propose Aeolus blockchain to achieve distributed execution of blockchain transactions. It is motivated by the performance evaluation of current blockchain systems that finds one of the bottlenecks in the transaction execution. To accelerate the transaction execution, Aeolus proposes a distributed blockchain transaction structure that enables the transaction to be executed on multiple servers. Aeolus also proposes distributed state update sharding as a "Master-Shards" architecture to keep the consistency of different clusters. Aeolus is implemented on Geth. On a test-bed of 132 servers, measured by the clients, Aeolus-Geth can achieve more than 100,000 TPS for ERC20 transactions that are extracted from the real-world blockchain. Its performance is 15.6 times that of the original Geth. It is also stable to continuously process ERC20 transactions for more than 8 hours.

In the future, besides the mentioned elastic scaling, the possible improvements are as follows: **(1) Efficient communication inside the cluster:** The communication in Aeolus causes a significant overhead on the execution master. An optional method is to make the shard server communicate with each other in the internal execution. **(2) Combined research on network sharding:** As the network among the peers can be the bottleneck, network sharding can be considered to reduce the overhead of peers to achieve further improvement. **(3) Customizable Dependency Handling Algorithm:** Traditional concurrency control solutions are with potential further improvement for blockchain transactions. Once the dependency can be handled by the developer, it could be more efficient, leading to higher throughput.

Acknowledgments The work described in this chapter is supported by the National Key R&D Program of China (2020YFB1006005), the National Natural Science Foundation of China (62032025), Alibaba Group through the Alibaba Innovative Research (AIR) programme, HK ITF Project (GHP05219SZ), and Hong Kong RGC Project (PolyU15222320).

References

1. H.-N. Dai, Z. Zheng, Y. Zhang, Blockchain for internet of things: A survey. IEEE Internet Things J **6**, 8076 (2019)
2. W. Chen, Z. Zhang, Z. Hong, C. Chen, J. Wu, S. Maharjan, Z. Zheng, Y. Zhang, Cooperative and distributed computation offloading for blockchain-empowered industrial internet of things. IEEE Internet Things J **6**, 8433 (2019)
3. Alicloud IoT Platform. https://www.alibabacloud.com/product/iot/ (2021)
4. P. Zheng, Z. Zheng, X. Luo, X. Chen, X. Liu, A detailed and real-time performance monitoring framework for blockchain systems, in *ICSE-SEIP* (2018)
5. S. Nakamoto, Bitcoin: A peer-to-peer electronic cash system. Decentralized business review (2008): 21260
6. V. Buterin: Ethereum 2.0 mauve paper. Ethereum developer conference. vol. 2. (2016)
7. E. Androulaki, C. Cachin, K. Christidis, C. Murthy, B. Nguyen, M. Vukolic, Hyperledger fabric proposals: Next consensus architecture proposal. https://github.com/hyperledger-archives/fabric/wiki/ (2016)
8. L. Luu, V. Narayanan, C. Zheng, K. Baweja, S. Gilbert, P. Saxena, A secure sharding protocol for open blockchains, in *ACM CCS* (2016)
9. ZILLIQA Team. The ZILLIQA Whitepaper. https://zilliqa.com (2017)
10. E. Kokoris-Kogias, P. Jovanovic, L. Gasser, N. Gailly, E. Syta, B. Ford, Omniledger: A secure, scale-out, decentralized ledger via sharding, in *IEEE SP* (2018)
11. J. Wang, H. Wang, Monoxide: Scale out blockchains with asynchronous consensus zones, in *USENIX NSDI* (2019)

12. M. Zamani, M. Movahedi, M. Raykova, Rapidchain: Scaling blockchain via full sharding, in *ACM CCS* (2018)
13. M.J. Amiri, D. Agrawal, A. El Abbadi, Parblockchain: Leveraging transaction parallelism in permissioned blockchain systems, in *IEEE ICDCS* (2019)
14. FISCO BCOS. https://fisco-bcos-documentation.readthedocs.io/ (2019)
15. Peercoin. https://github.com/peercoin/peercoin/ (2012)
16. Go Ethereum. https://github.com/ethereum/go-ethereum/ (2017)
17. M. Castro, B. Liskov, Practical byzantine fault tolerance, in *USENIX OSDI* (1999)
18. J.M. Faleiro, D.J. Abadi, J.M. Hellerstein, High performance transactions via early write visibility, in *PVLDB* (2017)
19. J.M. Faleiro, D.J. Abadi, Rethinking serializable multiversion concurrency control, in *PVLDB* (2015)
20. S. Mehrotra, R. Rastogi, Y. Breitbart, H.F. Korth, A. Silberschatz, Ensuring transaction atomicity in multidatabase systems, in *ACM SIGMOD/PODS* (1992)
21. P. Zheng, Z. Zheng, J. Wu, H.N. Dai, Xblock-eth: Extracting and exploring blockchain data from ethereum, in *IEEE OJ-CS* (2020)
22. Binance Smart Chain. https://github.com/bnb-chain/bsc/ (2021)
23. Solana Github. https://github.com/solana-labs/solana (2018)
24. A. Yakovenko, Solana: A new architecture for a high performance blockchain. Whitepaper (2018)
25. G. Wang, Z.J. Shi, M. Nixon, S. Han, Sok: Sharding on blockchain, in *ACM AFT* (2019)
26. C. Huang, Z. Wang, H. Chen, Q. Hu, Q. Zhang, W. Wang, X. Guan, Repchain: A reputation-based secure, fast, and high incentive blockchain system via sharding, in *IEEE IoTJ* (2020)
27. Y. Tao, B. Li, J. Jiang, H.C. Ng, C. Wang, B. Li, On sharding open blockchains with smart contracts, in *ICDE* (IEEE, 2020)
28. H. Huang, X. Peng, J. Zhan, S. Zhang, Y. Lin, Z. Zheng, S. Guo, Brokerchain: A cross-shard blockchain protocol for account/balance-based state sharding, in *IEEE INFOCOM* (2022)
29. H. Dang, T.T.A. Dinh, D. Loghin, E.C. Chang, Q. Lin, B.C. Ooi, Towards scaling blockchain systems via sharding, in *ACM SIGMOD* (2019)
30. H. Huang, Z. Yue, X. Peng, L. He, W. Chen, H.N. Dai, Z. Zheng, S. Guo, Elastic resource allocation against imbalanced transaction assignments in sharding-based permissioned blockchains, in *IEEE TPDS* (2022)
31. J. Hellings, and M. Sadoghi, Byshard: Sharding in a byzantine environment, in *VLDB* (2021)
32. D.V. Medhane, A.K. Sangaiah, M.S. Hossain, G. Muhammad, J. Wang, Blockchain-enabled distributed security framework for next-generation IoT: an edge cloud and software-defined network-integrated approach. IEEE Internet Things J 7, 6143 (2020)
33. A.K. Sangaiah, D.V. Medhane, G.B. Bian, A. Ghoneim, M. Alrashoud, M.S. Hossain, Energy-aware green adversary model for cyberphysical security in industrial system, in *IEEE TII* (2019)
34. B. Jia, X. Zhang, J. Liu, Y. Zhang, K. Huang, Y. Liang, Blockchain-enabled federated learning data protection aggregation scheme with differential privacy and homomorphic encryption in IIoT, in *IEEE TII* (2021)
35. Y. Li, C. Chen, N. Liu, H. Huang, Z. Zheng, Q. Yan, A blockchain-based decentralized federated learning framework with committee consensus. IEEE Netw. **35**, 234 (2020)

Chapter 7
Elastic Resource Allocation in Sharding-Based Blockchains

Huawei Huang, Zhengyu Yue, Xiaowen Peng, Liuding He, Wuhui Chen, Hong-Ning Dai, Zibin Zheng, and Song Guo

7.1 Overview

Motivation In the sharded blockchain, the blockchain nodes are divided into a number of smaller committees [1], each is also called a network shard. In each committee, local consensus can be achieved with a set of designated transactions using a specified consensus protocol such as Practical Byzantine Fault Tolerance protocol (PBFT) [2]. Thus, the sharded blockchain can improve the blockchain TPS by exploiting the concurrent transaction processing in parallel shards. Several representative examples of sharded blockchain protocols include Elastico [1], Omniledger [3], RapaidChain [4], and Monoxide [5].

In this chapter, we consider the Unspent Transaction Output (UTXO)-based transaction model. In the hash-based sharded blockchains [1, 3, 4], imbalanced

© 2022 IEEE https://doi.org/10.1109/TPDS.2022.3141737.

H. Huang (✉) · W. Chen · Z. Zheng
GuangDong Engineering Technology Research Center of Blockchain, Sun Yat-Sen University, Guangdong, China
e-mail: huanghw28@mail.sysu.edu.cn; chenwuh@mail.sysu.edu.cn; zhzibin@mail.sysu.edu.cn

Z. Yue · X. Peng · L. He
School of Computer Science and Engineering, Sun Yat-Sen University, Guangzhou, China

H.-N. Dai
Department of Computing and Decision Sciences, Lingnan University, Tuen Mun, Hong Kong
e-mail: hndai@ieee.org

S. Guo
Department of Computing, The Hong Kong Polytechnic University, Hung Hom, Hong Kong, China
e-mail: song.guo@polyu.edu.hk

© The Author(s), under exclusive license to Springer Nature Singapore Pte Ltd. 2023
W. Chen et al. (eds.), *Blockchain Scalability*,
https://doi.org/10.1007/978-981-99-1059-5_7

transaction assignments in some committees can be induced either by the abnormal transaction execution [6] or by a low-quality even a malicious transaction assignment strategy [7]. Referring to Elastico [1], committees work on different disjoint sets of transactions assigned according to the committee ID. However, if a malicious transaction assignment strategy [7] aims to create a blockchain shard with low-speed transaction processing, the TPS of the entire blockchain can be degraded drastically. For example, reference [7] mentioned that a malicious transaction assignment may strategically put a large number of transactions to a single shard. Such a *single-shard flooding attack* [7] can be realized through manipulating the hash value of transactions.

Specifically, the last s bits of a transaction's hash specify which committee ID that the transaction should be assigned to. However, the attacker with enough UTXO addresses can create a huge number of malicious transactions towards the target shard. Let D be the ID of the target shard and $\mathcal{A}$ be the set of attacker's UTXO addresses. Hash function $\mathcal{H}(\cdot)$ adopts SHA-256, and O is the set of attacker's available addresses that can be generated arbitrarily by public-private key pair. Then, Eq. (7.1) in [7] shows how to generate malicious transactions in a sharding blockchain consisting of 2^s shards: **for** TX.$in \in \mathcal{A}$,

$$\textbf{while } \mathcal{H}(\mathcal{H}(\text{TX}))\&\left(0^{256-s}\|1^s\right) \neq D \textbf{ do } \text{TX}.out \overset{@}{\leftarrow} O, \tag{7.1}$$

where $\overset{@}{\leftarrow}$ denotes choosing a single element from the given set O. In order to know the impact of such malicious transaction assignment. We implement the malicious TX-generation code given as Eq. (7.1) in Python and run the code using 12 operating-system threads on an AMD Ryzen 9 3900X 12-core processor. When the number of shards is 16, the TX-generation code can generate 8,038,886 TXs per second, among which 502011 TXs can be assigned to the target shard. Then, we conduct a group of simulations using 8 million Bitcoin TXs by injecting them into the TX-sharding system at the best fixed rates. Figure 7.1a demonstrates the time-varying queue size of the target shard under attacking in a 16-shard blockchain system. We evaluate the performance of queue size while varying the ratio of malicious TXs from 0 to 0.5. The TX rate is fixed to 4000 TPS, which is the best throughput of the 16-shard blockchain system. We observe that the queue size of the shard under attacking increases until all malicious TXs are injected. The results show that a larger ratio of malicious TXs implies a faster increase pace of the shard's queue size. Then, Fig. 7.1b illustrates the target shard's queue size versus different numbers of shards when the ratio of malicious TXs is fixed to 20%. The results show that a larger number of shards are more vulnerable in single-shard flooding attacks. In this chapter, we call such single-shard flooding attack the *bursty-TX injection* attack.

In summary, the bursty-TX injection can bring a large-size queue to a target blockchain shard, and thus cause a large congestion in that shard. Therefore, a critical issue is to maintain each shard in a stable status such that the imbalance of transaction's assignment can be quickly mitigated to guarantee low transaction confirmation latency in the shards suffering from the bursty-TX injection attack.

Fig. 7.1 The motivation examples: the impact of single-shard flooding attacks [7] (also called *bursty-TX injection attacks* in this chapter). (**a**) Queue size vs malicious-TX ratio in a 16-shard blockchain. (**b**) Queue size vs the # of shards with 20% malicious TXs

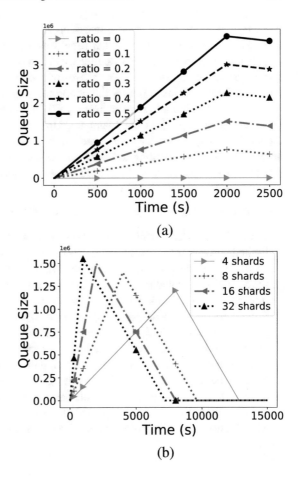

Challenges We assume that the permissioned sharded blockchain executes in a cloud platform, which is either implemented in the local datacenter or rented from a popular cloud provider such as Alibaba cloud or Amazon cloud. In the context of such *permissioned* blockchain, the malicious transaction assignment strategy [7] may inject a large number of bursty transactions to some target shards. Furthermore, the resource budgets in a permissioned blockchain are much more limited than that in a permissionless blockchain. This is because the resources of a permissionless blockchain (e.g, Bitcoin blockchain) are provided by a wide range of miners all over the world. In contrast, the resources in a cloud-based permissioned blockchain are provided by the local datacenter or by the commercial cloud platform provider. Thus, a challenge is how to maintain shards stable in a resource-limited permissioned blockchain while taking the threat of the bursty-TX injection attack into account.

On the other hand, although the existing state-of-the-art blockchain sharding studies [1, 3–5] have proposed a number of transaction-processing solutions in the context of sharding-based blockchains, we still have not yet found any available solutions to solving the stability issue aforementioned. Therefore, a new strategy that can handle the imbalanced transaction assignments occurred in the shards of a permissioned blockchain is in an urgent need. To this end, we formulate the congestion of the permissioned sharded blockchain as the stability issue in a multi-queue system. In this system, some shards may congest if they are assigned a large number of transactions either by the abnormal transaction execution [6] or by the malicious transaction assignment strategy [7]. To alleviate the congestion occurred in some shards, we adopt the Lyapunov Optimization framework [8] to address the stability issue. Our idea emphasizes on how to efficiently allocate blockchain-network resources according to the observed status of each shard's Memory Pool (shorten as *mempool*), so as to minimize the operation cost while simultaneously keeping the sharded blockchain stable.

Contributions The contributions are stated as follows.

- In the PBFT-based permissioned blockchain, we study how to allocate budget-limited network resources to blockchain shards in an elastic manner, such that the transaction processing can be maintained stable in those blockchain shards, under the condition of imbalanced transaction assignments or even under the bursty-TX injection attacks. We formulate this problem using the Lyapunov Optimization framework. We then devise a *drift-plus-penalty* (DPP)-based algorithm striving for the near-optimal resource-allocation solution.
- We rigorously analyze the theoretical boundaries of both the system objective and the shard's queue length, while utilizing the proposed DPP algorithm.
- Finally, the numerical simulation results show that the proposed DPP algorithm can maintain a fine-balanced tradeoff between resource consumption and queue stability. In particular, the DPP-based algorithm can also well handle the bursty-TX injection attack in two representative scenarios.

7.2   Related Work

Transaction Processing Several studies investigate the transaction processing of blockchains using queueing theory. The representative studies are reviewed as follows. In [9], the authors focus on how to develop queueing theory of blockchain systems. They devised a Markovian batch-service queueing system with two different service stages, i.e., the mining process in the miners pool and the creation of a new block. Besides, they adopted the matrix-geometric solution to obtain stable condition of the system. Then, Ricci et al. [10] introduced a simple queueing-theory model to show the delay experienced by Bitcoin transactions. The proposed model associates the delay of transactions with both transaction fee and transaction value. Their result indicates that users typically experience a delay slightly larger than the residual lifetime of the total duration between block generations. Memon et al. [11] implemented the simulation of mining process in Blockchain-based systems using queuing theory. Kawase et al. [12] considered a queueing model with batch service and general input to understand the stochastic behavior of the transaction-confirmation process. In [13], the authors applied Jackson network model on the whole Bitcoin network where individual nodes operate as priority M/G/1 queueing systems. The usefulness of this model is demonstrated by efficiently computing the forking probability in Bitcoin blockchain. Although these previous works reviewed above adopted the traditional queueing theory to depict transaction's processing, they cannot offer available solutions to handling the stability problem for network shards when the bursty-TX injection attack occurs. In contrast, the approach we propose in this chapter utilizes the Lyapunov optimization framework to resist the bursty-TX injection attack for the permissioned sharded blockchain.

Resource Allocation Several previous studies paid attention to the resource allocation of blockchain networks. For example, Jiao et al. [14] considered deploying edge computing services to support the mobile blockchain. The authors proposed an auction-based resource-allocation mechanism for the edge-computing service provider. Luong et al. [15] developed an optimal auction by exploiting the deep learning technique for the edge-resource allocation in the context of mobile blockchain networks. Fang et al. [16] proposed a queue-based analytical model to solve the resources allocation problem in PoW-based blockchain networks. These previous works focus on the resource allocation for traditional blockchain networks. In contrast, the resource-allocation model we propose in this chapter aims at the PBFT-based permissioned sharded blockchain by exploiting the queuing-based theory. More importantly, the proposed resource-allocation mechanism can particularly maintain the stability for each network shard.

7.3 System Model and Problem Formulation

7.3.1 Sharding-Based Permissioned Blockchain

Suppose that an enterprise needs to build a permissioned blockchain using the sharding technique. All blockchain nodes are executing in a local cloud platform. Those blockchain nodes are managed using sharding protocol, in which the local consensus is achieved by exploiting PBFT protocol. Thus, the natural goals of operating such a permissioned blockchain include: to keep the blockchain stable while processing transactions, and to consume the minimum resources while maintaining the local cloud platform. The cloud resources mainly include the computer power measured in the number of CPU cores, the network bandwidth, as well as the storage space provided by the cloud-platform virtual machines.

As shown in Fig. 7.2, the transaction-sharding protocol mainly includes the following stages: (1) the blockchain network is divided into different committees (or called network shards); (2) each committee then independently processes different sets of assigned transactions in parallel to achieve a high throughput of transaction processing; and (3) collation blocks are aggregated to perform the final PBFT

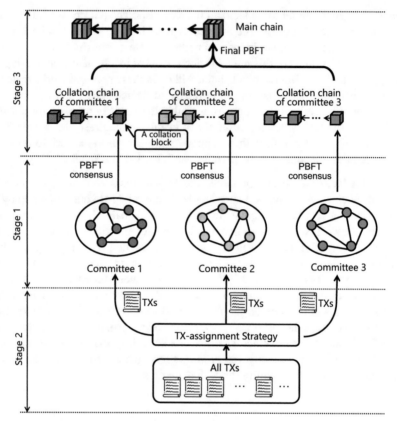

Stage 1: Formation of *network shards* (i.e., *committees*);   Stage 2: TX assignment;
Stage 3: Formation of the final block.

Fig. 7.2 A PBFT-based sharded permissioned blockchain, in which transactions are assigned to different committees (network shards) according to their hash values

towards the formation of a new block on the main chain. Referring to the classic blockchain sharding protocol [1], the computing power is mainly used to perform the PoW-based committee formation, while the network bandwidth is exploited to run the PBFT consensus protocol for generating new blocks.

7.3.2   Blockchain Shards

In a sharding-based blockchain network, several groups of transactions are allocated to different network shards for processing. The blocks generated in each shard chain are called *collation blocks*, which are verified by all miners (also called *collators*) in this shard. The collators of each shard are selected by the block validator in the entire blockchain network through validator manager contract (VMC) [17], which is the core of a sharding mechanism.

Each shard holds a memory, i.e., the local mempool in each shard, where the arrived transactions are stored tentatively and waiting to be processed by the committee. When a new transaction is assigned to a network shard, it will be validated by the committee node that the transaction first arrives at. After validation, this transaction will be stored in the mempool and then be broadcast to other committee nodes; otherwise, the transaction will be rejected. At the beginning of each epoch, the miners in a network shard will select a set of transactions from the local mempool to generate a *collation block*. When a miner wins the mining in each epoch, it will broadcast the new collation block to its committee peers, which then validate the new block. Afterwards, the new block will be added to the shard's collation chain and all the transactions contained in this collation block will be removed from the local mempool of this shard.

7.3.3 Arrived Transactions in Each Network Shard

Under the same UTXO-based transaction model presented in [1, 3, 4], we consider that committees (network shards) work on disjoint sets of transactions. In each network shard, since the propagation time for spreading new transactions is much shorter than the time spending on achieving consensus towards the collation block, the propagation time of new transactions is negligible in our system model. Thus, new transactions are viewed as that they arrive at all committee nodes within a network shard simultaneously. After transaction's propagation, all committee nodes in this shard share the same set of transactions. That is, they hold the identical view of the local mempool. Therefore, the mempool can be viewed as a single-server queue which stores the assigned transactions waiting to be processed by the multiple nodes in the shard. In this queueing model, transactions arrive randomly following a Poisson distribution. When being packed to a collation block, the transactions contained in the block will be removed from the mempool. We call this removing action the transaction's dequeueing. In each epoch, all committee members generate a new collation block when they reach an agreement based on the PBFT consensus protocol. Every shard's queue represents the condition of the local mempool. Based on the queueing model aforementioned, a blockchain sharding network can be viewed as a multi-queue system shown in Fig. 7.3.

7.3.4 Threat Model of Bursty-TX Injection Attack

Blockchain is typically implemented using conventional hardware, software and networks. Even a theoretically secure blockchain sharding protocol can be vulnerable to various attacks. Similar to the single-shard flooding attack presented

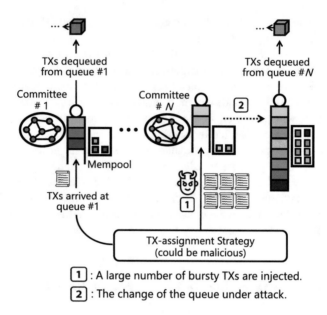

Fig. 7.3 Multi-queue model and the bursty-TX injection attack in the sharded blockchain

in [7], we consider that the hash-based transaction assignment strategy could be malicious. In most hash-based sharded blockchains [1, 3, 4], the several ending bits of a transaction decide which network shard to place. Through manipulating the transaction's hash, the malicious transaction assignment strategy can inject a large-volume bursty transactions in a target shard at a specified epoch. The large amount of transactions injected to a target shard can cause the effect of denial-of-service (DoS) attack [18] in the target. When such an attack occurs, the transactions submitted by blockchain users may congest in the shard's mempool. Thus, the service quality of the blockchain system degrades drastically, because the user's transactions suffer from large confirmation latency in the shard under attack. Especially in the context of transaction-sharding protocol like Elastico [1], the target shard suffered from such bursty-TX injection attack can delay the generation of the local collation block, and then postpone the creation of the final block in the main chain.

7.3.5 Problem Formulation

We consider that the permissioned sharded blockchain studied in this chapter runs in a time-slotted environment. All timeslots are indexed by $t \in \{0, 1, 2, 3, ...\}$, and the length of a timeslot is longer than the time of forming a collation block. We summarize important symbols and notations in Table 7.1. Let $I = \{1, 2, 3, ..., N\}$ be the set of mempool queues, thus each queue is indexed by $i \in I$. Then, K denotes the number of all types of aforementioned resources that can be allocated to the permissioned sharded blockchain.

We then use a vector $\mathbf{p}_i(t) \triangleq [p_i^1(t), p_i^2(t), p_i^3(t), \cdots, p_i^K(t)]$ to represent the total resources that can be allocated to shard $i \in I$ at timeslot t. Note that, $p_i^k(t)$, $k \in [K]$, denotes the amount of the kth resource invested on the shard $i \in I$ to generate a collation block in timeslot $t \in T$. Each type of the kth resource has a maximum budget denoted by $P_{\max}^k$. In order to represent the significance of each type of resources, we devise a weight vector $\mathbf{w} \triangleq [w_1, w_2, w_3, \cdots, w_K]$, where w_k indicates the weight of the kth resource.

In every timeslot $t \in T$, we assume that $B_i(t)$ is the amount of transactions (TXs) processed by shard $i \in I$. The value of $B_i(t)$ is closely associated with the allocated resource $\mathbf{p}_i(t)$. Referring to [16], the data amount processed by shard $i \in I$ at timeslot t is calculated as follows.

$$B_i(t) = \sum_{k=1}^{K} \left[w_k p_i^k(t) \right]^\alpha, \forall i \in I, t \in T, \tag{7.2}$$

where $\alpha \in [0, 1]$ is a normalized parameter associated with the consensus speed of the PBFT protocol. In reality, α could be the normalized degree of network connectivity in a peer-to-peer blockchain network. The larger α is, the easier a collation block is generated with the given same amount of resources.

At the beginning of a timeslot, a set of TXs will be assigned to each network shard. The TXs arrived in shard $i \in I$ at timeslot $t \in T$ are denoted by $A_i(t)$. Afterwards, the committee nodes in the shard will choose a subset of TXs from the local mempool to participate in the consensus process. The verified transactions will be packed into a new collation block. Then, we use $Q_i(t)$ to represent the queue length of shard i in the beginning of timeslot t. Thus, the queue-length evolution can be expressed as:

$$Q_i(t + 1) = \max\{Q_i(t) - B_i(t) + A_i(t), 0\}, \forall i \in I, t \in T. \tag{7.3}$$

On the other hand, to represent the investment cost on the consensus of the sharded permissioned blockchain, we define $c_i(t)$ as the numerical resource consumption by the network shard $i \in I$ in timeslot $t \in T$:

$$c_i(t) = \sum_{k=1}^{K} p_i^k(t), \forall i \in I, t \in T. \tag{7.4}$$

Objectives of Blockchain-Network Operator From the viewpoint of the operator of a permissioned sharded blockchain, the objectives are twofold: (1) to pursue a high speed of TX processing, and (2) to lower the operating cost in terms of resource consumption during the TX processing. Those two objectives seem conflict with each other. The operator has to maximize the payoff of transaction

Table 7.1 Symbols and notations

I	The set of queues, $|I|(= N)$ represents the size of I
T	The set of all timeslots, $t \in T$
K	The # of all types of resources, $k \in \{1, 2, 3, ..., K\}$
$\mathbf{p}_i(t)$	The vector of resources allocated for shard $i \in I$ at t
$p_i^k(t)$	The k-th resource allocated to shard $i \in I$ at timeslot t
$P_{\max}^k$	The budget of the k-th resource
w_k	The weight of the k-th resource
$\mathbf{Q}(t)$	Vector of actual queues, $\mathbf{Q}(t) = [Q_1(t), Q_2(t), ..., Q_N(t)]$
$Q_i(t)$	The queue length of shard $i \in I$ at timeslot t
$A_i(t)$	The arrival transactions of queue $i \in I$ at timeslot t
$B_i(t)$	The dequeued transactions of queue $i \in I$ at timeslot t
R	The reward to measure each unit of dequeued data
V	The parameter measuring the weight of penalty
α	The parameter reverse to the consensus difficulty
$L(\mathbf{Q}(t))$	The Lyapunov function of $\mathbf{Q}(t)$
$\Delta(\mathbf{Q}(t))$	The Lyapunov drift, $\Delta(\mathbf{Q}(t)) = L(\mathbf{Q}(t + 1)) - L(\mathbf{Q}(t))$
$\mathbf{Z}(t)$	Vector of virtual queues, $\mathbf{Z}(t) = [Z_1(t), Z_2(t), ..., Z_K(t)]$
$z_k(t)$	The increment arrived in virtual queue k at timeslot t
$\boldsymbol{\Theta}(t)$	The concatenated vector $\boldsymbol{\Theta}(t) = [\mathbf{Q}(t), \mathbf{Z}(t)]$

processing while using a limited amount of resources. To integrate those two conflict goals together, we devise a penalty function $pen(t)$, which is calculated by the total resource consumption defined in Eq. (7.4) minus the TX-processing payoff. To measure the payoff while processing a unit of data dequeued from $B_i(t)$, we also define a constant R as the TX-processing reward parameter. Here, we clarify the simplification to measure each transaction equally as the reward parameter R when calculating the payoff of dequeued transactions. This is because the unique value of each transaction is blind to the proposed resource-allocation method. Only the number of transactions in each shard can be observed by the proposed method taking the transaction's privacy into account in the context of permissioned blockchain. Therefore, our system model treats every transaction equally and calculates the payoff of transaction's processing using the constant reward parameter R. In practice, R can be configured according to the empirical preference of the blockchain network operator, when he/she defines the relative weights of two penalty terms $c_i(t)$ and $B_i(t)$. Then, the penalty function can be written as follows:

$$pen(t) = \sum_{i=1}^{N} [c_i(t) - B_i(t) \cdot R]$$

$$= \sum_{i=1}^{N} \sum_{k=1}^{K} p_i^k(t) - R \cdot \sum_{i=1}^{N} \sum_{k=1}^{K} \left[w_k p_i^k(t) \right]^{\alpha}, \forall t \in T. \tag{7.5}$$

Recall that a sharded permissioned blockchain network can be viewed as a multi-queue system as shown in Fig. 7.3. Besides the objective to minimize the penalty defined in Eq. (7.5), the network operator also intends to guarantee that each shard queue is in a stable condition during a long period, even under the large-volume bursty-TX injection attack. Using the notion of *queue stability* defined in [8], the multi-queue system is strongly stable if it satisfies:

$$\lim_{t \to \infty} \frac{1}{t} \cdot \frac{1}{N} \sum_{\tau=0}^{t-1} \sum_{i=1}^{N} \mathbb{E} \{Q_i(\tau)\} < \infty. \tag{7.6}$$

The basic idea to prove the Ineq. (7.6) is that in a multi-queue system, the assigned TXs in each queue will not be accumulated to infinity in the long run. Therefore, to keep the multi-queue system stable, each shard needs to process the TXs arrived in the queue with sufficient allocated resources. In this way, every TX assigned to this network shard can be processed in time. With the objective function and the constraints described above, we propose the following resource allocation problem for the sharded permissioned blockchain network.

$$\textbf{min} \quad \overline{pen}$$

$$\textbf{s.t.} \quad \sum_{i=1}^{N} p_i^k(t) \le P_{max}^k, \forall k \in [K], t \in T. \tag{7.7}$$

Queue stability depicted by Ineq. (7.6).

$$\textbf{Var:} \quad \mathbf{p}_i(t), \ \forall i \in I, t \in T.$$

In next section, we design an adaptive resource allocation algorithm that can find a near-optimal solution to problem (7.7).

7.4 Dynamic Resource-Allocation Algorithm

To address the proposed resource-allocation problem (7.7) in the context of maintaining the stability of the multi-queue sharded permissioned blockchain, we design a dynamic resource-allocation algorithm using the stochastic Lyapunov optimization technique [8]. In practice, the proposed algorithm can execute in the same manner of the sharding protocol.

7.4.1 Algorithm Design

Since the PBFT-based sharded blockchain is viewed as a queueing system with $N > 0$ queues, we define $\mathbf{Q}(t) = [Q_1(t), Q_2(t), ..., Q_N(t)]$ as the vector of queue backlogs of all network shards. To quantitatively measure the *size* of the vector $\mathbf{Q}(t)$, a *quadratic Lyapunov function* $L(\mathbf{Q}(t))$ is defined as follows:

$$L(\mathbf{Q}(t)) \triangleq \frac{1}{2} \sum_{i=1}^{N} Q_i(t)^2, \forall t \in T. \tag{7.8}$$

We then define a *one-timeslot conditional Lyapunov drift* $\Delta(\mathbf{Q}(t))$ as follows:

$$\Delta(\mathbf{Q}(t)) \triangleq L(\mathbf{Q}(t+1)) - L(\mathbf{Q}(t)), \forall t \in T. \tag{7.9}$$

This drift is in fact the change in the Lyapunov function (7.8) over one timeslot. Suppose that the current queue state in timeslot t is $\mathbf{Q}(t)$, we have the following lemma.

Lemma 7.1 (Lyapunov Drift) *Given the quadratic Lyapunov function (7.8), and assuming $L(\mathbf{Q}(0)) < \infty$, for arbitrary non-negative constants $B > 0$ and $\epsilon > 0$, the following drift condition holds:*

$$\lim_{t \to \infty} \frac{1}{t} \cdot \sum_{\tau=0}^{t-1} \sum_{i=1}^{N} \mathbb{E}\{Q_i(\tau)\} < B/\epsilon. \tag{7.10}$$

Lemma 7.1 tells that if the drift condition Ineq. (7.10) holds with $\epsilon > 0$, then all queues are strongly stable with the queue backlog bounded by B/ϵ. The proof of lemma 7.1 follows the same routine shown in [8], we omit the proof detail because of the space limitation.

Next, we need to handle the first constraint of problem (7.7) to ensure that the total consumption of the k-th resource should be restricted by the budget $P_{\max}^k$. To solve this issue, we transform the inequality constraints into a queue stability problem. By defining virtual queues $Z_k(t)$ for all $k \in [K]$, the update equation of $Z_k(t)$ is written as:

$$Z_k(t+1) = \max\{Z_k(t) + z_k(t), 0\}, \forall k \in [K], t \in T, \tag{7.11}$$

where $z_k(t) = \sum_{i=1}^{N} p_i^k(t) - P_{\max}^k$, $\forall k \in [K], t \in T$. The initial length of the virtual queue $Z_k(0), \forall k \in [K]$ is 0.

Insight Equation (7.11) indicates that $Z_k(t+1) - Z_k(t) \geq z_k(t)$. By summing the inequality above over timeslots $t = 0, 1, ..., T-1$, and dividing both sides by T, we have $\frac{Z_k(T) - Z_k(0)}{T} \geq \frac{1}{T} \sum_{t=0}^{T-1} z_k(t)$. With $Z_k(0) = 0$, take expectation on both sides and let $T \to \infty$, the result is $\limsup_{T \to \infty} \frac{\mathbb{E}\{Z_k(T)\}}{T} \geq \limsup_{T \to \infty} \overline{z_k}(t)$, where $\overline{z_k}(t)$ is the time-average expectation of $z_k(t)$. If virtual queue $Z_k(t)$ is mean-rate stable, we get $\limsup_{T \to \infty} \overline{z_k}(t) \leq 0$, which implies that the constraint of resource restriction in problem (7.7) is satisfied.

With the objective to maintain both the actual and virtual queues, we combine both of them to devise a concatenated vector $\Theta(t) = [\mathbf{Q}(t), \mathbf{Z}(t)]$, which can be updated using both Eq. (7.3) and (7.11). Then, the Lyapunov function of $\Theta(t)$ is defined as:

$$L(\Theta(t)) \triangleq \frac{1}{2} \sum_{i=1}^{N} Q_i(t)^2 + \frac{1}{2} \sum_{k=1}^{K} Z_k(t)^2, \ t \in T. \tag{7.12}$$

If we successfully make $L(\Theta(t))$ maintain a small value for each timeslot t, both the actual queues $\mathbf{Q}(t)$ and virtual queues $\mathbf{Z}(t)$ can be "squeezed" to a small space of queue backlogs. In the following, we present how to achieve such goal using the technique of *Lyapunov drift* [8].

Lemma 7.2 (Optimality Over Resource Allocation) *Let* $\mathbf{p}^* = [\mathbf{p}_1^*, \mathbf{p}_2^*, \mathbf{p}_3^*, ..., \mathbf{p}_N^*]$ *be the optimal resource allocation solution to problem (7.7). Suppose the sharded blockchain system satisfies the boundedness assumptions[8] and the law of large numbers. If the problem is feasible, then for any* $\delta > 0$, *there exists a stationary randomized policy that makes the resource allocation depend only on the state of multi-queue system, such that* $pen(t) < pen^*(t) + \delta$ *and* $A_i(t) < B_i(t)$, *where*

$$pen^*(t) \triangleq \sum_{i=1}^{N} \left[c_i^*(t) - B_i^*(t) \cdot R \right], \forall t \in T. \tag{7.13}$$

The proof of lemma 7.2 is given in [8]. The next step is to minimize a concatenated vector $\Delta(\Theta(t))$, which is defined as the *Lyapunov drift* of $\Theta(t)$, and $\Delta(\Theta(t)) = L(\Theta(t+1)) - L(\Theta(t))$. It should be noticed that minimizing the *Lyapunov drift* of $\Theta(t)$ would enforce queues towards a lower congestion. However, only focusing on the drift part may incur a large penalty $pen(t)$. Thus, we then propose a dynamic resource allocation algorithm based on the *drift-plus-penalty* (DPP) technique [8] to maintain the stability of a multi-queue blockchain system, and to minimize $pen(t)$ simultaneously. To achieve the goal, we integrate the penalty function into the Lyapunov drift $\Delta(\Theta(t))$. In every timeslot t, we try to minimize the following *drift-plus-penalty*:

$$\Delta(\Theta(t)) + V \cdot pen(t)$$

$$= \Delta(\Theta(t)) + V \cdot \sum_{i=1}^{N} [c_i(t) - B_i(t) \cdot R], \forall t \in T, \tag{7.14}$$

where V is a weight parameter representing how much we emphasize on minimizing the penalty $pen(t)$. When $V = 0$, the objective is to minimize the drift alone. Thus, to provide guarantees on $pen(t)$, we consider $V > 0$, which indicates a joint optimization taking both the system stability and the resource consumption into account.

Lemma 7.3 (Drift Boundary) *The boundary of the drift-plus-penalty expression shown in Eq. (7.14) satisfies:*

$$\Delta(\Theta(t)) + V \cdot \sum_{i=1}^{N} [c_i(t) - B_i(t) \cdot R]$$

$$\leq B + V \cdot \sum_{i=1}^{N} [c_i(t) - B_i(t) \cdot R]$$

$$+ \sum_{i=1}^{N} Q_i(t) [A_i(t) - B_i(t)] \tag{7.15}$$

$$+ \sum_{k=1}^{K} Z_k(t) z_k(t), \forall t \in T,$$

where the positive constant B exists and is bounded by:

$$B \geq \frac{1}{2} \sum_{i=1}^{N} \mathbb{E} \left\{ A_i(t)^2 + B_i(t)^2 | \Theta(t) \right\}$$

$$+ \frac{1}{2} \sum_{k=1}^{K} \mathbb{E} \left\{ z_k(t)^2 | \Theta(t) \right\}$$

$$- \sum_{i=1}^{N} \mathbb{E} \left\{ \min\{Q_i(t), B_i(t)\} \cdot A_i(t) | \Theta(t) \right\}.$$

Proof Exploiting the definition of *Lyapunov drift*, we have:

$$\Delta(\Theta(t)) = L(\Theta(t+1)) - L(\Theta(t))$$

$$= \frac{1}{2} \sum_{i=1}^{N} \left[Q_i(t+1)^2 - Q_i(t)^2 \right]$$

$$+ \frac{1}{2} \sum_{k=1}^{K} \left[Z_k(t+1)^2 - Z_k(t)^2 \right]$$

$$\overset{(a)}{\leq} \frac{1}{2} \sum_{i=1}^{N} \left\{ [Q_i(t) - B_i(t) + A_i(t)]^2 - Q_i(t)^2 \right\}$$

$$+ \frac{1}{2} \sum_{k=1}^{K} \left\{ [Z_k(t) + z_k(t)]^2 - Z_k(t)^2 \right\}$$

$$= \sum_{i=1}^{N} \left\{ \frac{1}{2} [A_i(t) - B_i(t)]^2 + Q_i(t) [A_i(t) - B_i(t)] \right\}$$

$$+ \sum_{k=1}^{K} \left\{ \frac{1}{2} z_k(t)^2 + Z_k(t) z_k(t) \right\}$$

$$\leq B + \sum_{i=1}^{N} Q_i(t) [A_i(t) - B_i(t)]$$

$$+ \sum_{k=1}^{K} Z_k(t) z_k(t), \forall t \in T,$$

where the inequation (a) follows from Eqs. (7.3) and (7.11). When adding $V \cdot \sum_{i=1}^{N} [c_i(t) - B_i(t) \cdot R]$ on both sides of the above derivation, the inequation (7.15) holds. □

Because the arrival new TXs $A_i(t)$ in timeslot t is independent of $\Theta(t)$, minimizing the right-hand-side (RHS) of Ineq. (7.15) for each timeslot t is equalized to solving the original optimization problem (7.7). Thus, we expand the RHS of Ineq. (7.15) and rearrange the objective as:

$$\begin{aligned} \mathbf{min} \quad & \Psi(\mathbf{p}_i(t)) \\ \mathbf{Var:} \quad & \mathbf{p}_i(t), \ \forall i \in I, t \in T, \end{aligned} \tag{7.16}$$

where $\Psi(\mathbf{p}_i(t)) = \sum_{i=1}^{N} \sum_{k=1}^{K} (Z_k(t) + V) p_i^k(t) - (Q_i(t) + V R) [w_k p_i^k(t)]^\alpha$.

Algorithm 1: Drift-plus-penalty resource allocation

   Input : T, V, R, α
   Output: $\mathbf{p}_i(t), \forall i \in I, t \in T$
1 $\mathbf{Q}(0) \leftarrow \emptyset, \mathbf{Z}(0) \leftarrow \emptyset$;
2 for $\forall t \in T$ **do**
3   Invoking Algorithm 2 $(t, \mathbf{Q}(t), \mathbf{Z}(t), V, R, \alpha)$ to get the optimal
       resource allocation $\mathbf{p}_i(t), \forall i \in I$.
4   Update the actual and virtual queues $\mathbf{Q}(t)$ and $\mathbf{Z}(t)$ according to Eq.
       (7.3) and Eq. (7.11), respectively.

Algorithm 2: Resource allocation per timeslot

   Input : $t, \mathbf{Q}(t), \mathbf{Z}(t), V, R, \alpha$
   Output: $\mathbf{p}_i(t), i \in I$
1 for $\forall i \in I, \forall k \in [K]$ **do**
2 $p_i^k(t) \leftarrow \sqrt[\alpha-1]{\dfrac{Z_k(t)+V}{\alpha(w_k)^\alpha[Q_i(t)+VR]}}.$

Note that, problem (7.16) is a linear programming and $\Psi(\mathbf{p}_i(t))$ is a convex function, through partially differentiating $\Psi(\mathbf{p}_i(t))$ by $p_i^k(t)$ and rearranging terms, then we get:

$$\frac{\partial \Psi(\mathbf{p}_i(t))}{\partial p_i^k(t)} = Z_k(t) + V - \alpha(w_k)^\alpha (Q_i(t) + VR)[p_i^k(t)]^{\alpha-1}. \tag{7.17}$$

From Eq. (7.17) we can find a real-numbered valley point $p_i^k(t) = \sqrt[\alpha-1]{\dfrac{Z_k(t)+V}{\alpha(w_k)^\alpha[Q_i(t)+VR]}}$ ($\forall i \in I, \forall k \in [K]$), which is the optimal resource allocation solution to the optimization problem (7.7). Then, given Eq. (7.17), the *DPP*-based resource-allocation algorithms are presented as Algorithms 1 and 2.

7.4.2 Algorithm Analysis

In this section, we analyze the performance guarantee of the proposed DPP-based algorithm.

7.4.2.1 Upper Bound of System Objective

First, Theorem 7.1 tells that the proposed DPP algorithm can ensure the system objective guaranteed within an $O(1/V)$ distance to that of the optimal solution to problem (7.7).

Theorem 7.1 *Suppose that problem (7.7) is feasible and there exists an optimal resource allocation solution which can obtain an optimal value pen*, and $L(\Theta(0)) < \infty$. For any $V > 0$, the time-average penalty yielded by the proposed Algorithm 1 satisfies:*

$$\limsup_{t \to \infty} \frac{1}{t} \sum_{\tau=0}^{t-1} \sum_{i=1}^{N} [c_i(\tau) - B_i(\tau) \cdot R] \le pen^* + \frac{B}{V}, \tag{7.18}$$

where B is depicted in Lemma 7.3.

Proof Integrating the result of Lemma 7.2 into the RHS of Eq. (7.15), and let $\delta \to 0$, we have:

$$\Delta(\Theta(\tau)) + V pen(\tau)$$

$$\le B + V \cdot pen^* + \sum_{i=1}^{N} Q_i(\tau) [A_i(\tau) - B_i(\tau)] \tag{7.19}$$

$$+ \sum_{k=1}^{K} Z_k(\tau) z_k(\tau),$$

where $\Delta(\Theta(\tau)) = L(\Theta(\tau + 1)) - L(\Theta(\tau))$.

Taking expectations on both sides, and summing the inequation (7.19) over $\tau \in \{0, 1, ..., t - 1\}$, it yields:

$$\mathbb{E}\{L(\Theta(t))\} - \mathbb{E}\{L(\Theta(0))\} + V \sum_{\tau=0}^{t-1} pen(\tau)$$

$$\le B \cdot t + Vt \cdot pen^* + \mathbb{E}\left\{ \sum_{\tau=0}^{t-1} \sum_{i=1}^{N} Q_i(\tau) [A_i(\tau) - B_i(\tau)] \right\} \tag{7.20}$$

$$+ \mathbb{E}\left\{ \sum_{\tau=0}^{t-1} \sum_{k=1}^{K} Z_k(\tau) z_k(\tau) \right\}.$$

Equation (7.3) implies that $Q_i(\tau) \ge 0$. Referring to Theorem 4.5 of [8] and the requirement of system stability, we have $\mathbb{E}\{A_i(\tau)\} - \mathbb{E}\{B_i(\tau)\} \le 0$. Equation (7.11) secures $Z_k(\tau) \ge 0$. Since $z_k(t)$ denotes the inequality constraint in problem (7.7), we have $\mathbb{E}\{z_k(\tau)\} \leq 0$. The Lyapunov function $L(\Theta(t)) \geq 0$ is due to Eq. (7.12). With those inequalities illustrated above, rearranging the terms of Ineq. (7.20) and dividing both sides by $V \cdot t$, we have:

$$\frac{1}{t}\sum_{\tau=0}^{t-1} pen(\tau) \leq pen^* + \frac{B}{V} + \frac{\mathbb{E}\{L(\Theta(0))\}}{V \cdot t}. \tag{7.21}$$

Then, taking a $\limsup_{t \to \infty}$ and invoking Eq. (7.5), the conclusion of Theorem 7.1 holds.   □

7.4.2.2 Upper Bound of the Queue Length of Shards

In this part, we analyze the congestion performance (measured in *queue length*) of network shards when adopting the proposed Algorithm 1. First, we give Assumption 7.1.

Assumption 7.1 (Slater Condition [8]) *For the expected arrival rates $A_i(t)$ and process rates $B_i(t)$, there exists a constant $\epsilon > 0$, which satisfies $\mathbb{E}\{A_i(t)\} - \mathbb{E}\{B_i(t)\} \leq -\epsilon$.*

We see that such Slater Condition [8] is related to the system stability. Using this condition, we then have the following theoretical upper bound of queue length.

Theorem 7.2 *If problem (7.7) is feasible and Assumption 7.1 holds, then the proposed Algorithm 1 can stabilize the multi-queue blockchain system, and the time-average queue length satisfies:*

$$\limsup_{t \to \infty} \frac{1}{t}\sum_{\tau=0}^{t-1}\sum_{i=1}^{N} \mathbb{E}\{Q_i(\tau)\} \leq \frac{B + V(pen^* - pen^{min})}{\epsilon},$$

where B is defined in Lemma 7.3 and pen^{min} is the minimum resource consumption yielded by all the feasible solutions.

Proof Referring to Ineq. (7.20), we separate the actual queues apart from the inequation. Given $L(\mathbf{Q}(t)) \geq 0$, we have:

$$-\mathbb{E}\{L(\mathbf{Q}(0))\} + V\sum_{\tau=0}^{t-1} pen(\tau)$$

$$\leq B \cdot t + Vt \cdot pen^* + \mathbb{E}\left\{\sum_{\tau=0}^{t}\sum_{i=1}^{N} Q_i(\tau)\left[A_i(\tau) - B_i(\tau)\right]\right\}.$$

Exploiting Assumption 7.1, we then have:

$$- \mathbb{E}\{L(\mathbf{Q}(0))\} + V \sum_{\tau=0}^{t-1} pen(\tau)$$

$$\leq B \cdot t + Vt \cdot pen^* - \sum_{\tau=0}^{t} \sum_{i=1}^{N} Q_i(\tau)\epsilon.$$

Rearranging terms and dividing both sides by $t \cdot \epsilon$, we get:

$$\frac{1}{t} \sum_{\tau=0}^{t} \sum_{i=1}^{N} Q_i(\tau)$$

$$\leq \frac{B \cdot t + \mathbb{E}\{L(\mathbf{Q}(0))\} + Vt \cdot pen^* - V \sum_{\tau=0}^{t-1} pen(\tau)}{t \cdot \epsilon}$$

$$\leq \frac{B + V(pen^* - pen^{min})}{\epsilon} + \frac{\mathbb{E}\{L(\mathbf{Q}(0))\}}{t \cdot \epsilon}.$$

Finally, we take a lim sup as $t \to \infty$ to conclude the proof. $\qquad \square$

Insights Theorems 7.1 and 7.2 show that the proposed DPP-based algorithm has an $O(1/V) \sim O(V)$ tradeoff between resource consumption and queue-length performance. As the TX processing delay is proportional to the queue's length, thus the proposed algorithm can make a fine-balanced cost-delay tradeoff for the permissioned sharded blockchain.

7.5 Performance Evaluation

In this section, we conduct numerical simulations to evaluate the proposed *DPP Res. Allocation* algorithm in the context of PBFT-based sharded permissioned blockchain.

7.5.1 Basic Settings for Numerical Simulation

In simulations, the sharded blockchain network consists of a varying number of N network shards.

Dataset For simulations, we generate numerical synthesized transaction dataset as the arrived TXs $A_i(t)$ for each network shard $i \in I$ at each timeslot $t \in$

$\{1, 2, ..., 1000\}$ timeslots. The integer value of $A_i(t)$ is randomly distributed within the range $[5, 25]$.

Resources Network shards consume the cloud-platform resources to strive for consensus. We consider two types of resources in our simulation. The first type is the computing power (measured in the # of CPU cores). The second type is the network bandwidth, measured in Kbit/Second (Kb/s). Recall that we have mentioned that the computing power is mainly for committee formation and the network bandwidth is for PBFT consensus in Sect. 7.3.1. The weights of those two resources are variable depending on different network configurations. How to set the weights of different resources is not the focus of this chapter. Thus, we set the weights of the two types of resources to 5 and 3, respectively. Other weight settings can be also evaluated similarly and thus omitted.

Other Parameters We then fix $R = 5$ to denote the reward of dequeueing each unit of TX data. The consensus parameter α for all network shards is set to 0.5. The total simulation duration is set as 1000 timeslots.

7.5.2 Metrics

To compare the performance of algorithms, we focus on the following metrics.

- **Queue Length**. The backlog of each queue which represents the number of unprocessed TXs in the mempool of each shard.
- **Computing-Power Consumption**. The consumption of computing-power for the all shards spending on processing TXs in each timeslot.
- **Network Bandwidth Consumption**. The bandwidth consumption for all network shards to process TXs waited in mempool per timeslot.

7.5.3 Baselines

We consider the following baselines for the comparison with the proposed algorithm.

- **Top-S Res. Allocation** [19]. This baseline equally allocates each type of resource to the queues that locate in the top-S percentage of all network shards with respect to (w.r.t) their queue length.
- **Longest-First Res. Allocation** [20]. This baseline always allocates each type of resource to the queue that has the longest queue among all network shards w.r.t their queue length.
- **Average Res. Allocation**. This strategy allocates each type of available resources to all network shards on average at each timeslot.

- **Random Res. Allocation**. The last baseline allocates each type of available resources with a random amount to every network shard at each timeslot.

7.5.4 Performance Analysis

7.5.4.1 Effect of Tuning Parameter V

The first group of simulations evaluates the effect of parameter V. Firstly, we fix $N = 4$ and set V to 50, 100, and 150 in different executing cases. In addition, to study the effect of dynamically tuning parameter V, we also implement a codebook-based method referring to [21]. In such codebook-based approach, V is adaptively varied within the range [50, 150] according to the changes of shard's queue backlog and the resource consumption. The goal is to maintain a balanced trade-off between those two objective terms. For example, when the queue length of shards is observed too large, V is tuned to a small value accordingly. When too many resources are consumed by network shards, V is then tuned to a large value. For all network shards, the total computing-power budget and the total network bandwidth budget are set to 200 CPUs and 100 Kb/s, respectively. From Fig. 7.4a–c, we can observe that the proposed *DPP Res. Allocation* can stabilize all queues of network shards, since the length of 90% of all queues is within 40 while varying the parameter V. Secondly, the virtual-queue technique can keep the two types of resources under their given individual budgets. Finally, we find that a larger V leads to a lower resource-consumption in terms of both computing-power and network bandwidth consumption. Thus, the resource consumption illustrates an $O(1/V)$ ratio. However, a large V increases the queue length and thus causes larger waiting latency for TXs. Therefore, the queue length shows an $O(V)$ ratio. Those observations match the insights disclosed in the end of Sect. 7.4.2. In contrast, the codebook-based method has a similar resource-consumption performance with other cases under fixed V, but yields a more narrow range of queue length than other three cases. In conclusion, the

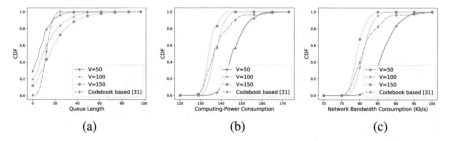

(a) (b) (c)

Fig. 7.4 Performance evaluation while varying parameter V. (**a**) CDF of the queue length of all network shards per timeslot. (**b**) CDF of the computing-power consumption of all network shards per timeslot. (**c**) CDF of the network bandwidth consumption of all network shards per timeslot

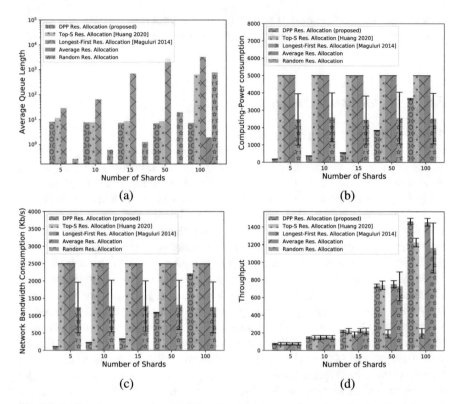

Fig. 7.5 Performance comparison with baseline algorithms. (**a**) The average queue length of each shard per timeslot v.s. the # of shards. (**b**) The computing-power consumption of all shards per timeslot v.s. the # of shards. (**c**) The network bandwidth consumption of all shards per timeslot v.s. the # of shards. (**d**) The throughput (total dequeued TXs in each timeslot) of all shards per timeslot v.s. the # of shards

tradeoff between the resource consumption and the queueing delay of TXs should be made carefully by tuning the parameter V.

7.5.4.2 Performance Comparison with Baselines

Through Fig. 7.5, we compare the proposed *DPP Res. Allocation* algorithm with the three baselines aforementioned. The budgets of computing-power and network bandwidth resources are set to 5000 CPUs and 2500 Kb/s, respectively. The number of network shards varies from 5 to 100. For the *Top-S Res. Allocation*, we set S to 50%.

Interestingly, from Fig. 7.5a, we observe that when the shard number is smaller than 100, *Top-S Res. Allocation* has the similar queue length as the proposed *DPP Res. Allocation* does. However, when the shard number reaches 100, the *Top-S Res. Allocation* strategy cannot maintain the stable queue length anymore, because the

Top-S strategy only focuses on allocating resources for the queues that locate at the top *S* percentage of all w.r.t queue length. When the number of network shards grows large, the resources are not able to fulfill the requirement of maintaining short queues for network shards. As for the *Longest-First Res. Allocation*, it can only maintain stable queue length when the number of shards is less than 10. When the number of shards exceeds 15, the average queue length of *Longest-First Res. Allocation* soars to about 700. Therefore, this strategy fails to guarantee a stable queue length. The reason is that this baseline allocates all available resources to the longest queue every timeslot. Thus, other queues are ignored, making the average queue length grows sharply.

On the other hand, when the number of shards is less than 50, *Random Res. Allocation* yields a shorter queue length than *DPP Res. Allocation*. This is because *Random Res. Allocation* can provide sufficient required resources to all network shards with the given budgets. However, once the number of shards exceeds 50, the average queue length indicated by *Random Res. Allocation* increases drastically from 20 to 780, as shown in Fig. 7.5a. Since the queue length grows exponentially under the *Random Res. Allocation* strategy when the number of shards increases, its low resource-consumption properties shown in Fig. 7.5b and c are meaningless.

In the case of *Average Res. Allocation* strategy, we see that the queue length is even lower than that of *Random Res. Allocation* when the number of shards is small, and still maintains a very low level when the blockchain has 100 network shards. However, such low-level queue length is achieved by supplying all the available resources (i.e., the full computing-power budget shown in Fig. 7.5b and the full network-bandwidth budget shown in Fig. 7.5c) to all network shards. Therefore, the *Average Res. Allocation* strategy cannot achieve a balance between resource consumption and queue's stability.

In contrast, the proposed *DPP Res. Allocation* algorithm can always maintain a stable queue length shown in Fig. 7.5a when the number of shards varies from 5 to 100. Also, Fig. 7.5b and c demonstrate that *DPP Res. Allocation* requires a linearly-growing resource consumption when the number of shards increases from 5 to 100. Even though when the shard number reaches 100, the average resource consumption of *DPP Res. Allocation* is still lower than that of the other three baselines including *Top-S*, *Longest-First* and *Average Res. Allocation*.

Regarding throughput (calculated by the total # of dequeued TXs in each timeslot), Fig. 7.5d shows that when the shard number is less than 15, five strategies have similar throughput. However, when the number of shards exceeds 50, the throughput of *Longest-First Res. Allocation* is significantly lower than other four baselines. The reason is that *Longest-First Res. Allocation* only serves the shard having the most congested memory pool whenever the shard number varies. When the shard number reaches 100, the throughput of the proposed *DPP Res. Allocation* is higher than that of *Top-S* and *Random Res. Allocation* schemes, and is similar to that of *Average Res. Allocation*. Considering the throughput performance shown in Fig. 7.5b and c, it's not hard to see that the *DPP Res. Allocation* has the most efficient resource utilization among the five algorithms.

In summary, the proposed *DPP Res. Allocation* attains a fine-balanced tradeoff between queue stability and resource consumption comparing with other baselines.

7.5.4.3 Continued Bursty-TX Injection Attacks Against All Shards

In this part, we compare the performance under the continued bursty-TX injection attack of the proposed *DPP Res. Allocation* with two baselines, i.e., *Top-S* and *Longest-First Res. Allocation*. Since the other two baselines (*Average* and *Random Res. Allocation*) have very low efficiency on resource consumption, we omit their comparisons in this group of simulation. The budgets of computing-power and network bandwidth resources are set to 5000 CPUs and 2500 Kb/s, respectively. The number of shards is set as 100. The parameter S is fixed to 50% for *Top-S Res. Allocation*. To simulate the continued bursty-TX injection attack, we keep injecting a number of TXs to each network shard with a rate 25 TXs/timeslot between the 100-th and the 150-th timeslot.

Figure 7.6a demonstrates the performance of queue length of three strategies under the continued bursty-TX injection attack. We can see that the proposed *DPP*

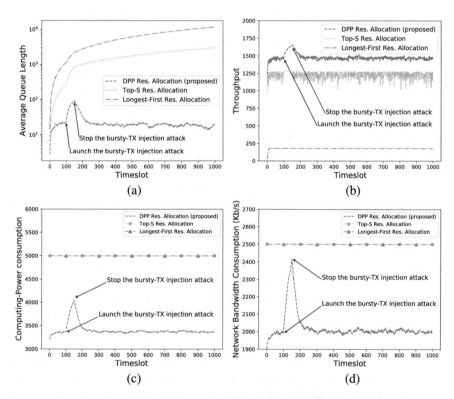

Fig. 7.6 Performance evaluation under the continued bursty-TX injection attack against all network shards. (**a**) The average queue length of each baseline under continued bursty-TX injection attacks. (**b**) The throughput (total dequeued TXs in each timeslot) of each baseline under the bursty-TX injection attack. (**c**) The computing-power consumption of each baseline under the bursty-TX injection attack. (**d**) The network bandwidth consumption of each baseline under the bursty-TX injection attack

Res. Allocation can quickly process the large number of injected TXs and maintain a short queue length in the 50 timeslots under attacking. In contrast, for the *Top-S* and *Random Res. Allocation* baselines, the average length of shard's queue has already become extremely congested even before we launch the continued bursty-TX injection attack at the 100-th timeslot.

In terms of throughput, Fig. 7.6b shows that the proposed *DPP Res. Allocation* can always have the maximum throughput comparing with the other two baselines. As shown in Fig. 7.6c and d, *DPP Res. Allocation* requires the lowest resource consumption among the three algorithms. The reason is described as follows. Unlike *Top-S Res. Allocation* and *Random Res. Allocation*, the proposed algorithm does not have to utilize all of the available resources in every timeslot. When the continued bursty-TX injection attack begins, although *DPP Res. Allocation* tends to utilize a suddenly increasing resources, it can quickly enforce shard queues to return to stable status when the attack stops at the 150-th timeslot.

7.5.4.4 Drastic Bursty-TX Injection Attack Against A Single Shard

Under the similar settings to that of the previous group of simulation, we are also interested in the performance of the three algorithm under the drastic bursty-TX injection attack against a specified network shard. The only difference is the implementation of the drastic injection attack. To simulate such the drastic bursty-TX injection attack, we inject 3000 TXs to only a single network shard at the beginning of the 100-th timeslot.

Figure 7.7 shows the evaluation results of the drastic bursty-TX injection attack. In contrast with the other two baselines, we observe the similar performance of the proposed DPP-based algorithm, in terms of average queue length, throughput, and the resource consumption. Comparing with the previous group of simulations, although the increases of both queue length and resource consumption are more sharp, the absolute values of those metrics are very similar to those of the continued injection attack. Importantly, the throughput of DPP-based algorithm still demonstrates the best among the three algorithms.

Thus, in summary, the proposed *DPP Res. Allocation* algorithm can maintain the stable queue length under both the continued and the drastic bursty-TX injection attacks, and illustrates a more efficient resource consumption than other two baselines.

7.6 Conclusion

System stability is critical to the key performance of the sharding-based blockchain. We study how to maintain stable queues for network shards by proposing a fine-grained resource-allocation algorithm for the PBFT-based sharded permissioned blockchain. Based on the multi-queue analytical model, we adopt the stochastic

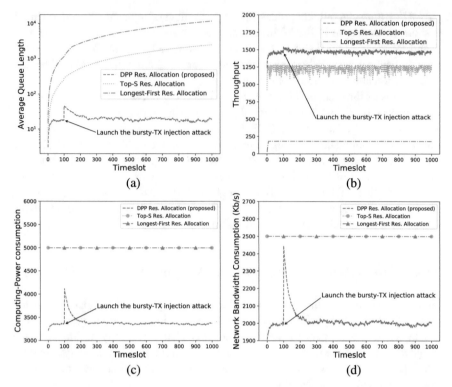

Fig. 7.7 Performance evaluation under the drastic bursty-TX injection attack against a single network shard. (**a**) The average queue length of each baseline under a drastic bursty-TX injection attack. (**b**) The throughput (total dequeued TXs in each timeslot) of each baseline under the bursty-TX injection attack. (**c**) The computing-power consumption of each baseline under the bursty-TX injection attack. (**d**) The network bandwidth consumption of each baseline under the bursty-TX injection attack

optimization technique to help us jointly consider both the resource consumption and the queue stability when allocating network resources to each blockchain shard. Through the proposed theoretical framework, we can choose how much we emphasize on resource-consumption or queue stability by dynamically tuning a weight parameter V. We also rigorously analyze the theoretical upper bounds of system objective and shard's queue length of the proposed DPP-based algorithm. Finally, the numerical simulation results show that the proposed DPP-based algorithm can effectively stabilize shard queues while requiring a reasonable level of resource consumption. Under two representative cases of bursty-TX injection attacks, the evaluation results demonstrate that the proposed DPP-based algorithm can well alleviate the imbalanced TX assignments with much shorter queue length, higher throughput, and lower resource consumption, comparing with other baselines.

Acknowledgments This Work is partially supported by National Key R&D Program of China (No.2020YFB1006005), National Natural Science Foundation of China (61902445), Guangdong Basic and Applied Basic Research Foundation (2019A1515011798), Guangzhou Basic and Applied Basic Research Foundation (202102020613), Pearl River Talent Recruitment Program (No. 2019QN01X130), CCF-Huawei Populus euphratica forest fund (CCF-HuaweiBC2021004), Hong Kong RGC Research Impact Fund (RIF) with the Project No. R5060-19, General Research Fund (GRF) with the Project No. 152221/19E, 152203/20E, and 152244/21E, the National Natural Science Foundation of China (61872310), and Shenzhen Science and Technology Innovation Commission (R2020A045).

References

1. L. Luu, V. Narayanan, C. Zheng, K. Baweja, S. Gilbert, P. Saxena, A secure sharding protocol for open blockchains, in *ACM SIGSAC Conference on Computer and Communications Security (CCS'16)* (ACM, 2016), pp. 17–30
2. M. Castro, B. Liskov et al., Practical byzantine fault tolerance, in *OSDI*, vol. 99 (1999), pp. 173–186
3. E. Kokoris-Kogias, P. Jovanovic, L. Gasser, N. Gailly, E. Syta, B. Ford, Omniledger: A secure, scale-out, decentralized ledger via sharding, in *IEEE Symposium on Security and Privacy (SP)* (2018), pp. 583–598
4. M. Zamani, M. Movahedi, M. Raykova, RapidChain: scaling blockchain via full sharding, in *ACM SIGSAC Conference on Computer and Communications Security (CCS'18)* (2018)
5. J. Wang, H. Wang, Monoxide: Scale out blockchains with asynchronous consensus zones, in *16th USENIX Symposium on Networked Systems Design and Implementation (NSDI 19)*, Boston, MA, February (USENIX Association, 2019), pp. 95–112
6. L.N. Nguyen, T.D.T. Nguyen, T.N. Dinh, M.T. Thai, Optchain: optimal transactions placement for scalable blockchain sharding, in *IEEE 39th International Conference on Distributed Computing Systems (ICDCS)* (IEEE, 2019), pp. 525–535
7. T. Nguyen, M.T. Thai, Denial-of-service vulnerability of hash-based transaction sharding: Attacks and countermeasures. arXiv:2007.08600 (2020)
8. M.J. Neely, Stochastic network optimization with application to communication and queueing systems. Synthesis Lectures Commun. Netw. **3**(1), 1–211 (2010)
9. Q.L. Li, J.Y. Ma, Y.X. Chang, Blockchain queue theory, in *International Conference on Computational Social Networks* (Springer, 2018), pp. 25–40
10. S. Ricci, E. Ferreira, D.S. Menasche, A. Ziviani, J.E. Souza, A.B. Vieira, Learning blockchain delays: a queueing theory approach. ACM SIGMETRICS Perform. Eval. Rev. **46**(3), 122–125 (2019)
11. R.A. Memon, J. Li, J. Ahmed, A. Khan, M.I. Nazir, M.I. Mangrio, Modeling of blockchain based systems using queuing theory simulation, in *2018 15th International Computer Conference on Wavelet Active Media Technology and Information Processing (ICCWAMTIP)* (IEEE, 2018), pp. 107–111
12. Y. Kawase, S. Kasahara, A batch-service queueing system with general input and its application to analysis of mining process for bitcoin blockchain, in *IEEE International Conference on Internet of Things (iThings) and IEEE Green Computing and Communications (GreenCom) and IEEE Cyber, Physical and Social Computing (CPSCom) and IEEE Smart Data (SmartData)* (2018), pp. 1440–1447
13. J. Misic, V.B. Misic, X. Chang, S.G. Motlagh, M.Z. Ali, Block delivery time in bitcoin distribution network, in *IEEE International Conference on Communications (ICC)* (2019), pp. 1–7

14. Y. Jiao, P. Wang, D. Niyato, Z. Xiong, Social welfare maximization auction in edge computing resource allocation for mobile blockchain, in *IEEE International Conference on Communications (ICC)* (2018), pp. 1–6
15. N.C. Luong, Z. Xiong, P. Wang, D. Niyato, Optimal auction for edge computing resource management in mobile blockchain networks: A deep learning approach, in *IEEE International Conference on Communications (ICC)* (2018), pp. 1–6
16. M. Fang, J. Liu, Toward low-cost and stable blockchain networks, in *IEEE International Conference on Communications* (2020), pp. 1–6
17. H.W. Wang, Ethereum sharding: Overview and finality (2017). Accessed 8 Sept 2019
18. D. Dasgupta, J.M. Shrein, K.D. Gupta, A survey of blockchain from security perspective. J. Banking Financial Technol. **3**(1), 1–17 (2019)
19. H. Huang, S. Guo, W. Liang, K. Wang, Y. Okabe, Coflow-like online data acquisition from low-earth-orbit datacenters. IEEE Trans. Mobile Comput. **19**(12), 2743–2760 (2020)
20. S.T. Maguluri, R. Srikant, Scheduling jobs with unknown duration in clouds. IEEE/ACM Trans. Netw. (ToN) **22**(6), 1938–1951 (2014)
21. J. Koo, J. Yi, J. Kim, M.A. Hoque, S. Choi, Seamless dynamic adaptive streaming in LTE/Wi-Fi integrated network under smartphone resource constraints. IEEE Trans. Mobile Comput. **18**(7), 1647–1660 (2019)

Chapter 8
Dynamic Sharding: A Trade-OFF Between Security and Scalability

Jianting Zhang, Zicong Hong, Xiaoyu Qiu, Yufeng Zhan, Song Guo, and Wuhui Chen

8.1 Overview

The blockchain has been considered as a revolutionary technology for implementing distributed ledgers with its high security and decentralization such as Bitcoin [1] and Ethereum [2]. In a blockchain, participants that do not trust each other can maintain a distributed ledger to guarantee a trustworthy and decentralized

J. Zhang
School of System Science and Engineering, Sun Yat-sen University, Guangzhou, China
e-mail: zhangjt26@mail2.sysu.edu.cn

Z. Hong · Y. Zhan · S. Guo
Department of Computing, The Hong Kong Polytechnic University, Hung Hom, Hong Kong, China
e-mail: zicong.hong@connect.polyu.hk; song.guo@polyu.edu.hk

X. Qiu
School of Computer Science and Engineering, Sun Yat-sen University, Guangzhou, China
e-mail: qiuxy23@mail2.sysu.edu.cn

W. Chen (✉)
GuangDong Engineering Technology Research Center of Blockchain, Sun Yat-sen University, Guangdong, China
e-mail: chenwuh@mail.sysu.edu.cn

© The Author(s), under exclusive license to Springer Nature Singapore Pte Ltd. 2023   193
W. Chen et al. (eds.), *Blockchain Scalability*,
https://doi.org/10.1007/978-981-99-1059-5_8

environment. However, it is still challenging for blockchain systems to deal with large-scale networks without compromising security and decentralization, in terms of both the number of nodes and transaction throughput. For example, Hyperledger achieves end-to-end throughput of more than 3500 transactions per second (TPS) but its network scale is less than 100 [3], while Ethereum can support thousands of blockchain nodes but only process 14 TPS [2].

To enhance the scalability of blockchain, sharding is widely considered as a promising solution [4]. Recently, several blockchain sharding systems, including Elastico [5], OmniLedger [6], RapidChain [7], Monoxide [8] and OptChain [9], have showed a breakthrough for the scalability of blockchain. In a sharding system, the system will be partitioned into independent smaller parts called *shards* (or *committees*), any of which maintains a separated ledger by nodes within the shard. The participants of different shards can process transactions in parallel, which means multiple blocks can be created and validated in parallel in the whole system and the transaction throughput can be improved prominently. In the meantime, sharding allows a large number of blockchain nodes to participate without increasing the overhead of communication, computation and storage because of smaller committees. However, the environment of a practical blockchain system is dynamic, i.e., blockchain nodes can join and leave the system and the malicious attackers can actively corrupt honest nodes, which can dynamically influence the number of nodes in the blockchain system. There still exists several challenges for sharding when dealing with the dynamic environment and we conclude three following challenges.

(1) Setting re-sharding interval: Because sharding partitions the blockchain system into smaller shards, the malicious attack targeted to a shard as well as the leaving of honest nodes in the shard can make the fault tolerance for the consensus of the shard be exceeded more easily, i.e., $\frac{1}{4}$ in Proof-of-Work [10] and $\frac{1}{3}$ in Practical Byzantine Fault Tolerance protocol (PBFT) [11]. Thus, it needs to do re-sharding (also called shard reconfiguration) periodically to guarantee the security of the sharding system. However, the re-sharding interval is difficult to set properly under the dynamic environment. Less frequent re-sharding can save more time for the consensus process, but it increases the risk of the sharding system. More frequent re-sharding can decrease the risk of the sharding system, but it intervenes the consensus process because validators stop processing consensus and suffers from extra cost for the communication and computation of re-sharding operation.

(2) Controlling shard number: Since most of the sharding systems use Byzantine Fault Tolerance (BFT)-based consensus protocol as their intra-committee protocol, the shard size is limited in a small number due to the communication overhead, i.e., $O(n^2)$ communication complexity per block in a shard with n nodes for PBFT [11]. The performance of the system degrades as a result of the increased size of each shard [12]. However, the probability of forming an unsafe shard will be high if the shard size is small. Therefore, if the shard number is fixed, the performance and security of the sharding system will be unstable and hard to make a trade-off when the number of nodes fluctuates in a dynamic environment.

(3) Adjusting block size: In the blockchain sharding systems, transactions need to be packed into blocks for verification and processing. A bigger block can pack more transactions, thereby increasing the transactions throughput. However, because each new block needs to be broadcast to all members within the shard during its consensus, a bigger block also incurs a significant communication overhead and increases the latency of each consensus round when the shard size is big. Therefore, the block size needs to be adjusted based on the dynamic environment to achieve the maximum transactions throughput.

Therefore, the re-sharding interval, shard number and block size should be adjusted dynamically according to the dynamic environment in a sharding system. However, all existing blockchain sharding systems adopt the static sharding policy, i.e., the fixed re-sharding interval, fixed shard number and fixed block size, and cannot efficiently deal with the real-world scenarios. This motivates us to design a dynamic sharding system to balance the performance and security under the dynamic environment of the blockchain system.

We propose SkyChain, the first dynamic public blockchain sharding protocol that enables blockchain system to automatically make shards based on the current system state. SkyChain can enhance the performance without compromising security when the blockchain system state changes. Specially, since the dynamic characteristic of blockchain sharding systems can be modelled as a Markov Decision Process (MDP) and the environment in blockchain system is in high dimension, we utilize a deep reinforcement learning (DRL) approach to acquire optimal sharding policies in different environment states. DRL can learn the characteristics of blockchain sharding system from previous experience and take a proper sharding policy based on the current network state to acquire a long-term reward. To train this DRL-based sharding model, we propose an optimization framework to evaluate the performance and security, which guarantees that the final sharding policies made by the trained agent are beneficial to balance the performance and security of blockchain. We summarize the main contributions of this chapter as follows.

- We present the first dynamic sharding-based framework in a public blockchain that can maintain a long-term balance between performance and security under the dynamic environment of blockchain systems.
- We propose an adaptive ledger protocol that guarantees the ledgers to be merged or split efficiently and without conflict according to the dynamic sharding result.
- We quantify a general sharding system and design a DRL-based sharding approach to dynamically adjust re-sharding interval, shard number and block size under the dynamic environment of blockchain systems.
- Experimental results show that SkyChain achieves a dynamic blockchain sharding system with improved performance and security.

8.2 System Overview

In this section, we present the system model and threat model and then describe the DRL-based sharding model in our system.

8.2.1 System Model

Since the permissionless blockchain allows all nodes to join in the system, it must require every node who wants to take part in Byzantine consensus network to establish an identity through a Sybil-resistant identity generation mechanism (e.g., PoW, PoS) [13, 14]. As most of previous work does [5–7], in our sharding system, nodes get their identities by solving a computationally-hard puzzle related with the randomness created in last shard reconfiguration. This is because solving PoW requires enough computation, resulting that the malicious processors can only create limited identities with their limited computation. Similar to most sharding system, we adopt a BFT-based consensus as the intra-consensus protocol.

In order to reach a consistency within a fixed time, we adopt the synchronous model to propagate the messages between honest nodes. A network is considered synchronous if the message sent by one node can reach all nodes in the network within a fixed bound delay Δ[15]. Since Δ is normally in the scale of minutes [6], it is not suitable to use synchronous model within a consensus round. Thus, we use partially synchronous model in intra-committee consensus protocol, which means committee can achieve responsiveness with an optimistic time-outs. Besides, there is an *identity chain* in our system, the main responsibility of which is to store the registry of validators and reorganize validators into shards.

8.2.2 Threat Model

We consider Byzantine fault-tolerant model as the fault model in our system, where the corrupt nodes can act in any arbitrary manner, e.g., modifying messages, sending incorrect or invalid messages, or doing nothing after receiving messages from other honest nodes. Similar to other work [5–7, 16, 17], the adversary is mildly adaptive during an epoch. In other words, it will take the adversary some time to corrupt the honest nodes. We assume that the total number of the malicious nodes is less than ns at any moment, where n represents the total number of blockchain nodes and $s = \frac{1}{4}$ indicates the Byzantine fault tolerance of the system while the committee Byzantine fault tolerance is $f = \frac{1}{3}$ [6]. We also adopt the view-change protocol [11, 18] for nodes to choose a new leader when the primary node is faulty.

8.2.3 DRL-Based Sharding Model

Unlike other sharding protocols whose sharding policies are fixed regardless of the changing of system state, we consider the dynamic change of blockchain environment, where we make different sharding policies to guarantee the trade-off between performance and security.

To achieve this goal, we use a DRL approach to help the system dynamically make sharding policy in reconfiguration period. DRL is a distinctive type of machine learning, which combines deep learning (DL) with the reinforcement learning (RL) to maximize the cumulative reward from the interactions between the *agent* and the *environment* in high-dimensional data [19]. In our system, the environment in DRL is dynamic blockchain environment and the agent is maintained by each of nodes. Note that an epoch in blockchain sharding system in this chapter is equal to an epoch in DRL.

Our framework can be illustrated as Fig. 8.1. We briefly introduce our framework as follows and the details will be shown in Sect. 8.5. At the end of epoch t, the transactions pool and the number of nodes for next epoch are used as the state s_t in DRL. The agent then chooses an action a_t, i.e., re-sharding interval, shard number and block size for next epoch, based on a neural network and then enters the next state s_{t+1}. After that, the agent obtains a reward from the environment and stores the transition (s_t, a_t, r_t, s_{t+1}) into the buffer. At the same time, the agent randomly batches a constant number of previous transitions to update its neural networks, which guarantees that the agent can keep selecting an action to maximize the long-term reward regardless of the infinite dynamic environments.

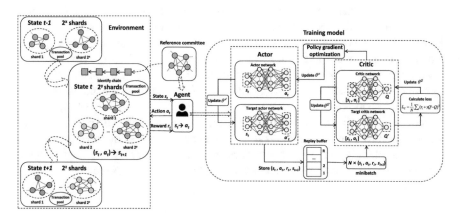

Fig. 8.1 SkyChain: DRL-based dynamic sharding framework

8.3   Adaptive Ledger Protocol

In this section, we propose an *adaptive ledger protocol* to guarantee the ledgers to be merged and split efficiently and without conflict according to the re-sharding result.

8.3.1   State Block

To tackle the issues of efficient isolation for dynamically changing ledgers and rapidly bootstrapping for reconfiguration nodes (i.e., new nodes or swapping nodes that are switched from original shard to another shard), we introduce *state blocks*. Reconfiguration nodes can get the entire state of a shard's ledger rapidly from the state blocks. Compared to transaction blocks that store transaction data, state blocks merely record the latest information of all accounts of a shard's ledger, including account addresses and account states (a data structure containing balance, nonce and storage root like [2]). Let sb_i^t denotes the state block of shard i at epoch e_t. Then, sb_i^t can be created by its related committee in the following steps: At the beginning of reconfiguration period, the committee's leader traces previous blocks since last state block, and creates a mapping between addresses and account states. Next, the state root of last transaction block is put in the header of sb_i^t, and the mapping between addresses and account states are used as the body of sb_i^t. Then, the leader gossips sb_i^t and the members of committee i run the intra-committee consensus protocol to agree on this state block. After that, the body of sb_i^{t-1} can be discarded to save the storage.

Another important reason to use state blocks is that they can simplify ledgers merging and splitting as subsidiary blocks. Since the number of system validators is dynamic, for example, some validators crash or leave during consensus period while some new nodes join in the system to participate in the consensus period of next epoch, it is crucial to adjust the shard size or shard number. When the number of system nodes declines, the size of a committee is so small that the malicious nodes can corrupt committees in a short time. It will threaten the security of blockchain systems. Consequently, we need to enlarge the size of committee by merging two or more committees into one. Note that the number of shards is cut down at the same time. In addition, when the number of system nodes increases, we can split a shard into more shards to get a higher throughput under the premise of security.

8.3.2   Ledgers Merging and Splitting

As Fig. 8.2a illustrates, we use various colors differentiate ledgers (i.e., green blockchain and blue blockchain respectively represent the ledger maintained by shard i and shard j at epoch e_t). Let sb_i^t denote the state block of shard i at epoch

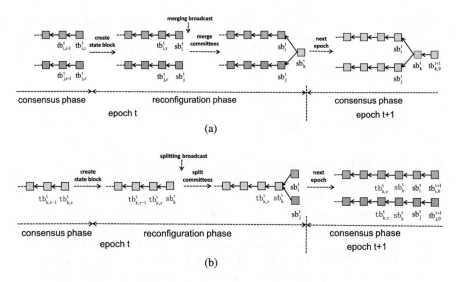

Fig. 8.2 Adaptive ledger protocol. (**a**) Ledgers merging process. (**b**) Ledgers splitting process

e_t and $tb_{i,r}^t$ denote the rth transaction block of shard i created at epoch e_t. Then, the procedure of merging ledgers can be described as follows. At the beginning of the reconfiguration phase at epoch e_t, shard i creates a state block sb_i^t that uses the hash of the last transaction block $tb_{i,r}^t$ as its previous hash, and adds it to the end of blockchain after reaching an agreement. Another shard j executes this process in the same way. After receiving an identity block broadcast by the reference committee, committees know which committee they will merge with and get the memberships' addresses of connected committee (i.e., the nodes in shard i and shard j realize they will be assigned into a same shard in the next epoch). Then, two shard's leaders sent the header of their state block to other nodes of shard i and shard j, and separately create a new state block sb_k^t whose state root is formed by hashing the state roots of sb_i^t and sb_j^t. After that, two shards collectively execute a consensus protocol to reach an agreement and the two chains are linked by sb_k^t. Finally, shard i and shard j are merged into shard k (denoted by yellow color in Fig. 8.2a). The validators of shard k consist of the original nodes in shard i and shard j, along with some new nodes verified during epoch e_t.

Ledgers splitting is similar to ledgers merging. As Fig. 8.2b shows, the procedure of splitting ledgers contains the following steps: After shard k reaching a consensus on the last transaction block $tb_{k,r}^e$ at the end of consensus phase of epoch t, it moves to shard reconfiguration phase. At the beginning of the reconfiguration event, the leader of shard k checks account information and consensus on a new state block sb_k^t. After receiving a identity block from the reference committee, the validators of shard k get their shard information in next epoch, including shard ID and addresses of members of shard. New leaders create new state blocks (i.e., sb_i^t and sb_j^t) based on identity block. Two node sets of shard k respectively choose one of the state blocks and execute a consensus protocol to add it to the end of blockchain. In this way, a chain could be divided into two chains, each of them maintains a disjoint ledger in back of the state block. Finally, they will respectively process different transactions in next epoch.

8.3.3 Shards Formation

Once a new identity block has been created by the reference shard, all nodes can update their identity chain and start to form new shards. To establish point-to-point connection with their shard peers, a naive solution is to ask each nodes to broadcast its identity and shard information to all nodes. This solution results in $O(n^2)$ communications, which is not scalable when the number of nodes n is large. To reduce the latency of connection establishment, we adopt a more efficient method to help nodes complete shards formation period, which has $O(n)$ complexity of communication. Our algorithm to form new shards is depicted in Algorithm 1.

At the beginning of each epoch, the reference shard has been formed from the current shard leaders and a group of full nodes that come from different shards. After entering shards formation period, the reference shard first generates a new identity block (line 2) based on DRL agent (see Sect. 8.5 for more details), and broadcasts it to the whole network (line 3). At the same time, the reference shard holds a leaders election (line 4), which will assign a portion of full nodes based on their shard information as the new shard leaders for next epoch. Then, these new shard leaders will inform their shard peers with a new leader verification (line 8). Every node can fast obtain other nodes' identities of new shard via new leaders, and then builds connections with them (line 9). After that, new shards have been formed and blockchain sharding system will enter next epoch.

Algorithm 1: Algorithm to form new shards for next epoch e_t

Input: q_{t-1}: number of pending transactions; n_{t-1}: number of nodes
Output: forming new reference shard and new shards

1 **Procedure** *ShardsFormation*:
2      $ib_t \leftarrow$ IBGeneration(q_{t-1}, n_{t-1})
3   BroadcastIB(ib_t)
4      $newRc \leftarrow$ LeadersElection()
5   **for** $l \in newRc$ **do**
6          $peers \leftarrow$ GetPeerID(l)
7   **for** $p \in peers$ **do**
8             $l.BroadcastIDs(p, peers)$
9   **end**
10   ConnectionBuild()
11   **end**

8.4   Blockchain Sharding System Analysis

In this section, we introduce the formal definitions of a blockchain sharding system
and some essential properties a robust blockchain sharding system should satisfy,
which are classified into performance properties and security properties. Then, we
concretely define the performance properties, i.e., efficiency and scalability, and
measure the performance from transaction throughput. Next, we analyze the security
properties, including availability, consistency and liveness. Finally, we formulate a
sharding optimization problem from the aspects of security and performance.

8.4.1   Definitions of Blockchain Sharding System

A blockchain sharding system containing k_t shards at epoch e_t can be denoted as
a collection of sets $S = \{S_1, S_2, \ldots, S_{k_t}\}$, where $S_i = \{n_{i1}, n_{i2}, \ldots, n_{i|S_i|}\}(1 \leq i \leq |k_t|)$, represents a transaction-processing shard (i.e., committee) which is
responsible for the verification and process of transactions. Let $n_t = \sum_{c=1}^{k_t} |S_c|$
denote the total number of nodes (validators in all shards) and $m_t = \frac{n_t}{k_t}$ represent
the average number of nodes per shard (i.e., shard size) at epoch e_t. Ledgers are
defined as a set $L = \{L_1, L_2, \ldots, L_{k_t}\}$, where $L_j(1 \leq j \leq |k_t|)$ is a valid ledger
that records transactions and the state of accounts. As introduced in Sect. 8.3, there
are two types of blocks in ledgers: transaction block tb^t and state block sb^t. The
former stores transaction data, while the latter records the latest information of all
accounts of a shard's ledger. Besides, in order to resist malicious attacks as Sect. 8.1
describes, shards have to be reconfigured every epoch. In SkyChain, every node
stores the latest identity blockchain B_r, as well as a transaction ledger maintained
by its shard. The reference shard C_r^t, which consists of every shard's leader and a
group of full nodes, helps coordinate re-sharding period and enhance consistency of
shards' states by maintaining the identity blockchain.

There are several critical components for a sharding system to complete.

(1) Intra-committee consensus. Since sharding technology partitions the
blockchain system into independent smaller parts, most blockchain sharding
systems adopt PBFT-based consensus protocol as their intra-committee
consensus. PBFT is composed of three main phases, i.e., pre-prepare T_{prep},
prepare T_{pre} and commit T_{com}. The communication complexity of PBFT T_{intra}

is proportional to shard size m_t. Specifically, intra-committee consensus latency can be computed by

$$
\begin{aligned}
T_{intra} &= T_{prep} + T_{pre} + T_{com} \\
&= (\frac{S^B logm_t}{R_t} + t_v) + (\frac{S^H logm_t}{R_t} + t_v) \\
&\quad + (\frac{S^H logm_t}{R_t} + t_v + t_a) \\
&= 3t_v + t_a + \frac{S^B logm_t}{R_t} + \frac{2S^H logm_t}{R_t},
\end{aligned}
\tag{8.1}
$$

where t_v is validation time of every phase, t_a is the cost that the new block is appended to a blockchain, S^B is the average size of transactions, S^H is the block header size and R_t is data transmission rate. Note that a full new block is broadcast only at the beginning of the consensus stage, i.e., in pre-prepare phase, while the later two phases broadcast block header instead. Besides, messages are received by overall nodes in $O(logm_t)$ times gossip at most [7].

(2) Cross-shard transactions. Those transactions whose senders and receivers are recorded in different shards are called cross-shard transactions. Cross-shard transactions require related shards to communicate with each other. Generally, relay transactions are created to guarantee the atomicity for processing cross-shard transactions. Let R_n be the average number of relay transactions and P_c be the probability of cross-shard transaction for a original transaction in the sharding system. Then, we can utilize the expected number of transactions for processing an original transaction R_p to calculate the practical transaction rate P_r by

$$
\begin{aligned}
P_r &= \frac{1}{R_p} \\
&= \frac{1}{1 \times (1 - P_c) + (1 + R_n) \times P_c} \\
&= \frac{1}{1 + R_n P_c}.
\end{aligned}
\tag{8.2}
$$

For example, in Monoxide [8], where $R_n = 1$ and $P_c = 1 - \frac{1}{k_t}$, if the system has processed 1000 transactions with 3 shards, the practical number of transactions being processed is $1000 \times P_r = 1000 \times \frac{1}{1+1\times(1-\frac{1}{3})} = 600$.

(3) Re-sharding. The purpose of re-sharding is to guarantee the security of the sharding system. In SkyChain, ledgers merging process and ledgers splitting process may happen during reconfiguration period. Therefore, the overhead of reconfiguration can be measured by the complexity of adaptive ledger protocol, which is proportional to the change of the number of shards $|\Delta k_t|$,

intra-committee consensus and randomness generation algorithm (detailed in Sect. 8.4.2).

Since sharding technology is an extension for blockchain, which aims to enhance the scalability of classic blockchain, a blockchain sharding system should preserve the intrinsic properties of blockchain. Besides, sharding introduces some new challenges, e.g., easier malicious attack, cross-shard transactions verification and re-sharding overhead. We conclude that a robust blockchain sharding system should uphold the following properties: efficiency, scalability, availability, consistency and liveness. Further, efficiency and scalability belong to performance properties, while availability, consistency and liveness are security properties. We measure the performance and security by defining and formulizing these properties.

8.4.2 Performance Analysis

Intuitively, efficiency indicates the overhead of bootstrap during reconfiguration period. Scalability expresses the ability of parallel processing that a sharding system can obtain in comparison to a non-sharding blockchain system with the increase of nodes.

Definition (Efficiency) Efficiency is measured by the re-sharding latency T_{res}, which indicates how long does a blockchain system take to reconfigure shards and enter the next epoch. □

In SkyChain, the adaptive ledger protocol is divided into four stages to complete reconfiguration period, as described in Sect. 8.3:

1. **Update**. Shards creates state blocks and update their ledgers respectively, denoted as T_s.
2. **Randomness generation**. The reference shard generates a randomness for next epoch, denoted as T_r.
3. **Identity block creation**. The reference shard agrees on a new identity block that includes epoch randomness and sharding policy for next epoch. This part is denoted as T_i.
4. **Adjustment**. Nodes spontaneously form predetermined shards for the next epoch based on the new identity block. This part is denoted as T_a.

At the beginning of reconfiguration period of epoch e_t, each leader of shards traces all valid transaction blocks since the state block sb^{t-1} of previous epoch e_{t-1}. Then the leader gathers the balance of all accounts, and writes these information into the body of a new state block sb^t which will be broadcast to other nodes after that. The main activity of update stage is to reach a round of intra-committee consensus, and thus we can make $T_s = T_{intra}$. Similarly, the latency of identity block creation T_i is equal to T_{intra}. Besides, since randomness generation algorithm is fixed, the latency of randomness generation stage can be considered as a constant κ. At the end of each epoch, a new identity block ib_{t+1} is broadcast to all network nodes, and new leaders will communicate with their own shards' nodes based on this new identity block. Then, nodes discover other nodes of the same shard and form new shards for next epoch. Obviously, more shards need more time to adjust. Using $|\Delta k_t|$ as the independent variables, we define a function $\mathbf{T}(|\Delta k_t|)$ to estimate the complexity of adjustment stage by

$$T_a = \mathbf{T}(|\Delta k_t|) = \alpha |\Delta k_t| + \beta, \tag{8.3}$$

where $\alpha > 0$ is a control factor. β indicates the cost that a portion of nodes are selected to be reshuffled from one shard to another shard.

Finally, we can conclude the re-sharding latency T_{res}^t at epoch e_t as

$$\begin{aligned} T_{res}^t &= T_s + T_r + T_i + T_a \\ &= \kappa + 2T_{intra} + \mathbf{T}(|\Delta k_t|). \end{aligned} \tag{8.4}$$

Definition (Scalability) Parameterized by k_t (the number of shards), it indicates a blockchain system can either adopt a large number of nodes or improve transaction throughput. □

Blockchain sharding system performs better on scalability property compared to a non-sharded blockchain system. On the one hand, scaling the size of system depends on three factors of a node: communication, computation and storage. In a blockchain sharding system, the network is partitioned into smaller parts where each node only maintains its own shard's ledger, which leads to the decrease of the overhead of communication, computation and storage. On the other hand, each shard processing transactions in parallel can scale transaction throughput in proportion to the number of shards k_t. We define a throughput scaling factor ω_t as parallelism of transactions processing at epoch e_t, which represents how many blocks can be created at the same time. Apparently, the throughput scaling factor ω_t is equal to k_t for a blockchain sharding system.

To measure the performance of a blockchain sharding system, we first define the length of epoch e_t as T_e^t. Each epoch consists of two periods: consensus period and reconfiguration period. We define the consensus period of shard S_i contains r_i^t rounds, in which S_i creates one new block within latency $T_{intra,i}$. Then we can easily get r_i^t by

$$r_i^t = \frac{T_e^t - T_{res}^t}{T_{intra,i}}. \tag{8.5}$$

Furthermore, the number of transactions Ω_i^t that shard S_i can process during epoch e_t is calculated by

$$\Omega_i^t = \frac{S^B}{S^T} r_i^t = \frac{S^B}{S^T} \frac{T_e^t - T_{res}^t}{T_{intra,i}}, \tag{8.6}$$

where S^T denotes the average size of one transaction. Next, the total number of transactions Ω^t processed by a blockchain sharding system during epoch e_t is

$$\Omega^t = \sum_{i=1}^{k_t} \Omega_i^t = \frac{S^B(T_e^t - T_{res}^t)}{S^T} \sum_{i=1}^{k_t} \frac{1}{T_{intra,i}}. \tag{8.7}$$

Considering the influence of cross-shard transactions as described in Sect. 8.4.1, we measure the performance of a blockchain sharding system by computing the practical transaction throughput O:

$$O = \frac{\Omega^t P_r}{T_e^t} = \frac{S^B(T_e^t - T_{res}^t)}{S^T T_e^t (1 + R_n P_c)} \sum_{i=1}^{k_t} \frac{1}{T_{intra,i}}. \tag{8.8}$$

8.4.3   Security Analysis

Similarly, we first introduce the definition of security properties, and then evaluate security of a blockchain sharding system via formulating these properties.

Definition (Availability) Parameterized by λ (shards formation security parameter) and ϵ (the average attack ability of a malicious node), it indicates that a shard is not controlled by malicious nodes and all transactions recorded in chain are valid.   □

Availability ensures that transactions can be correctly verified via historical data (i.e., old transactions which have been successfully recorded into ledger). Besides, since cross-shard transactions verification need different shards to exchange messages, availability protects safe shards from deception of unsafe shards. We define two attacks that may destroy the availability property of blockchain sharding system.

(1) **Unsafe shard formation attack**. The system will become unsafe if there is at least one unsafe shard because other secure shard is possible to validate transactions related with the corrupt shard. We use the hypergeometric distribution to compute the probability of the faulty system, i.e., the probability of forming at least one unsafe shard with m_t nodes and more than $m_t f$ malicious nodes in it. Specifically, we use X to be a random variable that indicates the number of malicious nodes assigned to a shard. Let $F = sn_t$ denote the number of overall malicious nodes in the blockchain sharding system with n_t nodes and s system Byzantine fault tolerance. Consequently, the probability of faulty system is:

$$P[X \geq \lceil m_t f \rceil] = \sum_{x=\lceil m_t f \rceil}^{m_t} \frac{\binom{F}{x}\binom{n_t - F}{m_t - x}}{\binom{n_t}{m_t}}. \tag{8.9}$$

We consider it unacceptable that a fault shard exists in sharding system. To keep the probability of unsafe shard formation negligible, we define a security parameter λ to bound the probability of unsafe shard formation. We think it is secure enough if the following inequality is satisfied.

$$P[X \geq \lceil m_t f \rceil] < 2^{-\lambda}. \tag{8.10}$$

For example, $\lambda = 5$ means that a sharding system is safe if the probability of forming a corrupt shard is less than 2^{-5}.

(2) **Corruption attack**. There are three models of corruption attack: (1) Static, where attackers can only corrupt nodes at a predefined time [5]; (2) Mildly adaptive, where attackers can slowly corrupt a portion of the honest over time during consensus periods [6, 7]; (3) Fully adaptive, where attackers can corrupt nodes at any time [20]. SkyChain assumes the corruption attack is mildly adaptive, which means a malicious node has limited attack power ϵ_t to attack honest nodes during the consensus period of epoch e_t. We consider a blockchain sharding system safe at epoch e_t if the following formulation is satisfied.

$$\epsilon_t n_t s (T_e^t - T_{res}^t) \leq m_t f, \tag{8.11}$$

where s is the resilience of the whole system and f is the resilience of a shard. This formula indicates that all attackers of a system cannot completely corrupt any one of safe shards before the blockchain sharding system enters re-sharding period.

Definition (Consistency) A blockchain sharding system is consistency if it satisfy:

(i) All nodes of one shard record the same ledger.
(ii) There is no more than one shard processing same transactions during any epoch, i.e., blocks created during same epochs are disjoint among different shards. □

Each shards only processes related transactions whose sender's addresses are recorded at the latest state block and forwards irrelevant transactions to other shards. If no shard is corrupt by the malicious attackers, the consistency property can be satisfied. To quickly help transactions to locate to which shard they should be processed within it, we adopt idea from the design of the inter-committee algorithm in RapidChain, where the complexity of routing transactions is $O(k_t)$ with k_t shards in the blockchain sharding system.

Definition (Liveness) Parameterized by γ (consensus rounds parameter) and d_k (block depth), it indicates that transaction blocks can be considered stable if there are at least γ consensus rounds at epoch e_t or d_k consecutive blocks behind them, i.e., these transaction blocks are ultimately accepted by all honest nodes. □

In a PoW-based blockchain system, the creation of a new blocks is random. Those miners who first solve a PoW puzzle have rights to propose a new block, and broadcast it to other nodes of network. Because of the network propagation delay, there may be several new blocks being created at the same time, which leads to the inconsistency of ledger. Therefore, a block and its transactions are confirmed by the network if there are d_k (e.g., $d_k = 6$ in Bitcoin [21]) or more blocks have been mined after it in a PoW-based blockchain system. Note that $gamma = 0$ in non-sharded blockchain systems because there is no epoch in them.

In contrast, PBFT-based blockchain systems pack only one block at every round. The new block is determined if the current leader is honest. When the current leader is corrupt or crash, the new block cannot reach an agreement and becomes a pending block. It will trigger a view change protocol [18], in which the new leader re-propose the pending blocks. Generally, a PBFT-based blockchain system can eventually achieves liveness if it has less than mf malicious nodes with m total nodes and f resilience. However, in a blockchain sharding system that adopts PBFT-based protocol as intra-committee consensus, the pending blocks may become invalid because shards have been adjusted at next epoch, resulting that a subset of transactions of pending blocks should be processed in different shards. Thus, it request the latency of consensus period must be long enough to execute a view change and at least one consensus round to re-propose the pending blocks when the initial leader is corrupt or crashed. We assume the latency of view change t_{vc} is less than the latency of a consensus round T_{intra}, then the consensus period needs to contains at least γ (e.g., $\gamma = 2$) consensus rounds. Note that $d_k = 0$ in a blockchain sharding system whose intra-committee consensus is PBFT-based consensus. Finally, we conclude that a blockchain sharding system is liveness if it satisfy

$$\gamma T_{intra}^t \leq T_e^t - T_{res}^t. \tag{8.12}$$

8.4.4   Problem Formulation

The performance of blockchain sharding system can be measured by transaction throughput. From Eqs. (8.1)–(8.12), we can conclude that the performance and security are contradictory objectives in the optimization problem. On the one hand, to improve transaction throughput, a blockchain sharding system can prolong the epoch length or decrease shard size, but leading to low security because it is easy to form a unsafe shard or corrupt a shard, according to Eqs. (8.8)–(8.11). On the other hand, if a shard consists of a large number of nodes, the blockchain sharding system can satisfy the security constraints to guarantee security, but leading to low transaction throughput with high consensus latency and less shard number, thus, compromising performance. From Eqs. (8.1), (8.8) and (8.12), we also find that block size can influence transaction throughput and security. When increasing block size S^B can enhance transaction throughput (Eq. (8.8)), it also leads the system not satisfy liveness property (Eq. (8.12)). Specifically, we conclude three influence factors about performance and security in a blockchain sharding system:

(1) Epoch length T_e^t: The effects of epoch length act in two ways. Increasing epoch length can bring an improvement of consensus rounds of an epoch (Eq. (8.5)), because the totally time spent in reconfiguration decreases within a certain period of time. However, it will increase corruption risk as the malicious nodes have more time to attack the honest nodes as illustrated in Eq. (8.11).

(2) Shard number k_t: Similarly, the number of shards may affect system throughput in two ways. On the one hand, increasing k_t can greatly improve transaction throughput because there are more shards to process transactions in parallel (Eq. (8.8)). Besides, a higher number of shards leads to smaller shard size. It can be able to shorten the intra-committee consensus time as m_t diminishing (Eq. (8.1)). On the other hand, the smaller m_t means that the shard can tolerate less faulty nodes and it is more possible to form an unsafe shard, which makes the blockchain sharding system loss availability property (Eqs. (8.9)–(8.11)).

(3) Block size S^B: It can be inferred from Eq. (8.6) that large block size can improve throughput because one block packs more transactions at the same time. However, from Eq. (8.1), we can find that the consensus latency is proportional to the block size, and then makes the blockchain sharding system loss liveness property (Eq. (8.12)). Thus, when increasing block size can improve transaction throughput, the consensus latency is prolonged, which eventually compromises security.

In our dynamic blockchain sharding system, we study to make a trade-off between performance and security by dynamically adjusting epoch length, the number of shards and block size. We use Eqs. (8.10)–(8.12) as the security constraints to maximize transaction throughput. Then, the problem formulation is as follows.

$$\max \quad O = \frac{S^B(T_e^t - T_{res}^t)}{S^T T_e^t (1 + R_n P_c)} \sum_{i=1}^{k_t} \frac{1}{T_{intra,i}} \tag{8.13}$$

$$s.t. \quad P[X \geq \lceil m_t f \rceil] < 2^{-\lambda},$$

$$\epsilon_t n_t s (T_e^t - T_{res}^t) \leq m_t f,. \tag{8.14}$$

$$\gamma T_{intra}^t \leq T_e^t - T_{res}^t.$$

It is crucial to set appropriate epoch length, shard number and block size. However, solving the above problem is difficult due to unawareness of future blockchain environment and nonlinear constraints. Thus, in the next section, we propose a deep reinforcement learning framework to dynamically adjust these parameters, so that it can reach the trade-off between security and scalability.

8.5 DRL-Based Dynamic Sharding Framework

In order to address the trade-off issue in dynamic blockchain systems, we utilize a deep reinforcement learning approach. Different from many static sharding approaches taking predefined rules, DRL strives to study a general sharding policy from past experience according to current blockchain environment and the given reward, which makes it adaptive to complex and dynamic blockchain environments. Considering that our action space is continuous, we use Deep Deterministic Policy Gradient (DDPG) algorithm [22] to train our model. To guarantee the truth and rationality of sharding policy made by the agent, we deploy the trained agent to the consensus layer. Then, the selection of actions can be agreed by a group of highly trusted nodes denoted by the reference committee. There are three key components in reinforcement learning, including state space, action space and reward function, we define them as follows.

8.5.1 DRL Model Design

(1) State Space: We consider a dynamic blockchain sharding system with n nodes, where the leaving of nodes can happen at all times and the joining of new nodes only happens during reconfiguration period. The state of transactions pool q denotes to the number of pending transactions. Thus, the state space at epoch e_t can be expressed by

$$s_t = [q, n]_t. \tag{8.15}$$

(2) Action Space: As discussed above, epoch length T_e, shard number k and block size S^B play a part in tackling the problem of trade-off in sharding system and change the blockchain environment. When we consider the arrival of nodes follows a distribution, epoch length will determine the number of system nodes in next epoch. Besides, shard number and block size can change the state of transaction pool by affecting the rate of processing transactions. Thus, they should be adjusted to adapt to the dynamic environment. We define the action space at epoch e_t as

$$a_t = [T_e, k, S^B]_t. \tag{8.16}$$

We need to scale action by defining a maximum action value because DDPG algorithm outputs an action range in continuous interval (e.g., $(-1, 1)$). We set the epoch length $T_e \in (0, Len)$ with the maximum epoch length Len. To guarantee the ledgers to be merged or split efficiently and without conflict, as described in Sect. 8.3, we set $k = 2^i, i = 0, 1, 2, \ldots, C$, where C is certain constant. We set $N_s = 2^C$ represents the maximum number of shards. Similarly, we define a value M to constrain the range of block size.

(3) Reward: Our optimization target is to obtain a sharding policy that could balance performance and security in every epoch. Since the scalability can be quantified easily with transaction throughput, we use transactions throughput as our reward function. Meanwhile, Eqs. (8.8), (8.10) and (8.11) are defined as three following constraint conditions

$$\Phi_1 : P[X \geq \lceil m_t f \rceil] < 2^{-\lambda},$$
$$\Phi_2 : \epsilon_t n_t s(T_e^t - T_{res}^t) \leq m_t f, \qquad (8.17)$$
$$\Phi_3 : \gamma T_{intra}^t \leq T_e^t - T_{res}^t.$$

Then, the reward r_t at epoch e_t can be defined as

$$r_t(s_t, a_t) = \begin{cases} 0, \text{ if one of } \Phi_1 - \Phi_3 \text{ dissatisfies,} \\ \frac{S^B(T_e^t - T_{res}^t)}{S^T T_e^t (1 + R_n P_c)} \sum_{i=1}^{k_t} \frac{1}{T_{intra,i}}, \text{ otherwise.} \end{cases} \qquad (8.18)$$

Since DDPG updates its model parameters according to every step reward that more reward represents better action, we set reward to be 0 when sharding policy has broken one of the constraints between security and confirmation latency, i.e., $\Phi_1 - \Phi_3$ cannot be satisfied completely.

8.5.2 DRL Training Methodology

Algorithm 2 shows the detailed training methodology of our DRL-based dynamic sharding framework. The agent maintains a sharding policy $\mu(s|\theta^\mu)$ (the actor network) and an evaluation of the value function $Q(s, a|\theta^Q)$ (the critic network) where θ^μ and θ^Q are the parameters of the actor network and critic network (Line 1). The agent uses the target network modified for actor-critic that are initialized as a copy of the actor and critic networks to calculate the target value for the updates of the networks (Line 2). To guarantee that the training samples are independently and identically distributed, DDPG uses a finite sized replay buffer for sampling (Line 3). At each timestep t, the agent selects and executes a sharding action a_t according to the current blockchain state s_t, then, applying a noise $\mathcal{N}$ for exploration (Line 9–11). After that, the blockchain environment will give the agent a reward which is measured by system security and throughput, and entering next state s_{t+1} (Line 12–15). The agent stores transition (s_t, a_t, r_t, s_{t+1}) in $\mathcal{N}$, then, batching a constant number of previous transitions from the replay buffer to calculate the loss function L_C and policy gradient $\nabla_{\theta^\mu} J$ for the update of the critic network parameters θ^Q and actor network parameters θ^μ (Line 17–21). Finally, DDPG use "soft" target updates to change the target network slowly: $\theta^{Q'} \leftarrow \tau\theta^Q + (1 - \tau)\theta^{Q'}$ and $\theta^{\mu'} \leftarrow \tau\theta^\mu + (1 - \tau)\theta^{\mu'}$ with $\tau \ll 1$ (Line 22).

Algorithm 2: DRL-based dynamic sharding framework for blockchain systems

---

1 **Initialize** critic network $Q(s, a|\theta^Q)$ and actor network $\mu(s|\theta^\mu)$ with weights θ^Q and θ^μ.
2 **Initialize** target critic network and target actor network with weights
   $\theta^{Q'} \leftarrow \theta^Q$ and $\theta^{\mu'} \leftarrow \theta^\mu$.
3 **Initialize** target network update rate τ, learning rate η, replay buffer $\mathcal{R}$.
4 **Set** training episode E and training steps T.
5 **for** *episode=1 to E* **do**
6   Initialize an exploration noise $\mathcal{N}$ for action exploration
7   Initialize environment and receive initial observation state s_1
8   **for** *t = 1 to T* **do**
9   Select action $a_t = \mu(s_t|\theta^\mu)$ according to s_t and the current policy
10   Apply noise $\mathcal{N}_t$ to action to get exploration action $a'_t = a_t + \mathcal{N}_t$
11   Execute a'_t to set next epoch length, shard number and block size
12   **if** *all constraints are satisfied* **then**
13   set reward r_t to be throughput
14   **end**
15   **else**
16   set reward $r_t = 0$
17   **end**
18   Observe next state s_{t+1} and termination condition *done*
19   Store transition $(s_t, a'_t, r_t, s_{t+1})$ in $\mathcal{R}$
20   Sample a random minibatch of N transitions (s_i, a_i, r_i, s_{i+1}) from $\mathcal{R}$
21   Set $y_i = r_i + \gamma Q'(s_{i+1}, \mu'(s_{i+1}|\theta^{\mu'})|\theta^{Q'})$
22   Update critic by minimizing the loss:
   $$L_C = \frac{1}{N}\sum_i(y_i - Q(s_i, a_i|\theta^Q))^2$$
23   Update the actor policy using the policy gradient:
   $$\nabla_{\theta^\mu} J \approx \frac{1}{N}\sum_i \nabla_a Q(s, a|\theta^Q)|_{s=s_i, a=\mu(s_i)} \nabla_{\theta^\mu}\mu(s|\theta^\mu)|_{s_i}$$
24   Update the target networks: $\theta^{Q'} \leftarrow \tau\theta^Q + (1 - \tau)\theta^{Q'}$
   $\theta^{\mu'} \leftarrow \tau\theta^\mu + (1 - \tau)\theta^{\mu'}$
25   **end**
26 **end**

8.5.3 DRL Deployment Methodology

In our blockchain sharding system, DRL agent is maintained by each blockchain nodes. Each new nodes must download the latest trained agent to reach a consistency before joining in the system. However, only the agents maintained by the members of reference committee can determine a sharding policy. At the beginning of each reconfiguration period, reference committee runs an intra-committee consensus protocol to agree a sharding policy for next epoch. Then, a new identity block consisting of the sharding information will be broadcast to other blockchain nodes, and appended to the identity blockchain. The sharding system will do re-sharding according to the sharding policy as shown in Sect. 8.3.

8.6 Evaluation

In this section, we evaluate the performance of our proposed algorithm in many aspects. We used Tensorflow to build our neural networks and implemented our algorithm with Python 3.6 in Windows Server 2016. We assume that each node has the same computing power in this system, that means each node can solve PoW puzzle and join in committees with the same probability. In a blockchain system, new blocks creation can be modeled as a Poisson process with time-dependent intensity [23], which means the decrease of transactions is also a Poisson process. Moreover, the amount of network pending transactions remains steady,[1] which means the arrival rate of transactions is approximately equal to the processed rate of transactions, i.e., the reduction rate of transactions. Thus, we model the arrivals of transactions in our blockchain sharding system as a Poisson process with arrival rate $\lambda_t = 10,000$. Each transaction must first enter and queue up in the transaction pool of infinite size to wait for being packed. According to the data about the historical changes of nodes number in Ethereum,[2] we can find that the number of nodes in blockchain dynamically changes all the time. In other words, the blockchain environment is dynamic with the joining or leaving of nodes. Thus, we assume that the change in the number of nodes Δ_N follows a Normal distribution with the variance $\sigma^2 = 100$ and the expectation $E_n = 0$, in which $\Delta_N > 0$ denotes new nodes joining while $\Delta_N < 0$ represents nodes leaving. The parameters setting used in the simulations are summarized in Table 8.1.

We design three baseline schemes to compare with our proposed scheme, including: (1) Proposed scheme with fixed epoch length. (2) Proposed scheme with the fixed number of shards. (3) Proposed scheme with fixed block size.

---

[1] https://cn.etherscan.com/chart/pendingtx.

[2] https://www.ethernodes.org/history.

Table 8.1 Simulation parameters

Parameter	Value
The initial number of nodes, N_0	10,000
The initial number of transactions, Q_0	2×10^8
The system Byzantine fault tolerance, s	$\frac{1}{4}$
The committee Byzantine fault tolerance, f	$\frac{1}{3}$
The security parameter, λ	5
Attack ability per malicious node, ϵ	1×10^{-5}
The latency for randomness creation, κ	0.5s
The parameter for adjustment stage, α	0.2
Reshuffle cost, β	2s
Validation time for messages, t_v	0.1s
Data transmission rate, R_t	10Mbps
Average block header size, S^H	10B
Average transaction size, S^T	64B
The latency for adding new block, t_a	0.2s
The consensus rounds parameter, γ	6
The maximum epoch length, Len	1000s
The maximum number of shards, N_s	64
The maximum block size, M	8MB

8.6.1 Convergence Analysis

We adopt the reward function in Eq. (8.18) to evaluate the transactions throughput. Figure 8.3 shows the convergence performance of our proposed DRL-based dynamic sharding scheme and other baseline schemes. We can see that the throughput of all schemes increases rapidly from a low level at the beginning of the learning process and becomes flattened after around 5000 training episodes. It illustrates that DRL-based dynamic sharding algorithm can make proper sharding policy according to different network environments to acquire a long-term reward in our sharding system. Figure 8.3 also shows the superior performance of our proposed scheme compared with other schemes, which means that epoch length, shard number and block size affect transactions throughput in our sharding system.

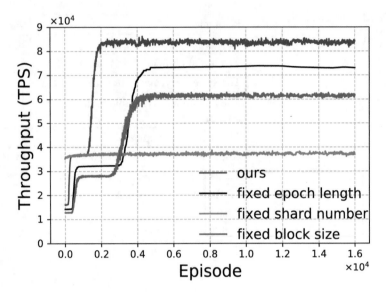

Fig. 8.3 Convergence performance of different schemes

8.6.2 Security and Latency Performance

We set the shards size $m = 80, 90, 110, 130, 150$ to calculate the probability of faulty system from Eq. (8.10). Figure 8.4 shows that the safe probability can reach 98% with the shards size $m = 150$ when the number of system nodes is lower

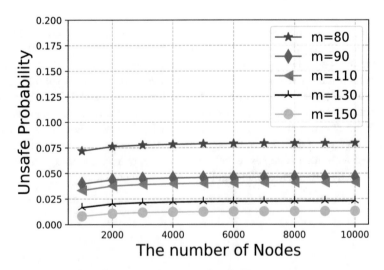

Fig. 8.4 The probability of insecurity with the number of nodes

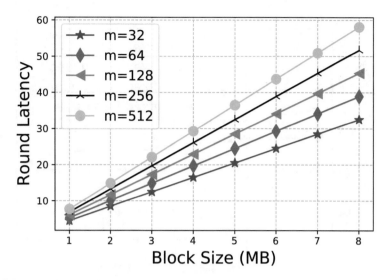

Fig. 8.5 Round latency with the block size

than 10,000. Besides, it can also be observed that the unsafe probability increases slowly with more and more new nodes joining in the system, which means the blockchain sharding system need to adjust the shards size to guarantee security when the number of system nodes changes.

Figure 8.5 shows the change of round latency, i.e., the intra-committee consensus time, when block size increases gradually, from which we can see that the consensus latency is related with block size and shards size. It reveals that block size can not be increased without limit since it will increase the time of new block added to blockchain, leading to Eq. (8.8) unsatisfied.

8.6.3 Throughput Comparison with the Baselines

We explore the effects of different system parameters on the performance of the blockchain sharding system in Figs. 8.6 to 8.11. Specifically, the throughput of our proposed DRL-based dynamic sharding framework is compared with that of the baselines with different thresholds of the consensus latency, security parameter, average transaction size, transmission rate, initial number of nodes and shard number limits.

Figure 8.6 illustrates the throughput with different limit ratios $\frac{1}{\gamma}$ of total consensus time of one epoch to consensus latency of a transaction where the ratio should satisfy Eq. (8.8). We can observe that throughput of the proposed scheme with fixed block size remains stable when the others decrease with the limit ratio increase. This is because the consensus latency of a transaction is limited

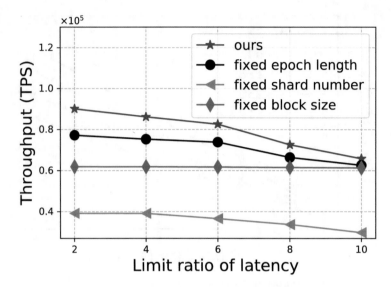

Fig. 8.6 The throughput with consensus rounds parameter γ

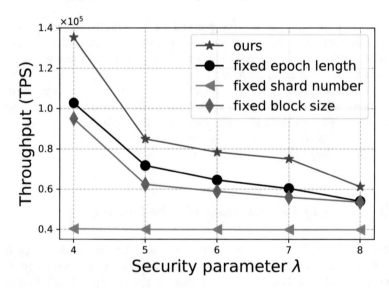

Fig. 8.7 The throughput with security parameter λ

more strictly by the constraint Eq. (8.8), causing a lower throughput calculated by Eq. (8.7). We also find that our proposed scheme perform better than other schemes regardless of the change of limit ratio of latency.

In Fig. 8.7, we discuss the impact of security parameter λ on throughput. The security parameter limits the number of shards since the shards size must be large enough to satisfy the shard-size security measured by Eq. (8.10). Therefore,

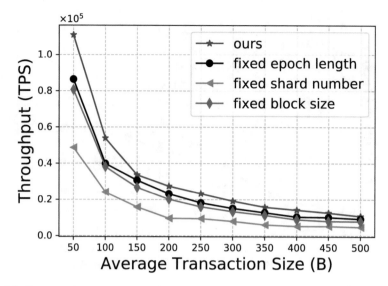

Fig. 8.8 The throughput with average transaction size

throughput decreases when the system need a higher probability of security (i.e., higher security parameter). Besides, we can also find that a slowly declined trend appeared with $\lambda \geq 5$, which means the system has a high probability of security when the shard size is large enough. Note that the throughput of the scheme with fixed number of shards change steadily because its shard size can ensure a low unsafe probability.

Figures 8.8 and 8.9 show the throughput with the transaction size and transmission rate, which makes sense when considering transaction sizes and transmission rate in a real scene due to the difference of transaction types and nodes. It is obvious that the throughput increases significantly with the decreasing transaction size and the increasing transmission rate. The reason is that one block can pack more number of transactions for smaller-size transactions and communicate faster for the higher transmission rate. In addition, we can see that our proposed scheme can achieve the highest throughput with the variation of parameters, then follows the fixed epoch length scheme, the fixed block size scheme and the fixed shard number scheme.

The effect of the initial number of nodes on throughput is depicted in Fig. 8.10. We can see that the throughput can be enhanced with nodes joining and stops increasing finally because of the limit shard number (here we set the maximum shard number to be 64). The increase of throughput is nonlinear with the increasing network nodes. This is because the consensus latency in one committee will increase when the shard size increases. This result indicates that we should adopt the dynamic sharding policy, instead of the fixed sharding policy, to create more shards for the improvement of the throughput when the network is large enough to guarantee each shard to maintain security.

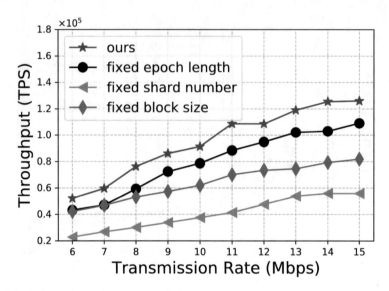

Fig. 8.9 The throughput with data transmission rate

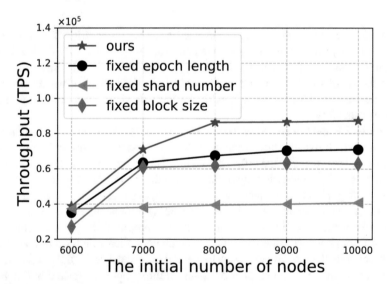

Fig. 8.10 The throughput with the initial nodes

The influence of changing the shard number can be illustrated in Fig. 8.11, which shows that the throughput can scale efficiently with the increasing number of shards. We can see that the throughput of our proposed scheme can reach 110,000 TPS when the maximum number of shards is 128. The fixed shard number scheme outperforms the fixed epoch length and the fixed block size when the maximum number of

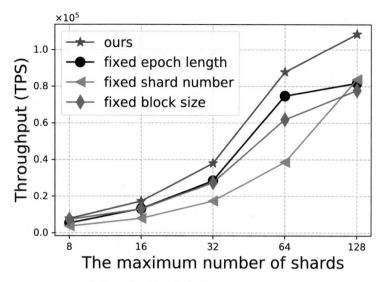

Fig. 8.11 The throughput with the maximum number of shards

shards is 128, but its throughput is still lower than our proposed scheme. This result indicates that our proposed scheme can better adapt different environments.

8.7   Conclusion

SkyChain is the first dynamic public blockchain sharding protocol that permits the system to dynamically shard to deal with the challenges of dynamic phenomenon in blockchain sharding systems. An adaptive ledger protocol was proposed to guarantee the ledgers to be merged or split efficiently and without conflict according to the dynamic sharding result. SkyChain adopts a DRL-based dynamic sharding approach to adjust the epoch length, shard number and block size to maintain a long-term balance between performance and security. In our proposed framework, we provide a quantitative measurement for the performance and security of sharding systems, which is also used to train our DRL agents. Experimental results demonstrate that our proposed framework can achieve a significant balance between performance and security than the baselines with different system parameters. In future work, we plan to consider more factors related with dynamic environment in the blockchain sharding systems and apply our DRL-based dynamic sharding framework to real

References

1. S. Nakamoto et al., Bitcoin: A peer-to-peer electronic cash system. Decentralized Business Review 21260 (2008)
2. G. Wood et al., Ethereum: A secure decentralised generalised transaction ledger. Ethereum Project Yellow Paper 151(2014), 1–32 (2014)
3. E. Androulaki, A. Barger, V. Bortnikov, C. Cachin, K. Christidis, A. De Caro, D. Enyeart, C. Ferris, G. Laventman, Y. Manevich et al., Hyperledger fabric: a distributed operating system for permissioned blockchains, in *Proceedings of the Thirteenth EuroSys Conference* (ACM, 2018), p. 30
4. G. Wang, Z.J. Shi, M. Nixon, S. Han, Sok: Sharding on blockchain, in *Proceedings of the 1st ACM Conference on Advances in Financial Technologies* (ACM, 2019), pp. 41–61
5. L. Luu, V. Narayanan, C. Zheng, K. Baweja, S. Gilbert, P. Saxena, A secure sharding protocol for open blockchains, in *Proceedings of the 2016 ACM SIGSAC Conference on Computer and Communications Security*, CCS '16, New York, NY (ACM, 2016), pp. 17–30
6. E. Kokoris-Kogias, P. Jovanovic, L. Gasser, N. Gailly, E. Syta, B. Ford, Omniledger: A secure, scale-out, decentralized ledger via sharding, in *2018 IEEE Symposium on Security and Privacy (SP)*, May (2018), pp. 583–598
7. M. Zamani, M. Movahedi, M. Raykova, Rapidchain: Scaling blockchain via full sharding, in *Proceedings of the 2018 ACM SIGSAC Conference on Computer and Communications Security*, CCS '18, New York, NY (ACM, 2018), pp. 931–948
8. J. Wang, H. Wang, Monoxide: Scale out blockchains with asynchronous consensus zones, in *16th USENIX Symposium on Networked Systems Design and Implementation (NSDI 19)*, Boston, MA, February (USENIX Association, 2019), pp. 95–112
9. L.N. Nguyen, T.D.T. Nguyen, T.N. Dinh, M.T. Thai, Optchain: Optimal transactions placement for scalable blockchain sharding, in *2019 IEEE 39th International Conference on Distributed Computing Systems (ICDCS)* (IEEE, 2019), pp. 525–535
10. I. Eyal, E.G. Sirer, Majority is not enough: Bitcoin mining is vulnerable, in *Financial Cryptography and Data Security*, ed. by N. Christin, R. Safavi-Naini (Springer, Berlin Heidelberg, 2014), pp. 436–454
11. M. Castro, B. Liskov, Practical byzantine fault tolerance, in *Proceedings of the Third Symposium on Operating Systems Design and Implementation*, OSDI '99 (USENIX Association, 1999), pp. 173–186
12. H. Dang, T.T.A. Dinh, D. Loghin, E.C. Chang, Q. Lin, B.C. Ooi, Towards scaling blockchain systems via sharding, in *Proceedings of the 2019 International Conference on Management of Data* (ACM, 2019), pp. 123–140
13. J.R. Douceur, The sybil attack, in *International Workshop on Peer-to-peer Systems* (Springer, 2002), pp. 251–260
14. J. Newsome, E. Shi, D. Song, A. Perrig, The sybil attack in sensor networks: analysis defenses, in *Third International Symposium on Information Processing in Sensor Networks, 2004. IPSN 2004*, April (2004), pp. 259–268
15. R. Pass, L. Seeman, A. Shelat, Analysis of the blockchain protocol in asynchronous networks, in *Annual International Conference on the Theory and Applications of Cryptographic Techniques* (Springer, 2017), pp. 643–673
16. R. Pass, E. Shi, Hybrid consensus: Efficient consensus in the permissionless model, in *31st International Symposium on Distributed Computing (DISC 2017)* (Schloss Dagstuhl-Leibniz-Zentrum fuer Informatik, 2017)
17. E.K. Kogias, P. Jovanovic, N. Gailly, I. Khoffi, L. Gasser, B. Ford, Enhancing bitcoin security and performance with strong consistency via collective signing, in *25th USENIX Security Symposium (USENIX Security 16)*, Austin, TX, August (2016, USENIX Association), pp. 279–296
18. M. Castro, B. Liskov, Practical byzantine fault tolerance and proactive recovery. ACM Trans. Comput. Syst. (TOCS) 20(4), 398–461 (2002)

19. V. Mnih, K. Kavukcuoglu, D. Silver, A.A. Rusu, J. Veness, M.G. Bellemare, A. Graves, M. Riedmiller, A.K. Fidjeland, G. Ostrovski et al., Human-level control through deep reinforcement learning. Nature **518**(7540), 529 (2015)
20. Y. Gilad, R. Hemo, S. Micali, G. Vlachos, N. Zeldovich, Algorand: Scaling byzantine agreements for cryptocurrencies, in *Proceedings of the 26th Symposium on Operating Systems Principles* (2017), pp. 51–68
21. A. Tomescu, S. Devadas, Catena: Efficient non-equivocation via bitcoin, in *2017 IEEE Symposium on Security and Privacy (SP)*, May (2017), pp. 393–409
22. T.P. Lillicrap, J.J. Hunt, A. Pritzel, N. Heess, T. Erez, Y. Tassa, D. Silver, D. Wierstra, Continuous control with deep reinforcement learning. Preprint. arXiv:1509.02971 (2015)
23. D. Kraft, Difficulty control for blockchain-based consensus systems. Peer-to-Peer Netw. Appl. **9**(2), 397–413 (2016)

Chapter 9
A Scalable and Secure Framework for 5G Networks Applications

Sicong Zhou, Huawei Huang, Wuhui Chen, Pan Zhou, Zibin Zheng, and Song Guo

9.1 Overview

Machine learning has spawned a lot of useful applications, such as computer vision, and natural language processing, etc. However, the parties who benefit from the technology are mostly large organizations, e.g., commercial companies and research institutes. Individuals with limited computing-resource cannot take part in machine learning tasks.

In fact, the combined power of individuals has been much underestimated. Taking these advantages into account, distributed learning [1] enables individual devices to learn collaboratively.

0890-8044/20/ $25.00 © 2020 IEEE Digital Object Identifier: https://doi.org/10.1109/MNET.001.1900658.

S. Zhou
School of Computer Science and Engineering, Sun Yat-Sen University, Guangzhou, China

H. Huang (✉) · W. Chen · Z. Zheng
GuangDong Engineering Technology Research Center of Blockchain, Sun Yat-Sen University, Guangdong, China
e-mail: huanghw28@mail.sysu.edu.cn

P. Zhou
Hubei Engineering Research Center on Big Data Security, School of Cyber Science and Engineering, Huazhong University of Science and Technology, Wuhan, China
e-mail: panzhou@hust.edu.cn

S. Guo
Department of Computing, The Hong Kong Polytechnic University, Hung Hom, Hong Kong, China
e-mail: song.guo@polyu.edu.hk

© The Author(s), under exclusive license to Springer Nature Singapore Pte Ltd. 2023
W. Chen et al. (eds.), *Blockchain Scalability*,
https://doi.org/10.1007/978-981-99-1059-5_9

Generally, factors that affect an ideal distributed learning are included as follows:

- High availability: any device can perform learning anytime.
- High scalability: the learning framework should support high concurrency, high communication efficiency and low storage complexity.
- Decentralization: the intervention of a centralized third-party is minimum.
- Byzantine-resilient model safety: the future distributed learning should ensure byzantine-resiliency [2], which indicates that the distributed learning can endure arbitrary attacks on learning convergence.

Communication latency and bandwidth are still viewed as the bottleneck of distributed machine learning [3]. This situation makes distributed learning highly unavailable for the majority. With significantly improved network conditions, 5G technologies enable high availability.

As do all distributed systems, the learning system is prone to *byzantine attacks* [2], especially when the availability is high. Therefore, more sophisticated approaches that can ensure the byzantine-resilience are required.

Recently, byzantine-resilient machine learning under master/slave settings has gained much attention [4–6]. In a byzantine-resilient distributed-learning task, two things are risk-prone: (1) gradient aggregation, and (2) model parameters.

Conventionally, the byzantine-resilient distributed-learning tasks are conducted under centralized settings, in which the byzantine-tolerant components rely on a globally trusted third-party as the *parameter server*. The problem is that the workload-handling capacity of such centralized parameter server is usually a bottleneck while performing the distributed learning. Moreover, to provide reliable services against the vulnerability of single-point-of-failure (SPOF), the redundant deployment of resources is entailed at the centralized third-party. Therefore, the centralized byzantine-resilient learning induces a high operational-expenditure (OPEX).

To achieve high availability while fulfilling the requirement of OPEX-efficiency and byzantine-resiliency, the distributed learning system would ideally be decentralized. However, to the best of our knowledge, the byzantine-resilient learning with decentralized configuration has not been well studied.

To this end, this chapter proposes a sharding-based blockchain framework named PIRATE, for byzantine-resilient distributed-learning under the decentralized 5G environment to protect learning convergence. Decentralized convergence-security, and trusted credit feedback for candidate management are the key features of PIRATE.

9.2 Preliminaries of Distributed Machine Learning in 5G Networks

9.2.1 Consensus Protocols for Decentralized Learning in 5G

To achieve global agreement within a decentralized setting, a byzantine-tolerant consensus protocol for state machine replication (SMR) is needed [2]. The consensus protocol should ensure that honest nodes can reach agreement on the order and the correctness of model updates, even when a certain amount of byzantine effort exists. In this section, we first briefly review the existing byzantine tolerant consensus protocols towards SMR, and then analyze what protocol is applicable for decentralized learning in the 5G era. For brevity, we call the byzantine-tolerant consensus protocol the consensus protocol in the remainder of this chapter.

Consensus protocols can be categorized into 2 types: the competition-based and the communication-based. The leader of competition-based consensus, e.g., the Proof of Work (PoW) adopted by bitcoin [7], needs to earn his leadership through a "fair" competition. Communication-based consensus protocols (e.g., Hotstuff [8]) select leaders through a deterministic way, or based on an unbiased randomness generated collaboratively.

In the context of blockchains, for competition-based consensus protocols, blocks are appended on the chain *before* consensus while the communication-based protocols append blocks thereafter. For competition-based methods, larger scales inevitably incur higher chance of forking. Plagued by the byproduct, competition-based methods struggle to achieve a high scalability.

While communication-based consensus protocols have no concern of forks, they require multiple rounds of communication to reach agreement. The high communication overhead also hurts the scalability of communication-based protocols.

Sharding-based consensus protocols [9] can achieve scalable consensus in the permissionless blockchain. They benefit from the instant finality of the communication-based methods, and permissionless resiliency of the competition-based methods.

In 5G networks, we need a consensus protocol that is available for a large scale of participants. An ideal consensus protocol should be scalable and permissionless. Sharding-based protocols make full use of the integrated resources by splitting a workload and allocating tasks among multiple committees. Such scalable strategy can fit perfectly in distributed learning. However, permissionless distributed-learning is challenging due to the volatile states of participants. Thus, a consistent assessment of training-reliability is required for the learning system task to function efficiently. Accordingly, we adopt a permissioned version of sharding-based consensus protocol in our proposed framework.

9.2.2   Configurations of Distributed Machine Learning

Machine learning problems mostly rely on some optimization problems. In order to orchestrate a distributed optimization, as shown in Fig. 9.1, computing nodes need to carry out the following steps. First, each node computes local gradients. Then, nodes communicate with aggregator(s) to get a globally aggregated gradient for model update. Based on how they communicate, two typical styles of configuration have been proposed:

Master/slave style: A centralized parameter server aggregates gradients and sends the aggregated result to each computing node.
Decentralized style: All nodes are aggregators. In an Allreduce manner, nodes communicate with neighbors to exchange gradients.

We then discuss the superiority of decentralized style:

- **Communication efficiency**. A recent work [3] demonstrated that the decentralized settings can better exploit the bandwidth resource, avoid traffic jams and share workloads among peers than the centralized master/slave settings.
- **Cost efficiency**. When the scale of participation grows substantially, no single party should be responsible for maintaining the system. Analogous to the situation of cloud netdisk services nowadays, if a service provider plays such a dominant role, the OPEX cost of the centralized system eventually transfer to clients. As a feasible solution, service providers enforce clients to choose between low quality of service and expensive membership fee. This is an opposite of win-win for providers and clients, provided that there are better solutions.
- **Reliability**. The centralized design of master/lave settings suffer from SPOF problem. Once the centralized server is overloaded or under attack, the whole system ceases to function. Thus, the communication burdens and the attack risks on one single server impair the reliability of the system.

9.3   State-of-the-Art Studies of Byzantine-Resilient Machine Learning

9.3.1   Byzantine-Resilient Machine Learning

As the scale of participants grows, the behaviors of computing nodes become more unpredictable. The distributed stochastic gradient descent (D-SGD) [10] framework should tolerate byzantine attacks, i.e., arbitrary malicious actions to prevent convergence, such as sending harmful gradients and corrupting training models as shown in Fig. 9.2. Current studies on byzantine-resilient machine learning mostly focus on protecting gradient aggregation. However, the parameters of training models owned

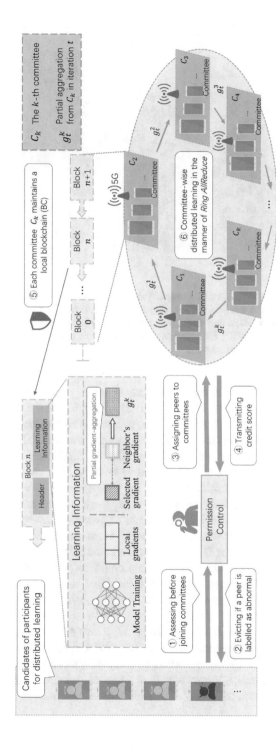

Fig. 9.1 The proposed PIRATE framework has two critical components: (1) permission control, and (2) blockchain-based learning committees for distributed SGD (D-SGD). Gradient aggregations and model parameters are protected by Hotstuff blockchain consensus protocol. Meanwhile, the permission control centre determines the joining and leaving of candidates

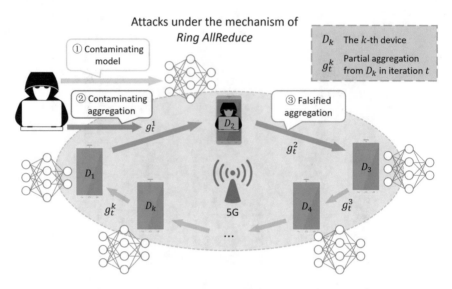

Fig. 9.2 While adopting the *Ring Allreduce* (https://github.com/baidu-research/baidu-allreduce) mechanism, malicious attackers can perform attacking from both inside and outside. ① Attackers from the outside can contaminate training models in target nodes. ② The outside attackers can also attack partial gradient-aggregation. ③ Byzantine computing nodes can send harmful aggregations that damage the convergence of learning tasks

by each data trainer are also vulnerable. We analyze existing frameworks that can protect both, and elaborate the protection of gradient aggregation in the next section.

A blockchain-based method, *LearningChain*, was proposed by Chen et al. [11], which is able to simultaneously protect gradient aggregations and model parameters, by storing them together on-chain. Exploiting the traceability of blockchain, erroneous global parameters can be rolled back to its unfalsified state. Historical parameter records cannot be falsified due to the tamper-proof characteristic of blockchain. They proposed "*l*-nearest gradients aggregation" to ensure that if byzantine computing nodes yield local gradients to prevent convergence of the learning algorithms, their effort would be mitigated. However, *LearningChain* still utilizes a master/slave setting for D-SGD where the parameter server is elected by PoW competition. In addition, the on-chain data could be potentially oversized, because all nodes would have to store all the historical model parameters and gradients. Such architecture is prone significant traffic congestion and substantial storage overhead.

In terms of reliability, rollbacks can possibly fail if two consecutive byzantine leaders collude. The essential problem is that, the model update is examined by only one leader when a proposal is submitted. In contrast, our proposed framework adopts a more decentralized setting, in which all nodes can naturally participate in validating the model updates, and every node maintains its own training model.

9.3.2   Byzantine Protection on Gradients

Before updating training models, computing nodes need to aggregate their local gradients. Aggregation solutions of simple linear combinations (e.g., averaging [12]) cannot tolerate one byzantine worker [4]. Thus, byzantine protection on gradients aggregation has gained much growing attention. Basically, the existing byzantine-based approaches can be classified into 2 categories: the tolerance-based and the detection-based.

Blanchard et al. [4] proposed a byzantine tolerant method called *Krum*. Instead of using a simple linear combination, Krum precludes gradients too far away from the majority and chooses one local gradient based on a spatial score. Experiments show that even with 33% of omniscient byzantine workers, the error rate is almost the same as that of 0%.

The tolerant approach *l*-nearest gradients proposed by Chen et al. [11] cannot guarantee safety against omniscient attacks. The aggregation solution is to aggregate *l* gradients closest, based on their cosine distances, to the sum of the received gradients. If an omniscient attacker manages to acquire all local gradients for other workers in time, the byzantine worker can yield a local gradient that changes the global aggregation arbitrarily [4].

One byzantine-detection method proposed by Li et al. [6] is designed for federated learning (FL). Existing byzantine-tolerant aggregation methods are mostly inefficient due to the non-identically and independently distributed training data. Experiments show that their detection-based method has a better performance than tolerance-based methods in FL. In their algorithm, a credit score was assigned by a pre-trained anomaly detection model to each local gradient. Since the weight of the local gradient was determined by the credit score, the weighted sum aggregation can filter out the byzantine local gradients.

Apart from detection methods, another machine learning method was proposed by Ji et al. [13] to learn the gradient aggregation. Different from the deterministic aggregation solution, they model the aggregation as a learning problem.

Tolerance-based methods are mostly designed under an independent identically distributed (i.i.d) assumption. Therefore, in the settings of FL where data is non-i.i.d, most tolerance-based methods do not perform well. However, tolerance-based methods have the benefit of simplicity that do not require additional training.

As shown in Table 9.1, we compare the performance of different protection approaches for gradient-aggregation under the normal setting and the FL setting.

9.3.3   Risks of Decentralization

In a decentralized scheme, every node has a greater impact on the global aggregation than a centralized scheme. As shown in Fig. 9.2, the existing protection methods are not applicable to the decentralized settings because of the following reasons.

Table 9.1 Gradient protection methods

Method types	The tolerance-based		The detection-based	The learning-based
Representative studies	Krum [4]	l-nearest gradients [11]	Anomaly detection [6]	Learning to learn[13]
Resiliency under 30% attack	High	Medium	Unknown	High
Resiliency under 30% attack (FL)	Low	Unknown	High	Unknown
Resiliency under majority attack	Low	Medium	Unknown	High
Resiliency under majority attack (FL)	Low	Unknown	High	Unknown
Computation complexity	$O(n^2)$	$O(n)$	$O(n)$	Model-related
Other functions except *aggregation*	None		Autoencoder training	Aggregator training

- Attacks on partial aggregation are detrimental. Every node aggregates a partial aggregation provided by another node. For byzantine nodes, they have more attack patterns, such as sending falsified partial aggregation results or sending nothing to stall the aggregation process. Thus, without a quorum of validators, partial aggregation process cannot be trusted.
- Anomaly detection [6] would be challenging. Credit scores cannot be trusted without proper validation mechanisms.
- Synchronization of model parameters could be a problem. Every node needs to maintain a local training model. Once contaminated by attackers, computing nodes will have no actual contribution to the holistic learning task.

As a solution, blockchain as a decentralized SMR system, can provide quorums of validators and practical synchronization mechanism to achieve byzantine-resiliency in decentralized learning.

9.4 Our Proposal—PIRATE: A Machine Learning Framework Based on Sharding Technique

9.4.1 Overview of PIRATE

Generally, we propose a framework of blockchain-based protection for the distributed machine learning named PIRATE, targeted for the convergence risks brought by decentralized D-SGD. PIRATE consists of two major parts, i.e., a permission control center and learning committees. The permission control center provides reliability assessment to candidates and assigns candidates into learning committees. Meanwhile, learning committees collaborate to solve a decentralized D-SGD problem with additional verification from blockchains and anomaly detection. As a result, malicious nodes are replaced and their harmful gradients are filtered.

9.4.2 Permission Control

In a distributed learning system with high availability, reliability assessment is essential, especially for mobile devices. Allowing devices in bad states to participate learning tasks would slow down the entire learning process. Thus, real-time reliability assessment and permission control are needed.

We propose a centralized solution for permission control. Figure 9.1 depicts the permission control of PIRATE. Before actually contributing to the global learning task, all candidates are assessed by a *permission control center* based on their computation ability, network condition, join/leave prospect and historical credit scores. Accordingly the permission control center determines whether a candidate can join a learning task and the workload to assign. If granted permission, candidates are to replace nodes with low accumulated credit scores during reconfiguration. During training, validated credit scores generated by committees are transmitted to the permission control center.

9.4.3   Sharding-Based Blockchain Protection Towards Decentralized Distributed-Learning

We propose a sharding-based blockchain mechanism for the protection of decentralized distributed-learning. We randomly split the computing nodes into multiple committees, in which partial aggregations are agreed. No longer centralized, the burden of aggregation workloads is mitigated.

Let n denote the total number of computing nodes, c denote the size of a committee. We then discuss the key actions of the learning committees.

Random Committee Construction All nodes would be assigned a random identity by the permission control center. According to the identities, committees of size c are formed. Every committee member knows the identity of all honest peers in their committee and their neighbor committees.

Intra-Committee Consensus Every committee maintains a separate blockchain with Hotstuff [8] to reach consensus on local aggregations, training models and credit scores. With an honest majority of members having agreed and partially signed (threshold signature) on the data, the data is tamper-proof.

Global Consensus In a committee-wise Ring Allreduce[1] manner, committees communicate locally-agreed aggregations and their threshold signatures with their neighbor committees. Since committee members know all honest members in their neighbor committees, by checking whether an aggregation is signed by an honest majority, committee members can verify the aggregation from neighbors. With $2(n/c - 1)$ consensus steps, every node would have a globally agreed aggregation, completing one iteration.

Reconfiguration After finishing a learning task, nodes with low credit scores in every committee are replaced. The permission control center would consider these nodes as byzantine nodes and replace them with new nodes. Following Bounded Cuckoo Rule [9], old and new nodes in a committee are randomly evicted to some other random committees. The random eviction rule provides join/leave attack protection while guaranteeing a same resiliency of 1/3 in each committee.

---

[1] https://github.com/baidu-research/baidu-allreduce.

9.4.4   Intra-Committee Consensus

As in Fig. 9.1, each committee maintains a blockchain to protect aggregations and training models within the committee. We adopt Hotstuff[8] as the consensus protocol of the blockchain. Figure 9.3 depicts the intra-committee consensus process. We define the process of finishing a partial aggregation a *step*, the process of finishing a model update an *iteration*.

When a local gradient is computed, members take part in repeated consensus steps. A consensus step (CS) includes:

- **Component 1**: local gradient selection,
- **Component 2**: neighbor committee aggregation,
- **Component 3**: aggregation of Component 1 and Component 2.

For component 1, committee members can either collaboratively select c^2/n local gradients, or coordinate in a round robin manner to choose c^2/n local gradients.

For component 2, members wait for the leader of the neighbor committee C_{i-1} to broadcast the tamper-proof neighbor aggregation from last step. Since the aggregation is an agreed result from the neighbor's last step, members of this committee C_i can verify the result by checking the threshold signature. If the leader of C_{i-1} chooses to withhold the result from C_i, members of C_i would send requests to a random member of C_{i-1} for the result.

Finally for component 3, having a neighbor committee aggregation and a set of local gradients, nodes aggregate them using the detection-based BFT aggregation [6]. A pre-trained anomaly detection model would assign a weight to each proposed gradient according to the anomaly score. Zero weight would be assigned to a proposed gradient if its anomaly score surpasses a threshold, thereby harmful gradients that hinders convergence are "filtered". Meanwhile, members are required to validate and store historical credit scores of each other until a new committee is formed. These verifiable credit scores are transmitted to the permission control center during reconfiguration.

After all components being executed, the incumbent leader broadcast the partial aggregation and a digital digest of training parameters for members to verify and agree on. Having sufficient signatures, the leader would broadcast the decided aggregation in its committee C_i and in the neighbor committee C_{i+1}.

With Hotstuff [8] a consensus step requires four phases of communication, i.e., PREPARE, PRE-COMMIT, COMMIT and DECIDE. Each phase is driven by a leader issuing a block containing verifiable threshold signatures.

As shown in Fig. 9.3, only 1/4 of blocks are generating aggregations. To address this issue, we can pipeline consensus steps to achieve a better performance. Each leader would be responsible for driving four consensus steps in different phases. In an ideal scenario where no byzantine leader is elected, every block generates an agreed aggregation in average.

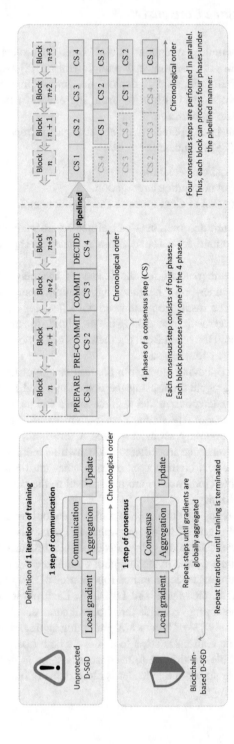

Fig. 9.3 We define the process of finishing a partial aggregation a *step*, the process of finishing a model update an *iteration*. A consensus step (CS) has 4 phases, each driven by leader. The protocol can be pipelined for performance enhancement, ideally executing 1 aggregation each block in average

Members are required to store one set (4 sets if pipelined) of gradients for validation, which is composed of its own local gradient, aggregation of the corresponding neighbor committee and an aggregation proposal from the incumbent leader.

9.4.5 Committee-Wise Ring Allreduce

In PIRATE, we adopt a committee-wise Ring Allreduce as the decentralized communication scheme. The committee-wise Ring Allreduce enables verification of aggregation in a fully decentralized setting. For classic Ring Allreduce, we refer our readers to baidu-allreduce (see footnote 1). The worker unit of committee-wise Ring Allreduce is no longer a processing unit, but an entire committee. Also, instead of segmenting one single gradient for transmission of each round as classical Ring Allreduce does, a committee transmits one whole gradient in each round (consensus step) by controlling the selection ratio n/c^2 to 1 (1/4 if pipelined). The selection ratio ensures that the amount of whole gradients to transfer equals to the number of committees. After $2(n/c - 1)$ rounds, all local gradients are aggregated.

9.4.6 Security and Complexity Analysis

9.4.6.1 Security Analysis of Convergence Attack

As shown in Fig. 9.2, various attack behaviors are considered. Training models and aggregations are two main targets of attack.

Training models are maintained by all computing nodes. Since training models are on-chain information, computing nodes can quickly recover an approved training model once it is contaminated. With Hotstuff [8], the recovery mechanism only fails if the committee is composed by over 33% of byzantine nodes.

Both local gradients and partial aggregations could be contaminated or falsified within a certain committee, either by outsiders or malicious participants.

When local gradients are contaminated, they would be effectively filtered by the gradient anomaly detection if the percentage of the contaminated gradients is less than 30% [6]. In terms of partial aggregations within committees, with each committee running consensus protocol that only approve aggregations with authenticators (i.e., threshold digital signatures), contaminated aggregations would not be accepted by committee members. And again, such mechanism only fails if the committee is composed by over 33% of byzantine nodes.

An authenticated partial aggregation is to be broadcast to members of the neighbor committee. Similar to the above mechanisms, passing partial aggregation to neighbors fails if the committee is composed by over 33% of byzantine nodes.

9.4.6.2   Security Analysis of Take-Over Attack

In terms of take-over attacks, we adopt the Bounded Cuckoo Rule for reconfiguration, which is proven to keep committees *balanced* and *honest* in [9]. *Balanced* refers that the number of nodes in the committee is bounded, and *honest* refers that the fraction of byzantine nodes is less than 1/3. Given the two properties, the reconfiguration mechanism shields the system from take-over attacks.

9.4.6.3   Computation Overhead

Extra computation cost mainly comes from generating digital digests and verifying them. We adopt Hotstuff as the consensus protocol, which has a complexity of $O(n)$[8]. Such overhead is insignificant compared to gradient broadcasting. For instance, generating a 100 MB Merkle tree with a 3.5GHz processor and PySHA-3 would roughly takes 1 second, and verifying the tree would take way less than 1 second [14].

9.4.7   Applications

9.4.7.1   Decentralized Federated Learning

In FL, data privacy are protected with differential privacy mechanisms. In terms of convergence safety, FL relies on byzantine-resilient centralized D-SGD algorithms like [6] for protection. However, most of these algorithms alone cannot provide protection in a decentralized setting. PIRATE solves this problem with blockchains. Meanwhile, with anomaly detection and consensus mechanisms of PIRATE, verifiable credit scores can be utilized as a powerful index for client selection, a crucial stage of FL.

9.4.7.2   Big Data Analysis for Consortium Blockchains

Consortium blockchains are widely used in industry organizations for the benefits of a shared governance. With PIRATE, organizations can continuously conduct secure big data analysis using decentralized D-SGD on the shared data. The learnt results are trustworthy in an environment where learning devices owned by different organizations do not have to trust one another. Each organization is required to maintain its own permission control centre. Utilizing the credit score feedback, each organization would always have their most reliable devices on duty.

9.5   Case Study

We implemented a prototype of PIRATE based on Hotstuff.[2] To further evaluate the performance of PIRATE in a large-scale scenario, we conducted a simulation.

9.5.1   Security

To demonstrate feasibility and verification-based security of PIRATE, we conducted an experiment on the prototype. As shown in Fig. 9.4 we experimented on 6 instances, four of which composes Committee1, and the rests are Neighbor1 and Neighbor2. In a committee-wise Ring Allreduce manner, Committee1 and its neighbors communicate with verifiable aggregations. The training process is omitted in the experiment for simplicity.

In Fig. 9.4 variables like hqc, b_lock and vheight, we refer our readers to [8]. Green colored line are the execution logs of intra-committee consensus phases, i.e., PREPARE, PRE-COMMIT, COMMIT and DECIDE. Other colored lines correspond to the verifiable decisions on aggregations of Committee1, Neighbor1 and Neighbor2. Contaminated decisions would be detected with the given information.

9.5.2   Performance Evaluation

We conducted a simulation for performance evaluation on pipelined PIRATE in a large scale scenario. On one machine, we ran 50–100 instances to simulate a single committee. According the selection ratio n/c^2, we can speculate the performance of 625–2500 nodes in total due to the concurrent nature of PIRATE. We assume devices spend a same amount of time for computing gradients. We simulate this process by having instances wait for a same amount of time to generate an equal-sized chunk of data (28 MB). Then, instances transmit chunks of data to simulate the decentralized D-SGD process of PIRATE. The machine is a mini PC (model serial number: NUC8i5BEK), with a quad-core i5-8259U processor (3.80 GHz). To simulate the network condition of 5G, we assume every message has a 10 ms latency. And the uplink bandwidth is uniformly-distributed ranging from 80 to 240 Mbps, while the downlink bandwidth is set to 1 Gbps.

We compare PIRATE with another blockchain-based D-SGD framework LearningChain without the presence of malicious node. We first compare the gradient storage overhead of the two frameworks. We then compare the iteration time measured by the time used to broadcast a block.

---

[2] https://github.com/hot-stuff/libhotstuff.

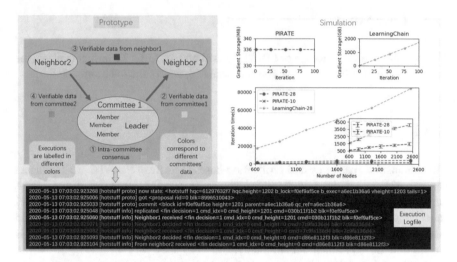

Fig. 9.4 Efficiency as shown in the right-top section, is evaluated with a simulation. The rest of the figure demonstrates how the prototype works. In the simulation section, the left-top figure: Gradient Storage of PIRATE vs. iteration with single gradient size of 28 MB. The right-top figure: Gradient Storage of LearningChain vs. iteration with the single-gradient size of 28 MB. The Bottom figure: Iteration time of PIRATE and LearningChain vs. number of nodes with the single-gradient sizes of 28 MB and 10 MB. In the prototype section, the upper part is the abstraction of the whole process. The lower part is the execution results recorded in a logfile

As Fig. 9.4 shows, gradient storage overhead for PIRATE are constant as iteration progresses, while LearningChain's storage has a linear growth. In each iteration, PIRATE stores only the leader's gradient, the neighbor committee's gradient and the local gradient itself has computed. In LearningChain, nodes are required to store the history of all leader-announced gradients, and the local gradients broadcast by all nodes.

Figure 9.4 shows that PIRATE outperforms LearningChain on iteration time. The major cost in each iteration is the broadcast of gradients. PIRATE shows a superior performance in terms of iteration time for each committee. This is because nodes are required to broadcast to only c members, meanwhile, consensus decisions are reached concurrently.

9.6   Open Issues

The open issues are envisioned as follows.

- **Decentralized Permission Control**. Candidates having inferior computation ability, bad historical credit scores and unstable network conditions can undermine the efficiency of distributed learning. Without a centralized permission control, reliability assessment is challenging, especially for realtime attributes.

Latency induced by decentralized communication and verification inevitably affects timeliness.

- **Protection Against Model Poisoning Attack**. When applied to FL, PIRATE faces a challenging issue of model-poisoning attack. The attack can be successful even for a *highly constrained* byzantine node [15]. By exploiting the non-i.i.d property of data shards, byzantine attackers can send poisoned local updates that do not hurt convergence. Such harmful local updates can still affect the global model that triggers misclassifying. The attack is also "sneaky" enough to bypass accuracy checks from central servers. In a decentralized environment, where nodes are less constrained in terms of communicating, computing and validating, model poisoning attack can be even more threatening.
- **Privacy Protection**. When computing nodes train their own data and upload training models for aggregations (like FL), it is possible for attackers to reconstruct the private data using gradient information. For privacy protection, differential privacy mechanism is widely used [11]. However, inevitably there is a trade off between a privacy budget and training accuracy. A well-balanced protection mechanism in both privacy and training accuracy is tempting.

9.7   Conclusion and Future Work

To guarantee the high availability of distributed learning in 5G era, a distributed-learning framework with high efficiency, decentralization and byzantine-resiliency is in urgent need. To fill this gap, we propose PIRATE, a byzantine-resilient D-SGD framework under the decentralized settings. Utilizing a sharding-based blockchain protocol, learning convergence can be well protected. A prototype is implemented to show the feasibility of the proposed PIRATE. The simulation results show that PIRATE scales better than the existing solution LearningChain. As future work, we will further analyze the robustness of PIRATE with extensive experiments.

Acknowledgments This work is partially supported by National Natural Science Foundation of China (61902445, 61872310, 61972448), partially by Fundamental Research Funds for the Central Universities of China under grant No. 19lgpy222, partially by the General Research Fund of the Research Grants Council of Hong Kong (PolyU 152221/19E), partially by Hong Kong RGC Research Impact Fund (RIF) with the Project No. R5034-18, and partially by Guangdong Basic and Applied Basic Research Foundation (2019A1515011798).

References

1. D.P. Bertsekas, J.N. Tsitsiklis, *Parallel and Distributed Computation: Numerical Methods*, vol. 23 (Prentice Hall, Englewood Cliffs, 1989)
2. L. Lamport, Time, clocks, and the ordering of events in a distributed system. Commun. ACM **21**(7), 558–565 (1978)

3. X. Lian, C. Zhang, H. Zhang, C.J. Hsieh, W. Zhang, J. Liu, Can decentralized algorithms outperform centralized algorithms? A case study for decentralized parallel stochastic gradient descent, in *Advances in Neural Information Processing Systems* (2017), pp. 5330–5340

4. P. Blanchard, E.M. El Mhamdi, R. Guerraoui, J. Stainer, Machine learning with adversaries: Byzantine tolerant gradient descent, in *Advances in Neural Information Processing Systems 30*, ed. by I. Guyon, U.V. Luxburg, S. Bengio, H. Wallach, R. Fergus, S. Vishwanathan, and R. Garnett (Curran Associates, 2017), pp. 119–129

5. Y. Chen, L. Su, J. Xu, Distributed statistical machine learning in adversarial settings: Byzantine gradient descent. Proc. ACM Meas. Anal. Comput. Syst. **1**(2), 44:1–44:25 (2017)

6. S. Li, Y. Cheng, Y. Liu, W. Wang, T. Chen, Abnormal client behavior detection in federated learning. Preprint. arXiv:1910.09933 (2019)

7. Nakamoto, S. (2008). Bitcoin: A peer-to-peer electronic cash system. *Decentralized business review*, 21260.

8. M. Yin, D. Malkhi, M.K. Reiter, G.G. Gueta, I. Abraham, Hotstuff: Bft consensus in the lens of blockchain. *arXiv preprint arXiv:1803.05069*. (2018)

9. M. Zamani, M. Movahedi, M. Raykova, Rapidchain: Scaling blockchain via full sharding, in *Proceedings of the 2018 ACM SIGSAC Conference on Computer and Communications Security* (ACM, 2018), pp. 931–948

10. M. Zinkevich, M. Weimer, L. Li, A.J. Smola, Parallelized stochastic gradient descent, in *Advances in Neural Information Processing Systems* (2010), pp. 2595–2603

11. X. Chen, J. Ji, C. Luo, W. Liao, P. Li, When machine learning meets blockchain: A decentralized, privacy-preserving and secure design, in *2018 IEEE International Conference on Big Data (Big Data)* (2018), pp. 1178–1187

12. B.T. Polyak, A.B. Juditsky, Acceleration of stochastic approximation by averaging. SIAM J. Control Optim. **30**(4), 838–855 (1992)

13. J. Ji, X. Chen, Q. Wang, L. Yu, P. Li, Learning to learn gradient aggregation by gradient descent, in *Proceedings of the Twenty-Eighth International Joint Conference on Artificial Intelligence, IJCAI-19*, International Joint Conferences on Artificial Intelligence Organization, 7 (2019), pp. 2614–2620

14. D. Koo, Y. Shin, J. Yun, J. Hur, Improving security and reliability in Merkle tree-based online data authentication with leakage resilience. Appl. Sci. **8**(12), 2532 (2018)

15. A.N. Bhagoji, S. Chakraborty, P. Mittal, S. Calo, Analyzing federated learning through an adversarial lens. Preprint. arXiv:1811.12470 (2018)